Lessons in Leadership

LESSONS IN
LEADERSHIP

My Life in the US Army
from World War II to Vietnam

GENERAL JOHN R. DEANE JR.

Edited by Jack C. Mason

 UNIVERSITY PRESS OF KENTUCKY

Copyright © 2018 by The University Press of Kentucky

Scholarly publisher for the Commonwealth,
serving Bellarmine University, Berea College, Centre College of Kentucky,
Eastern Kentucky University, The Filson Historical Society, Georgetown
College, Kentucky Historical Society, Kentucky State University, Morehead
State University, Murray State University, Northern Kentucky University,
Transylvania University, University of Kentucky, University of Louisville,
and Western Kentucky University.
All rights reserved.

Editorial and Sales Offices: The University Press of Kentucky
663 South Limestone Street, Lexington, Kentucky 40508-4008
www.kentuckypress.com

Library of Congress Cataloging-in-Publication Data

Names: Deane, John R. (John Russell), 1919–2013, author. | Mason, Jack C.,
    editor.
Title: Lessons in leadership : my life in the US Army from World War II to
    Vietnam / General John R. Deane Jr. ; Edited by Jack C. Mason, US Army
    Reserve (Ret.).
Other titles: My life in the US Army from World War II to Vietnam
Description: The University Press of Kentucky : Lexington, Kentucky, [2018] |
    Includes bibliographical references and index.
Identifiers: LCCN 2017044671 | ISBN 9780813174945 (hardcover : alk. paper)
    | ISBN 9780813174952 (pdf) | ISBN 9780813174969 (epub)
Subjects: LCSH: Deane, John R. (John Russell), 1919–2013. | Generals—United
    States—Biography. | Leadership—United States. | United States.
    Army—Officers—Biography. | United States. Army—Military
    life—Anecdotes. | History, Military—United States—20th
    century—Anecdotes.
Classification: LCC E745.D43 A3 2018 | DDC 355.0092 [B] —dc23
LC record available at https://lccn.loc.gov/2017044671

This book is printed on acid-free paper meeting the requirements of the
American National Standard for Permanence in Paper for Printed Library
Materials.

Manufactured in the United States of America.

Member of the Association of University Presses

Contents

Photographs follow page 90

Foreword

I did try to copy his style and techniques, and they were very helpful to me. I received accolades for my leadership, when I was really only copying what Uncle Jack had taught me.
—Lieutenant General Henry E. "Hank" Emerson

During my thirty-eight years of service in the United States Army and Army Reserve, I have traveled all over the world in many interesting assignments and run across many extraordinary characters. In one of the last tours of my career, I had the great fortune to meet General John R. "Jack" Deane Jr. while serving as his escort officer during a visit to Army Materiel Command (AMC) at Redstone Arsenal, Huntsville, Alabama.

General Deane had been invited to participate in an AMC Former Commander's Conference and to celebrate the new unveiling of the headquarters building and recent move from Fort Belvoir, Virginia, to Redstone Arsenal. As many soldiers will tell you, there is not a whole lot of upside to escort officer duty. Army senior leaders don't get where they are by being unassertive. If the tasking is done correctly and without incident, you have done your job. If something goes awry, there is a good chance you will hear about it later.

It so happened that on the day of his arrival at Huntsville, Deane had endured a series of long delays between connecting flights. He finally landed at 11:00 p.m., with the conference events scheduled to kick off at 7:00 the next morning. All I knew about my assignment was that I was escorting a ninety-two-year-old four-star general officer and thought to myself, "Well, should I have a wheelchair waiting at the ramp to whisk him off to his quarters for a much-needed rest before the start of a full day of activities?" I was surprised to encounter a distinguished gentleman in suit and tie, wheeling his carry-on luggage behind him as he strolled off the plane. Full of energy and wearing a big smile, he was in excellent shape and happy to have finally arrived. As the duty driver and I drove him to his quarters, he engaged both of us with many questions and concerns over the damage he viewed from recent tornadoes that had passed through the area.

After the short ride to the hotel, I dismissed the driver and got the general settled in his room. I thought, "Okay, that went well; at least he will get a couple of hours of rest before the conference starts." But Deane had other ideas. The Boston Red Sox were battling the Tampa Bay Rays in the playoffs and the game was in extra innings. He wanted to go down to the lobby bar and watch the game over a nightcap of Stolichnaya vodka. By the time I finally got home it was around 1:00 a.m. and I, a fifty-five-year-old, was beat. The next morning when I arrived to pick him up, Deane had already had breakfast and was mingling with several other former AMC commanders in the lobby.

I relate this story to make a point. Most of us have encountered individuals at some point in our lives who have clearly stood out among the rest. Deane was such a man. In my profession, a uniform, with its rank and awards displayed, demands respect, and the personality of the individual inside it is secondary. I immediately found that Deane, though an elderly gentleman thirty-five years retired from military life and without the trappings of a high-ranking uniform with prestigious awards, was still a commanding presence in a room. He had the personality to draw you in, and with his sharp wit and humor, he knew how to spin a tale. I witnessed his uncanny ability, in a lighthearted manner, to charm men and women alike; my wife, who has an innate ability to discern character, referred to him as a "rock star." Here was a man who had mastered the art of leadership and the ability to communicate and relate to anybody. He lived his life to the fullest.

How was Jack Deane able to rise so far and have such a successful career during his lifetime of service to the nation? I believe several factors came together to offer a chance for his leadership ability to be fully displayed and create an opportunity to rise to the very top of his profession. He had a very sharp mind, gifted with intelligence and the drive to succeed. His father, a career officer who served as General George Marshall's senior assistant, was the perfect role model; for as long as he could remember, Jack was surrounded by, and intimate with, men who would rise to become senior leaders in the US Army during World War II and afterward.

He had determined to make his career in the army from a very early age, and his foundation of training at West Point was just a continuation of what he had been subconsciously practicing since he was a child. Sterling character and a life guided by purpose prepared him to become an extraordinary leader. He was very comfortable with the military lifestyle, and when given the opportunity to lead men in battle, he did so with poise, skill, and bravery. Early in his career, he was fortunate to serve under two legendary soldiers, Terry Allen and James Gavin, who acted as mentors in guiding his career. Finally, he was lucky, escaping many dangerous situations during the course of his many wartime assignments.

Prodded by his family, Jack had written notes and collected stories and interviews over the years for the purpose of documenting his career, but other priorities always seemed to get in the way. When I met him, he was ninety-two, and I believe he felt there were much more valuable ways to spend his remaining days than to work on a book. He handed his material over to me, and we communicated every day or so by email. When I asked him to explain or expound on something, he replied in detail. Often he would send me additional stories to reinforce a point he was trying to make.

Deane's life and comments are interesting and enlightening. Every leader can draw lessons from his story. His thoughts and observations recorded in this book are taken from interviews and conversations conducted over the last thirty years, nearly until his death in 2013. They are as relevant today as they were when they were first recorded.

But in the end, Jack Deane's comments are just those of one man's journey through a lifetime of experiences in the army. He had his biases, and some may not agree with a few of his observations or criticisms, but they were always honestly expressed. He had strong opinions about people, and that is part of what makes his story so interesting. As Jack's close friend Hank Emerson was known to say, "During my career, I served under more than a couple of jerks. But I think you can learn as much from the negative experiences as you can from the positive, and you just tell yourself, if I get the chance, I am never going to do it like that."[1]

Lisa Deane, Jack's youngest daughter, sent me a personal note that helps to give a better understanding of the general's personal philosophy of life.

My father was already a general by the time I was old enough to really understand his role in our military or appreciate his wit in professional settings. I believe he was enormously influential to many in the military with less significant positions, whom he didn't know personally, as well as many people not in the military. And while these influences are not demonstrative of his wit, they were traits he learned probably from his military upbringing and through his own training.

These included the importance of giving thanks. He showed the importance of acknowledging thanks through his prolific note writing. Having been the recipient of many notes, I felt appreciated, which in turn taught me at a young age how important it is to write notes to others. Over the years many friends and colleagues have received a note from my dad and remarked how much it touched them.

He also strongly believed that making decisions was all about evaluating choices. There was always a lengthy evaluation of all of the facts and options before I was to make a decision. While the lengthy debate wasn't always appreciated, the results always seemed to be more sound. Whether it was his insistence that I jump out of the thirty-four-foot parachute tower at Fort Bragg (at the age of twelve) because it was the best way down (when the stairs looked more inviting) or the analysis of why I should take the bar exam despite no desire to practice law; his options and the rewards I felt later always made me realize it was worth it. By the time I was in college the shorthand directive for reminding me to weigh the options was his saying, "Remember pi r squared; the elements of an equation are not always easy, but looking at all the components is critical."

He was always engaged. When I ask anyone over the age of seventy-five what is new, the comments usually regard their latest blood pressure medicine or their flare-up with arthritis. Not with my dad. When asked what was new with him, it was usually about some young person he was guiding who was interested in West Point, the issues faced by the Maine lobstermen, or a great letter he received from my son Wes. It was never about how poorly he was feeling. I attribute this to his staying engaged with world events, keeping proficient in technology, and focusing on nutrition and healthy habits. This lesson of staying engaged has led me to really rethink how I want to live.

Deane's mind and memory remained sharp until the very end of his life, and I'm sure you will find his comments enlightening. His style of writing always told a story not as a way to brag of an accomplishment but as a way to relay an important point or lesson. As a member of what has been termed our "Greatest Generation," he lived his entire life guided by the ideals of West Point. He was truly a hero to his soldiers, his friends, and his family.

From Private to General: A Life of Leadership

John R. Deane Jr. lived a full life by anyone's measure. His entire ninety-four years of life revolved intimately around the military. Born into an army family after World War I, Deane had an adventurous childhood growing up at several army posts in the United States; he also spent two years in China. He experienced a year serving as an enlisted soldier before achieving his goal of attending the United States Military Academy. Upon graduation, his leadership abilities were quickly tested as he was immediately placed in an untried division entering combat for the first time.

He advanced rapidly in his chosen career and was awarded for his valor. He was fortunate in the fact that one of the army's most charismatic leaders, Major General Terry Allen, became one of his first mentors. After almost two hundred days of continual operations, he ended the campaign in Europe as a battalion commander. When he returned to postwar Germany on a new assignment, his background in intelligence led to the development of an important espionage program that successfully gathered information on the occupying Soviet forces in Germany and throughout Eastern Europe.

His next assignment, in Washington, set a pattern that would continue for the rest of his career: working in research and development areas interspaced with important operational assignments in the field. In the research and development office, he gained an expertise in budget systems and the process of how the army procured funding for long-range weapons programs. During this early phase of his career, Lieutenant General James Gavin became an important advisor and mentor.

These Pentagon tours in research and development were always split up by overseas operational assignments, which seemed always to place Deane in a critical command position in demanding situations. He served as the 2nd Battle Group, 6th Infantry commander in Berlin and was on the scene when the Soviets began construction of the Berlin Wall. He personally led the first foot patrol tracking the course of the wall as it was being erected.

While later serving as the assistant division commander of the 82nd Airborne Division, Deane was assigned the position of operational commander of the unit's brigades during the Dominican Republic intervention. This was followed by a tour as an assistant division commander of the 1st Infantry Division in Vietnam under Major General William DePuy and later, as commander of the 173rd Airborne Brigade. He led the Sky Soldiers in the only combat parachute jump of the Vietnam War.

As a senior leader, Deane rounded out his career as the commander of the 82nd Airborne Division, director of R&D assignments in the Pentagon, and deputy director of the Defense Intelligence Agency. His last assignment, which resulted in a promotion to four stars, came as the commander of Army Materiel Command. Senior Department of Defense leaders felt an "outside force" was needed to reinvigorate AMC, which was beginning to gather a reputation of unresponsiveness to its customers in the operational world. Deane was the perfect candidate, a highly successful combat arms officer who specialized in R&D environments. He worked at this effort until his retirement in 1977.

Deane's father and mother were both born and raised in San Francisco and went to college at the University of California at Berkeley. John Deane Sr. left school before graduating in order to enlist in the army at the start of World War I. He went to training camp with a selected group of enlisted men in a program that produced the officers known as "ninety-day wonders." A notable fact associated with this training was that one of Deane's tent mates was F. Scott Fitzgerald, later a noted novelist. At the conclusion of his training, Deane was commissioned a second lieutenant and assigned to the infantry.

Much to his disappointment, he did not serve overseas. He was stationed in Oregon, at Fort Custer, Michigan, and later in Panama as a platoon leader in the 14th Infantry Regiment. At the end of the war, with no outside connections that would guarantee employment and his wife pregnant, Lieutenant Deane decided to stay in the army, which he had grown to love, so that he could support his family. His acute intelligence and extroverted personality ideally matched his line of work and he thrived in his chosen profession. The Deanes' son, John R. Deane Jr., was born on June 8, 1919, in San Francisco, followed by a daughter, Peggy, in 1922.

The early part of John Deane Sr.'s career consisted of normal assignments and advanced schooling: basic and advanced infantry officer courses at Fort Benning, Command and General Staff College at Fort Leavenworth, and the Army War College at Fort McNair, Washington, DC. Command assignments included commander of Company G, 29th Infantry Regiment, Fort Benning, and Company I, 15th Infantry Regiment in Tientsin, China. Deane also served as an instructor at the Command and General Staff College.

On one occasion while serving in the 29th Infantry Regiment, then an instructor demonstration regiment for the Infantry School at Fort Benning, Captain Deane was conducting a field problem of a company in attack. Colonel George C. Marshall was on hand, observing the training. "By the grace of God, I think, I happened to do things, at least the way General Marshall wanted to have them done on that particular day, and he never did forget it," recalled Deane. "I think my experience was similar to many; the officers that Marshall met during his service, he never lost sight of."[2]

In November 1941, Deane was assigned as assistant secretary (later secretary) to the Army General Staff. In this position, he quickly became General Marshall's right-hand man in much of the intensive staffing and planning involved with mobilizing the country and equipping a first-class army to meet the growing threat in Europe. Marshall sat Deane down and described his expectations. Deane recalled, "Among other things, he said that every paper that comes to him will come through me, and he wanted me at least to be prepared to tell him what the paper was about; and if he wanted my opinion on it, he wanted my honest opinion on it. But, if he ever thought that I was saying something because I thought it was what he wanted to hear, then my usefulness to him would be finished. We had a very nice talk, and he indicated that he had confidence in me. He was a very kindly man, but he hated people to catch him at it."[3]

A large part of this job entailed developing a strategic vision and coordination of Allied military operations. Deane served as a key member on the army staff at every major head of state meeting the Allies conducted during the war: in Quebec, Casablanca, Teheran, Yalta, and Potsdam. As part of the US/UK Combined Chiefs of Staff, Deane worked closely with his British counterparts, and once opined, "They are all brilliant men and one must admit that at planning and negotiating, the British have it all over us. On the other hand, we can outperform them any day."[4]

Describing his father's service, Deane Jr. wrote, "Although Marshall had a reputation as a hard worker, I never heard my Dad complain about it. I do believe, from things I have heard, that he was not much for condoning mistakes and was not at all sympathetic to incompetence. I do not believe he ever called my Dad by his nickname, Russ, during their several years of serving together. He always called him 'Deane.' I do not think he had a close, warm relationship with many people."[5]

In 1943, at the request of Ambassador Averell Harriman, Major General Deane was sent to Russia to serve as the army attaché. His primary duties consisted of supervising the Lend Lease Program and coordinating Soviet and Western European Allies' military operations. Earning the respect of both Stalin and General Marshall, he served in this position until the defeat of Germany. By the end of the war, Deane was considered the army's most skilled and seasoned negotiator with the Soviet leadership.

After the Allied victory in World War II, Deane left Moscow to serve as the military liaison to the United Nations before retiring in March 1946. As a civilian, he wrote a best-selling book, *Strange Alliance,* which detailed his experiences and interactions with Russian leaders. Deane described the paranoia of the Soviet officers and their ingratitude for the huge amount of weapons and equipment that the United States provided under the Lend Lease Program. He prophesized that, with the encouragement of the West, in time the Russian people would bring down their government by themselves. The primary way to help accomplish this, he suggested, was through increased Western trade and communication with the Russian people.

It is worth noting that Lieutenant General Edward Rowny, who served as the military representative of the Joint Chiefs of Staff during the negotiations for the Strategic Arms Limitation Talks (SALT II) and later as chief of the US negotiating team of the Strategic Arms Reduction Treaty (START), believed that *Strange Alliance* was one of the best books ever written on how to negotiate with the Soviets. He drew heavily on Deane's book when he wrote his "Ten Commandments on Negotiating with the Soviets," published in the *New York Times* in January 1948.[6]

Although influential friends from the Roosevelt and Truman administrations offered high-paying jobs in New York, Deane opted for the position of head of the wine division of United Distillers, running Italian-Swiss Colony Wine Company, in order to be close to his native San Francisco. He became a driving force in the industry by pushing the California wine growers association into worldwide markets. After turning down feelers from the Truman administration to become director of the Central Intelligence Agency, he accepted a two-year stint as the CIA chief of station in London. "I was amazed that my father would turn down the opportunity to become the CEO of the Agency, only to accept the head of one of its many divisions, but my father explained that he had loved his time in London and had many friends there from World War II days. He thought my mother would love it. She had put up with all the unpleasantness of service in the army and now deserved the pleasure of a stint in London. That was his last public job."[7]

1

Growing Up as an Army Brat

My earliest recollections of army life come from growing up as a young boy at Fort Benning, Georgia. One year, there was very serious flooding on the Chattahoochee River and Upatoi Creek. The bridge across the Upatoi, at the main gate to Fort Benning, was probably twenty feet above the surface of the creek in normal times. Now the water had risen until it was only about five feet below the bridge. (The bridge to which I refer has long since been replaced by one that is much higher and sturdier.)

There was concern the bridge would wash out. Accordingly, the authorities decided that all the kids who were in school in Columbus at the moment should be returned to the post. I can remember that when the school bus reached the bridge after the ten-mile journey from Columbus, the situation was considered so serious that we were not permitted to cross. The kids dismounted and crossed on foot.

The flood waters remained high for several days, which meant we had an unexpected vacation. One day during this vacation, two of my pals and I went down to the Upatoi in a deserted area well up the creek from the bridge. As we approached the creek, we found a homemade canoe in the woods not far from the bank. It was made of canvas stretched over a frame of barrel staves. We decided to launch it and take a ride on the creek. I guess we were eleven or twelve years old then, but we considered ourselves mature outdoorsmen. There were no paddles, so we cut saplings to use as poles. We put the canoe in the water and got in. We used the poles to keep it fairly near the shore. One of my friends was in the front of the canoe and, as he tried to use his pole one time, it did not reach the bottom of the creek. The momentum of his thrust caused him to momentarily lose his balance. The canoe took on some water.

My buddies lost their nerve and jumped for the bank and scrambled ashore. Their action caused the canoe to take on more water and it began to sink. By this time I was too far from shore to jump. The water had become deeper, so my pole was useless. As the canoe settled deeper into

1

the water and began to go under, I tried to get out of it and swim for shore. I was a fairly strong swimmer, so I had no sense of fear at the moment.

From my earlier Berkeley, California, days, I still liked to wear corduroy trousers. I was wearing a brand-new pair my grandmother Deane had sent me from San Francisco. A nail in the framework of the canoe pierced my new cords just below my knee. The nail entered at such an angle that it would not free itself. The canoe, now completely submerged, began to pull me under.

I went to Sunday school every Sunday while I was at Fort Benning. When I visited my grandmother Wood in San Francisco, I accompanied her to Grace Episcopal Cathedral every Sunday. Despite the hours spent in these holy places, I did not think of myself as a particularly religious person. I believed there was a God, and I believed in God, but it was sort of a passing belief, or at least nothing substantial. When the canoe began to pull me under, however, I began to pray. I can't remember what I said or what my thoughts were, but I know I was praying in some sort of a fundamental way. It was natural, not something I had learned in Sunday school or elsewhere. Then, just as I thought I was going to go under, I found myself afraid, but not in a state of panic. I looked for some means to help myself to get out of the clutches of the sinking canoe.

Suddenly, right before me was the branch of a tree. It extended from its partially submerged trunk out over and just inches above the water. It was a substantial branch, probably three or four inches in diameter. Protruding vertically above this branch were several small branches, maybe an inch in diameter. I grabbed two of these and braced my forearms against the horizontal branch. I desperately kicked as hard and violently as I could and the nail ripped its way to the bottom of my trouser leg and tore the cuff.

Mother was not happy with the condition of my trousers when I returned home. She was not at all happy about my stupidity in going in that flooded creek, but underneath her scolding, I could tell she was really happy to see me home.

This event in my life brought a deep and abiding faith in God. I know I am always in his hands. He has saved me from death and disaster on countless occasions, many times in combat situations. I know he will continue to do so until he decides he wants me to enter his heaven.

Growing up on a military installation, young Deane came to visualize his future at an early age. One childhood incident he vividly remembered came when the Deane family was waiting at the local station at Fort Benning for the train that would take them away on leave. His father noticed *a young private from his company, looking somewhat disheveled, waiting for a train himself. Captain Deane knew that the soldier didn't have a pass and was therefore AWOL. As he talked to him, he learned that the young man had just received word that his mother was dying and, without thinking or even stopping to get any money for the trip, he ran off to take the next train to see her. Deane called his company duty officer to put the young soldier on emergency leave, and then gave him $20 out of his own pocket to get him home.*

My father and his friends, who were army officers, profoundly influenced me and my whole life. From the time I was perhaps ten years old, and living at Fort Benning, I observed my father and his friends and thought that they were a great group of people. I thought, "That's the kind of life I want to live." So that decided where I would go in life. It also gave me an inspiration, which led later to a philosophy: I tried to do things that I thought these people whom I admired would approve of. That profoundly influenced how I governed my life.

One of my father's friends gave me a set of books when I was about ten or twelve. The author was an army general officer named Paul B. Malone. The books dealt with a young man who had been a soldier in the Philippines and had subsequently won an appointment to West Point. Three of the books described his life at West Point. Reading them greatly influenced my desire to go to the military academy. From then on, everything I did was aimed at getting into the academy.

Between 1932 and 1934, my father was assigned as company commander of K Company, 15th Infantry Regiment, in Tientsin, China. We went from Fort Benning, stopping in San Francisco for a couple of weeks to visit my grandparents. My grandmother Deane was quite a sketch: an Irish lass of the first order, full of pep and joie de vivre, who loved to take a nip from time to time. After World War II, when she was a widow, every time I went to San Francisco, I would take her and her good friend Launa Goodwin out to lunch at the Palace Court in the Palace Hotel, a lovely European-style hotel. Launa was the widow of a great guy who had been a frontier fighter, among other romantic things, in his youth. Invariably, as soon as we were seated, I would ask if they would like a cocktail, knowing that they could scarcely contain themselves. They would always say that it was a little early in the day, but for me to go ahead. I would demur, saying that I did not want to drink alone. Thus began a back-and-forth banter lasting perhaps ten minutes and ending with us all ordering a drink, an outcome we all knew from the beginning was foreordained. It was always fun.

We sailed from San Francisco in the late summer of 1932 on the US Army Transport *Republic,* the largest ship in the Pacific at the time, much larger than the Matson Line and the Dollar Line ships that plied the Pacific waters between San Francisco and Honolulu. I do not recall the original name of the *Republic,* a ship that had belonged to the Germans before World War I and was seized by our government as a part of the reparations levied against the German government.

Traveling on the army transports was a combination vacation cruise and social gathering. The army was small in those days, so most people knew each other or had close mutual friends. Card games, especially bridge, parties, and other social activities began before the ship even left the dock at Fort Mason, the port of embarkation in San Francisco.

The arrival of the army transports in any port was always a festive occasion. Service people stationed in or near the port crowded the dock to meet friends they might not have seen for years. Bands played, paper tape and confetti filled the air. The passengers continuing on the voyage usually got off the ship to stay with friends during the layover. Our first port of call was Honolulu, where we were greeted not only by the band and a crowded deck, but by hula dancers and friends bearing leis. It was the first of many visits there, but I have little recollection beyond the hoopla that accompanied our arrival and departure.

In the dining room, the four of us—Dad, Mother, my sister Peg, and I—were seated at a table with Carl and Ann Fritzsche, a young couple Mother and Dad had met not long before we left Fort Benning.[1] Carl was a West Point graduate, class of 1928. He had been the NCAA heavyweight boxing champion while at the academy. He would have represented the United States in the 1928 Olympics had he not severed one of his tear glands playing lacrosse that spring. It did not heal in time for him to try out for the team. He played a considerable role in my life in later years.

Carl taught boxing classes each day on the trip for boys ranging in age from about nine to thirteen. The lessons culminated in a boxing exhibition conducted just prior to our arrival in the Philippines. We had a large audience of parents and people interested in something different for an evening's entertainment. Fortunately, out of deference to my parents, Carl matched me with a kid who did not have enough talent to make me look bad.

Our second stop was in Manila, where we stayed for several days. One of my shipmates who disembarked there, Willis D. "Crit" Crittenberger Jr., became a lifelong friend. Crit and I later went to Beanie

Millard's Prep School in Washington to prepare for the entrance examinations to West Point and subsequently became classmates at the academy. While we were in Manila, I spent a couple of nights at Crit's new home at Fort McKinley. I remember going to the club in Manila, perhaps an Officers' Club or just a club in which many army officers were members. It had a great swimming pool and snack bar.

Crit Crittenberger was the son of Major Willis Crittenberger, G2 (intelligence officer) of the Philippine Department. The younger Crittenberger, who retired from the army in 1978 as a major general, recalled that after traveling for three weeks aboard ship, sharing in all the activities twelve-year-old boys enjoyed, Jack and he had grown to become good friends. As the transport ship remained in Manila for several days unloading cargo, Crit invited Jack to stay at his family's new quarters. The two boys spent their time swimming, playing tennis at the Army Navy Club, and watching the ships in the bay as they came and sailed away. When the Republic was ready to depart, the Crittenberger family drove Jack back to the ship, where he embarked on the final leg of the voyage to China.[2]

As we sailed on to China from Manila, we encountered a typhoon, the Pacific version of a hurricane. We only touched the edge of the storm, but the seas became very rough. The ship's crew had to put ropes down the passageways so that we passengers had something to hang onto. There were not many people using the ropes because so many were seasick. Stub Oseth, who graduated a couple of years ahead of me at West Point, and I made our way back to the very stern of the ship. I am sure no one saw us or we would have been hustled back to where it was safe. We spent half an hour or so on the very lowest open deck. The stern of the ship would go down as the bow rose over the waves up front. We would go down so far that Stub and I could almost reach out and touch the water. Then we would go up so high that the propellers would come partially out of the water and we could hear them thrash about and the ship would vibrate. I would guess our vertical travel was something like one hundred feet since the stern was probably sixty feet above the water when the ship was in calm seas. When we finally went forward to go to lunch, I was beginning to feel a bit woozy. Mother was in bed, deathly seasick. Dad brought her a baked potato from the dining room. She could not eat it so Dad gave it to me. I devoured it and immediately felt fine.

When we finally reached our port at Chinwangtao, we boarded a train and traveled for three or four hours to our final destination, Tientsin. The house that had been rented for us was not ready, so we stayed with Captain and Mrs. Leeper and their daughter, Beth Ann. The Leepers were old friends of my parents and Beth Ann was the age of my sister, Peg. Shortly after our arrival, Beth Ann was diagnosed as having scarlet fever. The doctor ordered a precautionary inoculation for each of us. That was our trip and introduction to our two years in China.

Tientsin was divided into four sectors, large areas of the city—the British sector, the French, the Japanese, and the Italian. Each had military units stationed there. The Americans did not have a sector as such. They had a so-called compound, an area the equivalent of two or three city blocks, located in the British sector. This is where the troop barracks of the 15th Infantry Regiment and several recreational facilities were located. I have a vague recollection that we lived on Wellington Street. We went to school in an escort wagon that had been converted into sort of a bus. It was pulled by mules and driven by a tobacco-chewing mule skinner named Swayze.

There was a gymnasium where I learned to play basketball and a YMCA. The YMCA was a gathering place for the American kids. There were various games to be played there. I remember Battleship was one game that we played a lot. There was a library in the Y that had books of interest to youngsters. There was also a soda fountain that was the center of attention when we had a little money but did not have the time to go to Kiesling's.

Kiesling's was a real treat. It was a German bakery located in the British sector. It had been in existence since before World War I, when the Germans had a large presence in China. The adults used to gather there for tea. The kids went for the marvelous ice cream, ice cream sodas, malted milk shakes, and sundaes. In all these years, I have yet to discover an ice cream that beats my memories of Kiesling's.

In the summer months, the 15th Infantry Regiment sent contingents of troops to Chinwangtao for target practice. The camp where we stayed was several miles outside the village of Chinwangtao. The rifle range was constructed on the shore and the bullets went through the targets, out into the sea. During the winter, the regiment maintained a detachment in the village to keep the range and equipment stored there.

At the invitation of Carl Fritzsche, who commanded the detachment in Chinwangtao, I went there to hunt duck and geese with him one autumn. It was an interesting trip. We went hunting with a couple of sergeants. We stayed in the homes of Chinese in the area. We slept on Chinese beds, called *kangs,* which were sort of like an adobe box with a hole in one side and a convoluted flue system. We slept on top of this "box."

The Chinese landlord at each place would stuff *kaoliang*, sort of a sorghum-like growth, under the bed through the hole and light it. The ensuing fire would heat the bed up and get really warm. Although we would be sleeping in a bedroll, like the army had in those days, the forerunner of the sleeping bag, the bed would become uncomfortably warm. When you threw back the covers to cool off, you would freeze on top while burning up on the bottom.

One thing that really amazed me on the trip was the appetites of the sergeants. They would eat a dozen eggs for breakfast like it was nothing. Before that, I had never seen anyone eat more than two eggs at a single meal.

The families of the officers went to Chinwangtao for the whole summer. We lived in sort of camp-like structures with many rooms but no windows, just screens on the doors to keep out the insects. There was a central mess where we all ate. Once my mother took Peg and me on a short cruise to Shanghai, Japan, and back.

There was a magnificent beach where the kids and many of the wives spent a good part of each day and where those of dating age spent considerable time in the evenings. In the afternoons those who liked tennis could go to the town of Chinwangtao. I think we went by bus of some sort. The tennis courts were at a British club connected with the Brits involved with the port. The fondest recollection I have of that club was the ginger beer, something I had never had in the States, and rarely see here even now. After a tennis match in the hot sun, an icy-cold ginger beer was fantastic.

During the summer of 1932, Major Crittenberger arrived in China for an inspection visit and brought along his son in the hopes that his official duties as the intelligence officer might be easier with the Chinese and Japanese officials. Crit described Jack's devilish personality when the two reunited and resumed their adventures together.

On our first morning together, we mounted two separate rickshaws and off Jack flew, already knowing where he was going. In the heavily trafficked Chinese roads, he went faster than I did and kept going, not waiting for me to catch up. In short, he ditched me. I had enough sense to just keep going straight and eventually caught up with him. He was laughing very much at my worry about being lost in a Chinese city, with no Chinese-language ability. He was a good jokester.

After I caught up with Jack in our rickshaws, he led us into

the American infantry area and took me to a snack bar, where he
recommended a hamburger and Coke just to keep us fortified.
When my burger arrived he casually pushed over a bottle, which
he told me was a good English mustard that I should try. At his
suggestion, I slathered my hamburger with it, not knowing it
was a very hot mustard. With my first bite, I immediately had to
run to the bathroom. After I got back to the table, Jack was all
smiles, happy he'd pulled another one on me.[3]

I had learned to ride horses while living at Fort Benning between
1928 and 1931. They had riding classes for the kids every Saturday.
When you learned to ride well enough, you could sign out a horse from
the stable and go riding around the Benning reservation. My friends and
I did this a lot.

At Fort Benning, there were many equestrian events—hunts, horse
shows, and polo. In fact, some people said that Fort Benning, the home
of the infantry, was horsier than Fort Riley, the home of the cavalry. I
rode in the hunts and some of the horse shows. I did not play polo but I
frequently went out to watch the matches. I remember that Terry Allen
was one of the most outstanding players, and probably the wildest. He
later commanded the 1st Infantry Division in North Africa and Sicily and
became my commander in the 104th Infantry Division in Europe during
World War II.

While watching these polo matches, one of the attractions during
the games was the fact that mallets were frequently broken. The shaft
with the grip and the head of mallet, now two separate pieces, were discarded. The other kids and I would scoop up the pieces. There would be
a piece of shaft left in the head. We would remove it, then cut the shaft
with the grip to size and insert it into the head. A little glue and a wedge
held the shaft in the head and we had a short polo mallet. We would also
retrieve any discarded polo balls. With these and our homemade mallets, we played polo on our bicycles. These bicycle games and the games
I watched the officers play aroused my first interest in polo.

In Tientsin some of the officers played polo and, of course, all were
friends of my father. They included Charlie Royce, John Jeter, and Dud
Strickler. Charlie had been stationed at Fort Benning with Dad. His wife,
Daisy, was the granddaughter of Walter Reed, the army doctor. Daisy
ran a dancing class at Benning before she married Charlie. Since she was
a friend of Mother, I was enrolled in the class. I did not like this very
much. In fact, I hated it. This and the fact that all my transgressions were

reported to Mother did not put Daisy at the top of my list of favorite people. It was not really until we were all in China that I began to like her.

John Jeter was a lieutenant in my dad's company. Dud Strickler, by far the best polo player in Tientsin, was also a lieutenant. He was later killed by the Japanese on the Bataan Peninsula when the Japanese invaded the Philippines in the early stages of World War II. During those three months of fighting, Dud was twice awarded the Distinguished Service Cross.[4] One day, Dad told me that Dud had asked whether I might be interested in playing polo. My immediate response was that I would. Dud then took me, for the next week or two, to the polo cage to learn the fundamentals of hitting the polo ball.

The polo cage was a structure containing a mock-up of a horse, complete with saddle and reins, surrounded by chicken wire. The floor sloped from all sides toward the wooden horse. You sat on the horse with a polo mallet and hit polo balls. The balls would roll back to you on the sloped floors. You hit forward shots from both sides of the horse as well as shots to the rear. It was here that Dud taught me how to hold a mallet, how to swing properly to ensure hitting the ball and striking it with all the force possible.

I then graduated to the small Mongolian horses belonging to the 15th Infantry. First Dud taught me how to handle the horse, how to get it to stop sharply, how to get it to turn quickly to the right or left from a stop, and how to get it to "ride off," or push an opponent's horse off the line of the ball so that I could hit it or the opponent could not hit it. I learned the rules, all the fouls to be avoided, and who had the right of way in each situation. After two or three weeks of this, Dud decided I was ready for the real thing.

In those days in the army, mornings were spent in military training; afternoons were devoted to athletics. The officers coached, supervised, or played. Polo was one of the sports played exclusively by the officers. They played twice during the week, sort of practice matches, and then on Saturday afternoon in more formal matches. The formal matches were characterized by white riding breeches, team shirts, and our best helmets. The ladies and friends were present as spectators during these matches, and at the end of the matches, the players, their wives, and friends enjoyed cocktails. Ginger beer for me since I was only thirteen or fourteen at the time.

I played every day that I could in the practice matches. School interfered to some extent. I played occasionally in the Saturday matches. Even if I wasn't playing, I went out and watched to learn as much as I could. Playing on the small Mongolian horses was also helpful. I could

use the shorter mallet, which was easier to control. This was my introduction to polo. Later, at West Point, I played with some close friends.
George Brown and his younger brother Tim and I were on the football
team together at Immaculata High School in Leavenworth, Kansas.[5]
Ted deSaussure and I roomed together at Beanie Millard's, the West
Point Prep School in Washington, DC.[6] George and Ted were admitted
to the academy in the class of 1941. I failed the physical exam due to a
hernia, but passed it the following year and was admitted in the class
of 1942.

We had a marvelous polo pony at West Point, government owned, of
course. We used to play against some of the best players in the country;
fun for us, practice for them. All of them would have loved to have been
able to buy that horse from the army. George Brown played the horse
his senior year and I played him the next, my senior year. Polo brought
us all together and solidified our friendship. We stayed in touch through
the years.

At the close of 1934, the army selected Captain Deane to attend the
Command and General Staff College at Fort Leavenworth. After grad-
uating the course, Deane was chosen to stay on as an instructor. The
Deane family spent the next several years living at Fort Leavenworth and
John Jr. attended school at Immaculata High School, "a private Catho-
lic school run by a group of tough nuns who disciplined me from time to
time." Many students at the school came from army families stationed at
Leavenworth.

Here he met and became lifelong friends with the Brown family
and their sons, George and Tim. Both would graduate from West Point
and retire as general officers, Tim as a brigadier general in the army and
George, who rose to serve as the chairman of the Joint Chiefs of Staff, as
an air force general. All three successively served as captain of the polo
team in the year of their graduation, George Brown in 1941, Deane in
1942, and Tim Brown in 1943.

Upon his high school graduation, Deane enrolled at Beanie Mil-
lard's, a prep school in Washington, DC, that specialized in an intensive
cramming course that prepared young men to take the rigorous entrance
examination for West Point. Millard's was popular with military families
whose children were vying for an appointment to the military academy
but had been faced with many school changes and uneven instruction
over the course of family deployments.

Deane's scores in his first attempt at the entrance test were high
enough to receive a Presidential Appointment. Unfortunately, the failed

physical exam made him ineligible to enter the West Point class of 1941. Forced to wait until the following year, he decided to enlist in the army. My father was somewhat opposed to my decision. He felt that I might not get into West Point if I enlisted. When I entered the army, I took the examination again and earned the highest score for both the Presidential and Army Appointments. With no problem with the exams and completely healthy, I entered the West Point class of 1942.

Incidentally, the year that I spent as an enlisted man was probably the single most important year in my life. I learned more that year about leadership—about what men aspire to, what influences them, what motivates them—than in any other year in my life. I attribute this to my company first sergeant, First Sergeant Oliver, whom I vividly remember to this day.

I was initially assigned to G Company of the 16th Infantry Regiment at Governor's Island, New York. At that time, the 16th Infantry was a show regiment, the same thing that the 3rd Infantry is in Washington today. We paraded in New York, put on parades at Governor's Island, and so forth. We used to send out funeral details for veterans to provide firing squads. When veterans needed some kind of support at a function, the regiment would provide it. I can remember that the soldiers all liked to be assigned to either a Polish wedding or an Irish wake, because they got deeply involved in the festivities. The funerals weren't anything great, but the wakes and the Polish weddings were fantastic!

I stayed in Company G for a while. I learned how to shine my shoes. In those days we used to take all of the finish off a pair of shoes, then take a piece of bone or toothbrush handle and rub that shoe until it was as smooth as glass. Then we applied polish to it until you could see your face in it. We had a special kind of dye that made our shoes a certain color, and they were all alike. I had good officers there, though none that I can remember well.

I was soon transferred to A Company, 16th Infantry, which was stationed by itself at Fort Dix, New Jersey—then called Camp Dix. I was transferred to A Company because I had taken and passed the test to get into the West Point Prep School, which was located at Fort Dix. I learned a number of valuable lessons while I was stationed here.

My main influence was First Sergeant Oliver. He was well along in years; it seemed to me at the time that he was an old man, but he was probably only in his forties. The first sergeant was a very fine man of tremendous character. He was firm but at the same time very approachable. He was very considerate and concerned about the welfare of the soldiers in his company. This impressed me greatly, because we all sort of wor-shipped him.

I remember he was a fantastic rifle shot. When I was preparing to go on the range for the first time as a soldier, we used a .22-caliber rifle on a small target range. One day I was shooting and the first sergeant came over. He took my rifle and said, "You know, the importance of squeez-ing the trigger when you have a perfect sight picture can't be overem-phasized. That squeeze decides whether you'll hit the bull's-eye or you won't."

He was shooting standing up with no support. He waved the rifle back and forth through an arc of about six inches, and eventually it would go off. He would say, "Can you see where I hit?" I couldn't see, so I assumed he was hitting the bull's-eye. After the third shot, the target flopped down and was hanging by one tack. He had shot out the other three tacks! But he had demonstrated the importance of squeezing the trigger only when he had exactly the right sight picture. With that simple demonstration, I became an expert rifleman.

This was a very nice method of teaching. At the same time he gener-ated a lot of respect in his ability—without getting up there and saying, "Look what I can do." It was almost like a joke, but you learned some-thing from that. I saw him work with soldiers who got into trouble; he saw something in them that the officers didn't understand. He would plead their case with the officers to ensure they received a just punish-ment, but not one far beyond what was required in light of their particu-lar circumstances.

I had a company commander who was very much like First Ser-geant Oliver. He was also an older man—Captain O'Neil. One thing that impressed me about him was that he let the first sergeant handle the non-commissioned officers. Captain O'Neil didn't go down and run the pla-toons, squads, or individuals. He saw that the proper people ran those units, and he devoted his time to those responsibilities for which he had been made a captain.

After about six months of duty, I was assigned to the prep school, which took me out of the normal day-to-day soldier business. I was really just a student. This was also an interesting and useful experience.

At Fort Dix, in those days, there were no modern barracks. They were all old World War I buildings, ramshackle as could be and about to fall down. A number of parking garages were located near the prep school. I had a car parked down there that I used to drive back to New York on the weekends to see my parents when I could get away. One day, when I came to get my car, there was a truck parked across the front of the garage and I couldn't get out. The truck belonged to the guard detail, who were down the street having a beer or something. When I asked if they would move the truck, they handed me the keys and told me to go ahead and move it for them.

As soon as I started it up, an officer jumped up on the running board and ordered me out. It turned out that he ran the motor pool, and some of his vehicles had recently been stolen for short periods. Soldiers would just take them to do something they wanted to do, then return them. He thought that this was another case of an unauthorized use of a vehicle and decided to make an example of me and preferred charges.

Here I was, studying to go to West Point—my whole ambition in life—and I could see it going down the tubes pretty fast. So I went to my platoon sergeant of students and told him my problem. Without any doubt in me, or any question, or any concern about his own well-being, he successfully went to war for me and got me out of this situation. He was doing what you should do as an officer: take care of your soldiers. That was a lesson that was not lost on me, I can assure you.

During my enlistment, I had an operation to correct a hernia that had caused me to fail my physical exam the year before and I was assigned to light duties during my convalescence. During that period, my father was temporarily assigned from his position in New York to Fort Dix. They were having trouble constructing a rifle range down there that could handle the new ammunition that had just come into the army. This new ammunition had a greater range, so that all the barrier walls on the ranges had to be strengthened to keep the rounds from straying off the reservation.

My father was put in charge of the task, because someone had failed to perform it properly, and it was in danger of not being completed on time. I was assigned as his motorcycle driver. He rode in the sidecar and I drove the motorcycle. During this assignment, I witnessed something in my father that I had never experienced as a kid. His job was to get the range built on time, and there wasn't anything that was going to stop him.

I remember one morning when only about half of the dump trucks showed up to haul dirt. I drove my father back to the garage, and we found the rest of the trucks. The mechanics were all lying around drinking coffee, smoking cigarettes, and reading comic books. My father went to the head of the motor pool and said, "Where are my trucks?" The guy said, "We have to do normal maintenance." My father said, "You call that normal maintenance—all those guys sitting around doing nothing?" The guy started to stammer a little. My father said, "If those trucks are not out on the rifle range in an hour, I'm coming back, and when I do, I'll have your job." Very shortly, the dump trucks showed up at the range.

I had never heard my father talk in such a quiet but deadly voice before. I learned a lesson from that. You can't put up with incompetence. If you have a job to do, you just have to lay it to the incompetent people or get them out. Those were some of the major experiences I had as an enlisted man that had a bearing on my later life.

In our West Point class of 1942, two of us went on to become four-star generals: Lucius Clay, the son of famous General Lucius D. Clay, an air force general officer, and myself.[7] The lowest graduate in our class but the first guy who made general officer was Jack Crowley.[8] Jack was in my company and a good friend of mine. He was pretty bright but got hurt playing football or something in his plebe year. He was in the hospital for a while, missed a lot of classes, and got down to the bottom of the class. His decision to stay there was by design, not happenstance. To stay at the bottom, behind some of the really dumb guys, and not get kicked out was really a great feat. He accomplished it and later became the first of our class to make general.

A number of other men from the class of 1942 rose to become general officers. Tom Rienzi, who was a signal officer, rose to the rank of lieutenant general.[9] Bob Terry, also a signal officer, was a major general.[10] Danny Raymond, an engineer officer, retired as a major general.[11] Crit Crittenberger, whose father was also a general officer, retired as a major general.[12] I'm sure there are quite a number of others, but those come to mind immediately.

My roommate at West Point was James E. Josendale, or "Josy." We first became friends while attending the West Point Preparatory School together. Josy enjoyed lacrosse and, as a cadet sergeant in his first class year, was the bearer of the proud I Company guidon, which I commanded. He was also a Sunday school teacher and worked on the *Pointer* staff. Between classes, he would lay a doubled-up comforter on the springs of his bunk and say, "Wake me up in five minutes," and be asleep as the last word left his mouth. His dislike for studying and difficulty with spelling led to his revered "goat" standing near the bottom of our class.

He met his wife Dorothy while we were all in New Haven attending the Army-Yale football game in 1939. Dottie and a friend were in the car we flagged down and begged for a ride to the train station. Without that ride, Josy might never have met Dottie, and we would probably have missed the train formation. On the way to the station—whether it was love at first sight or the attraction of her LaSalle convertible—Josy asked Dottie to the academy the following weekend.

The two married the day after graduation. We were together again at the infantry basic course at Fort Benning, and from there, Josy reported to the 90th Infantry Division. When the 90th arrived in England in 1944, Josy volunteered to join the Office of Strategic Services (OSS) and spent the remainder of the war with the 9th Army OSS detachment in Europe. He resigned from the army in 1946 as a captain and went to work for Wire Rope Corporation of America, a business owned by Dottie's family. They lived in St. Joseph, Missouri, and during the 1950s, while Josy's classmates were attending the command and general staff course at Fort Leavenworth, he and Dottie would throw a great annual party. They would send a bus, complete with a bar and bartender, to Fort Leavenworth to pick us up and transport us to their country club in St. Jo. After dinner and a night of dancing, the bus would return us to Leavenworth.

I graduated from the United States Military Academy on May 29, 1942.[13] I immediately left for California with two classmates and a cadet going on yearling furlough. My classmates were Dick Clark and Jack Heard. The yearling I do not remember. We went in Dick's brand-new car. Dick Clark was in my company at the academy. At least the last two years there, our rooms were right across the hall from each other. Dick and his roommate, Bill Corley, and Josy and I became very close friends. Dick was one of my favorite classmates. He was a captain in the Air Corps and squadron commander. Unfortunately, he was killed during an air mission over Neustadt, Austria, in 1944. Survivors who bailed out of the crippled heavy bomber said he rode his ship to the ground after determining that all other members of the crew had bailed out safely.

Johnny Heard was the brother of Betty Heard, who was the reason for my trip to California. I was going to marry her at Camp Cook, where her father, Major General Jack Heard, was the commanding general of the 5th Armored Division. On the way to San Diego, we stopped in Gila Bend, then a very small town between Phoenix and Yuma. It was typical of the western towns you see in the cowboy movies. We went into the saloon to have a beer. There were two things that keep Gila Bend a vivid memory. First, the people there all had skin that looked like weathered leather. They looked completely dried out. Second, I thought to myself, "I hope I never have to come to a place like this again." But a year and a half later, I was back in the same desert, just a few miles away, on maneuvers with the 104th Infantry Division.

2

Terry Allen and the 104th Infantry Division

After my wedding, I returned to Fort Benning to take the infantry officer basic course and reported to my new unit, the 104th Infantry Division. Due to allocation of school slots in my division, after nine months as a platoon leader and executive officer I was sent back to Benning for the infantry advanced course. There were two of us I can recall from my regiment who had about the same length of service. The other fellow was Hugh Carey, who later became the governor of New York. Many of the other students in our class had several years of service. Many had been Reserve officers and had been on active duty for a year or two. Others were National Guard officers who had five or six years of experience before coming on to active duty. Hugh and I were the exception to the norms in terms of length of service.

In those days, the army tried to cram as much training as they could into you. If you were due to go overseas at some point, they wanted you to have all the training possible before you went. Because Hugh and I had become company commanders relatively quickly, our regimental commander wanted us to get the schooling that would help us. This schooling was a great help, as a matter of fact. When I came back from the school to the regiment, I immediately became the regimental S2 (intelligence officer). Hugh became the operations officer. We moved into positions that typically were filled by majors, and stayed in those slots as the regiment went into combat.

While we were at school, the whole division moved from Camp Adair, Oregon, to the desert in the eastern part of Oregon. We trained there until about November 1943. Then the whole division moved down to the California-Arizona maneuver area, about halfway between Phoenix and Yuma, in the desert. We trained down there until March or so and then moved to Camp Carson in Colorado, where we finished our training and went overseas.

As the new regimental S2, I studied manuals and lesson plans from Benning. The lieutenant who had been the S2 ahead of me had been an acting S2 for quite a long time, and he taught me a few things. The intelligence sergeant had certain experience and also helped me. From then on, you learned by the school of hard knocks.

I remember the first training exercise we had—the first after I came back and became the S2. I sent a patrol to get intelligence that was important in the planning of the next phase of the operation of the regiment. The patrol, for reasons I can't recall, didn't get back with the information in time to have any value to the regimental commander's decision about what to do next.

Brigadier General Bryant Moore, who had been a great hero as a regimental commander at Guadalcanal, was our assistant division commander.[1] He got up at the after-action critique and really hauled me over the coals in front of everybody for my failure to provide the regimental commander with the necessary information. I had not done my job as a regimental intelligence officer very well. That was a pretty motivational event. I decided that I didn't want that to happen again, so I worked at intelligence even harder from then on. That's how I learned.

I almost got pulled out of the division at one time, because General Wedemeyer needed an aide to go with him to Southeast Asia.[2] He and my father were good friends; he admired my father and figured that his son would probably be okay as an aide. Well, fortunately for me, in my view, I didn't get that job. With our decentralized promotion system at the time, the officer who did a really good job had a chance to progress; he didn't have to wait his turn in line and watch all the bums go through the upper echelons before he got his chance, just because they were a little more senior. Hugh Carey and I moved up to the rank of major in very short order. I don't say that to be boastful; I think we demonstrated our abilities later in life when he became governor of New York and I became a four-star general. It was obvious that we had some capability, and that was recognized in the early stages of our career.

Some of the broken-down National Guard captains in the division were not getting promoted, while Hugh, myself, and others like us were passing over them. With a centralized promotion system, they would just look at an officer and say, "Well, he has five years of service and needs to be promoted." So there were a few advantages to the promotion system we had in World War II.

My regiment, the 415th, deployed to Europe two months after D-Day. The 104th Infantry Division saw almost two hundred days of continuous fighting through Belgium and western Germany; we were never pulled off the frontlines. We deployed, I think, in August 1944, and entered combat in October.

My intelligence school training at Fort Ritchie helped me in a couple of respects. One, I learned something about the general methodology of running the S2 business. They also had an outstanding photo interpretation course there, and I learned to interpret photos. Both as the S2 of the regiment and later as a battalion commander, I found that I relied very heavily on photographs to give me an idea of what I might expect in the battle that we were planning for and were about to fight. That photo interpretation course enhanced my ability to read maps, to visualize things from a point of ten thousand or twenty thousand feet in the air, seeing what was on the ground, and visualizing what it was. That was very valuable to me.

So later, as a battalion commander, when we got prisoners, I'd go there and tell the interrogators the kind of questions I wanted asked. I even used to sit down with the prisoners and the interrogator over a map or some aerial photos of the positions that they had been in. Then I'd find out where the machine guns were, where they had laid minefields, where their barbed wire was, those things. So that came out of the school as well.

Our division shipped by rail from Camp Carson, Colorado, to Camp Kilmer, New Jersey. We moved to the ships just like you would in any military formation moving out to the field. Each company moved at a certain time and went to a certain ship and you got on it. Our regiment boarded the *Christobal*. They had rosters of where you were assigned to sleep and so forth. We left New York Harbor on August 27 to rendezvous with a large convoy. Some guys began to play poker; other guys got seasick.

I think the crossing took us ten days. We didn't really do much training on the ship. In the first place, we were pretty crowded. Secondly, there wasn't much space to do much training. In fact, a lot of people were sick. We encountered heavy weather and rough waters for most of the voyage. They had so many troops so crammed in on those ships that the odors made you sick just to go below deck. Once guys began to get sick, it got worse and worse. It was awful. I've never seen so many people get seasick.

I think we anchored off of Utah Beach on September 7, 1944. The

104th Infantry Division became the first American division to land in France directly from the States. The first job we had was guarding the lines of communications. We had people who rode the trains, people who went with convoys, and so forth. There was a lot of theft. Guys would steal a truck full of supplies: cigarettes, candy bars, food, and rations worth their weight in gold.

For a few weeks, we guarded supply lines and then we were assigned to the British I Corps, 1st Canadian Army, up in Belgium. We went with them through Belgium into Holland and helped to clear the areas north of Antwerp. Our division entered combat operations on October 25, 1944. When we finished that operation, we got far enough north that we were sent through Aachen, which had already been captured, into the line around Eschweiler. That was on the corridor that led to Cologne and later turned out to be the northern flank of the Bulge.

We continued to hold the northern flank during the Battle of the Bulge. Everything below us got pushed in. Then we continued to Cologne. Later we went up the Rhine, crossed, circled through the Ruhr Pocket, and headed east. We went through Leipzig and ended up on the Mulde River, which was a tributary of the Elbe. I guess we stopped there. When the war ended, my battalion was moved up to Magdeburg, at the confluence of the Mulde and the Elbe. We held that area for a while, and watched the Russians on the other side of the river.

Our regimental commander, Colonel John H. Cochran, was a student of warfare.[3] He was a bachelor married to the army. He didn't read novels; he read field manuals and military history. He believed strongly in the importance of intelligence to the commander. Accordingly, when he assigned Lieutenant Everett Pruitt as the platoon leader of the Intelligence & Reconnaissance (I&R) Platoon, he gave Pruitt the latitude to choose any soldiers in the regiment to fill the unit. Everett was an excellent choice to command this unit. His unselfishness and leadership ability were immediately evident to all. I would later recommend him for the Medal of Honor for leading a patrol on December 30, 1944, that stumbled into a minefield and suffered several casualties. Pruitt single-handedly fought a rear-guard action as the remainder of the patrol carried the wounded men to safety. He richly deserved the award, but the nomination was downgraded and he was awarded a Distinguished Service Cross (DSC) for his actions.

Pruitt was a world-class track star and a former member of the Pepperdine College four-hundred-yard relay team, which had set a world record a year or two earlier. He was in superb physical condition and he wanted physically fit, intelligent, self-confident men in his platoon. He believed college athletes would fit the bill. He had his choice of all the men assigned to the regiment.

Once he had selected his men, he trained them hard. His platoon could beat any kind of sporting team assembled from the rest of the entire regiment. They could outperform any other unit in any phase of military tasks. They worked together as a well-oiled machine.

During the patrol in which he would earn the DSC, we needed all the intelligence we could get on the enemy's position, his defenses, and any obstacles the regiment might encounter in our river crossing. This was needed to minimize casualties and allow an effective night attack, which was the hallmark of the Timberwolf Division.

Pruitt and his men planned a patrol across the Roer River to capture a prisoner. They had spotted a German bunker that appeared to be occupied by three German soldiers at night. This bunker was in the median between the lanes of an autobahn passing through the area, similar to our interstate highways. Using measurements obtained with an engineer transit, they calculated the distance from the river bank to the bunker. They laid out a course on the ground to the bunker. They used this course for several nights to practice getting from the river bank to the bunker.

Their means of crossing the river was a destroyed bridge on the autobahn. Pruitt took a patrol of eight men across the bridge and started for the bunker in the lead. He later told me all was going well when he heard an explosion behind him. Thinking one of his men had thrown a grenade, he rushed back to find out why. He found that one of his men had stepped on an antipersonnel mine known as the Schu-mine. The mine had cost the man his foot and had put the entire mission at risk.

Pruitt decided to have two men take the wounded man back to safety while he continued the mission with the other four. It was still not known that they were in a minefield. One of the two men who attempted to lift the wounded man was standing on a Schu-mine. The added weight on the mine caused it to detonate and he, too, lost a foot. Pruitt now had two men who could not move on their own. It would take two of the remaining men to carry each of their wounded friends. The second explosion had alerted the Germans and they sent out a patrol to investigate.

Realizing that the mission had been compromised and recognizing the danger to his men, Pruitt ordered one of the men to get back across the river to alert friendly forces as to what had happened. He ordered the rest of the men to help the wounded to safety while he covered them with fire. About this time a third man was incapacitated by a mine. Now there were three of the six remaining men helping the three wounded while Pruitt fought a rear-guard action alone.

We had planned artillery fires between the patrol and the Germans in the event the patrol was discovered. The patrol would fire a flare into the air to signal they wanted the artillery support. Pruitt fired the flare and the artillery began its protective fires. This slowed the German patrol momentarily, but they pressed on. Pruitt fought them every inch of the way. He withdrew a few yards at a time as his men made their way toward the bridge. Pruitt finally reached the end of the bridge and determined to make a last stand there until his men were safe.

He fired at the German patrol until he ran out of ammunition. Suddenly, in a scooped-out section of the concrete, he felt three grenades. Ignoring his own safety, he stood up and threw the grenades at the oncoming Germans and prepared to take them on in hand-to-hand combat. Pruitt was strong, athletic, and a tough cookie. I am sure he would have done well against them.

The grenades again slowed the Germans down. As they regrouped, Pruitt's men called out that they were safe. He made his way back to safety when he knew his men were safe. I never met a more courageous man. I recommended Pruitt for the Medal of Honor, a recognition he so richly deserved. Instead, he was awarded the Distinguished Service Cross, the second-highest award our nation bestows for gallantry in action against an armed enemy.

As my regiment was moving up in Belgium toward Holland, the Germans began falling back, but we did not know how far or when they might stop and make a stand. As the S2, it was my job to find out. I decided the best thing to do was to take the I&R Platoon and scout out the Germans. The I&R Platoon belonged to Lieutenant Pruitt, but on occasions, I led it on patrols.

We took off late at night with the idea of returning before dawn. There were twenty-four of us in six jeeps. We moved cautiously but with good speed. After we had gone about two miles, the lead jeep stopped suddenly. I was in the second jeep and jumped out to investigate. In the meantime, the platoon immediately dismounted from the jeeps and formed a perimeter out twenty-five to fifty meters from the road. They did this without command. It was a part of their training.

When I reached the lead jeep, I saw a German soldier in a foxhole beside the road. My adrenaline must have really been pumping because I reached down and pulled him right out of the hole. One of my clerks in the S2 section was Marty Glick. Marty was a Jewish kid from New York

who had been a music arranger for one of the big-time bands. His importance to me lay not in his musical abilities but in the fact that he could
speak Yiddish, broken German, or a combination of both. Anyway, he
could communicate with the Germans. We always took him on patrols
when we thought there might be a need for his limited but effective lin-
guistic abilities. I admired him. He would go with us despite a great fear
of what would happen to a Jewish soldier if captured.

Glick determined two things immediately. The German I had pulled
out of the hole had a companion who was also sleeping in the same hole.
We got him out too. He also found out that we were in the middle of a
German infantry company of about sixty men. Our mission was complete at this point. We knew where the enemy was. Now was the time to
get out.

I ordered the platoon sergeant to get the vehicles turned around and
then ran back to my jeep and radioed to regiment our location and the
fact that we had contacted a German unit of sixty men. About this time a
shot rang out near the rear of our column. As I ran back to find out what
had happened, I saw a German soldier who turned out to be an officer on
the bank, silhouetted against the sky with a grenade in his upraised hand.
I whirled and fired my carbine from the hip. I could hear, at least I thought
I heard, the shot thud into his stomach. Not knowing whether I had killed
him, and being fearful that he still might throw the grenade, I ran up the
bank and finished him off.

That was when I discovered he was an officer. He had a Luger pistol,
one of most prized trophies of the war. I took the pistol, which was stolen from me some years later, and continued to the rear of the column.
By this time, the firefight was building to a crescendo. I ordered the men
back to their vehicles. I quickly accounted for them all and then ordered
everyone to mount up and get going. Our original two prisoners had
been killed in the course of the action, and besides the officer I had shot,
the patrol had killed eleven other Germans. We had no idea how many
we wounded, but we did capture another prisoner. We brought him back
with us lying across the hood of my jeep. Our only casualty was our
medic, who was grazed across his left cheek by a bullet.

When we reached regimental headquarters, the assistant division
commander, Brigadier General Moore, was there conferring with Colonel Cochrane. They called me into the colonel's tent and had me describe
the events of the evening. For my actions, I later learned, General Moore
had directed the award of the Silver Star, my first decoration of the war.[4]

General Moore was later promoted to major general and left the

104th to command the 8th Infantry Division. Many years later, after I had moved to Gouldsboro, Maine, I happened to be driving down a street in the neighboring town of Ellsworth when I noticed Bryant E. Moore School. I couldn't believe my eyes; I went in and discovered that General Moore's hometown was just down the road from where we had decided to settle down and the local community had named the school after him.

On March 2, as the division was preparing a regimental attack before daylight, a German shell struck the command post of the 2nd Battalion, 414th Infantry, killing the battalion commander, Lieutenant Colonel Joseph M. Cummins Jr., and two visiting officers, the regimental commander, Colonel Anthony J. Touart, and Colonel George A. Smith Jr., the new assistant division commander. A bunch of other guys were in a cellar making plans for the operation when the shell came in. It was from a big railroad gun, like a 240 millimeter—just a tremendous hunk of metal. It didn't even explode, but it killed Tony Touart and a couple of his battalion commanders. So our regimental exec took over as the new regimental commander. One of our battalion commanders became the regimental exec. That left a battalion open.

Lieutenant Colonel Gerald Kelleher was promoted and assigned to command the 414th Infantry Regiment with the death of Colonel Touart, and Lieutenant Colonel Peter Denisevich, commander of the 2nd Battalion, 415th Regiment, was moved to the 415th Regiment as executive officer to replace him. Deane was chosen to replace Denisevich as commander of the 2nd Battalion.

I thought the only majors that really had much going for them at the time were Hugh Carey and myself. The other battalion execs were majors, but most of them were older guys. They had come up through the National Guard, but they weren't really all that great. As S2, I had been out and done a lot of patrolling. So I got the nod to get the battalion, because I had actual experience of running operations.

During the evening of March 2, 1945, elements of the 3rd Armored Division seized the town of Oberhausen on the outskirts of Cologne. As they moved forward to their new objectives at 0500 the next morning, elements of the 2nd and 3rd Battalions, 415th Infantry, arrived to replace them. The armored columns, in seizing Oberhausen during the night, bypassed scattered pockets of resistance. Major Deane, while on reconnaissance overlooking the edge of his objective, personally took nineteen prisoners.[5]

I led the battalion through Cologne. When we entered the city, I had issued orders to do certain things a certain way. One of my company execs, Bill Dyer (William Connell Dyer Jr., from Salem, Oregon), had been an acting company commander while his commander was wounded and off in a hospital; Dyer was sort of bitter about being put back in his old position of exec when his CO returned, but I didn't have another company to give him.

Contrary to our orders on how to proceed through Cologne, he grabbed a few guys and just took off. His group knocked off some snipers and went down to the Rhine River. I found out after they returned. On the one hand, of course, I was unhappy. He had disobeyed orders, and his actions could have cost his life and those of the men he took with him. On the other hand, the people at division had heard about the action and thought it was great that my battalion was the first to reach the Rhine and so forth.

When Bill Dyer got back to my command post, I took disciplinary action because of what he had done. At the same time, because of his courage, I gave him a medal. The people from headquarters were saying, "You have to send a bottle of water out of the Rhine to the commanding general." I didn't want to send soldiers back down to the Rhine just to get a bottle of water. Someone might get shot, and it wasn't worth sending a soldier down there again. So we got a beer bottle that was lying around someplace, went out to the rain barrel, filled it up, and sent it to the division commander.

A week or so later, I was at division headquarters for some meeting. Old Terry Allen, who was a tremendous leader, had this beer bottle sitting on his desk and was telling everybody that it was filled with water from the Rhine. Years later, after I got to know Allen well, I told him the truth. He always spoke highly of me, thought I was a good battalion commander, and always told people that I was one of the best battalion commanders that he ever had. I can remember that because it pleased me so much, especially coming from a man I loved, admired, and respected so greatly. I thought to myself that one of the reasons he was so good to me was that he saw himself in me when he was a young man in World War I.

Terry retired in El Paso. He told me early on that any time I came to El Paso or Fort Bliss, he wanted me to call him regardless of the hour, day or night. I visited Fort Bliss several times. I usually arrived in the late afternoon or early evening. When I called, he would tell me to go to the bar in the Officers' Club, pick up a bottle of scotch, and put it on his tab. He would meet me in an hour or so, and we would spend the evening and half the night consuming the entire bottle, talking about leadership, war situations, and so on. It was always a great experience for me.[6]

Once, while I was working as the executive officer to the secretary of the army, Frank Pace, we traveled to El Paso for a speech. Terry heard we were coming and called me to ask for some time with the secretary. I arranged a breakfast meeting. Terry wanted to talk to Pace because he wanted to be recalled to active duty and assigned to command a division in the Korean War, which was under way at that time. Terry had been jogging five miles every day and had been working out in the gym. He was in great shape. He wanted to get back in the action. Pace talked to Joe Collins, then the chief of staff, when we got back to Washington. Collins refused to go along with the idea for a variety of reasons, all of which I guess were sound.

I first saw Terry Allen when I was a kid of about ten at Fort Benning. My dad was the company commander of G Company, 29th Infantry Regiment at the time. Polo was a big sport among the officers then. Terry Allen was one of the polo players, perhaps the most outstanding and without question the most flamboyant. He rode a horse like it was part of him. He was daring—cutting in front of other riders, slamming into other players to keep them off the ball—just an exciting player, a man who loved life and lived right on the edge of it all the time.

When Terry took command of the 104th Division, he inherited a very well-trained unit, courtesy of "Doc" Cook, one of the George C. Marshall team that had brought the Infantry School to prominence at Benning in the late 1920's and early 1930's. The 104th Division, however, had no great spirit, drive, or pride. Terry Allen instilled that immediately. First of all, he built on the fact that our division shoulder patch bore the silver head of a timberwolf on a green background howling at the moon—presumably the moon, even though the moon was not part of the patch. We were the Timberwolves. No one else in the army was a Timberwolf. He signed all letters, directives, policies, and such not as "Terry Allen, Commanding General," as provided for in regulations, but as "Terry Allen, Chief Timberwolf."

The second big thing he did was to institute night training. He planned that when we went into combat, we would always attack at night, and we trained to do this. We trained to be comfortable operating in the dark, and we became known as the Night Fighters and were proud of that distinction.

Finally, and the greatest thing, was Terry's personality, his manner, his actions. When he came to see the troops, he did not come as the big-shot division commander, He came as a warrior just like them, a man who shared their accomplishments and their failures, their disappointments and their joys. He was easy to know. He had a devilish smile that said he liked life and fun just as much as they did. His smile conveyed the feeling that he was happy as hell to be with his soldiers, so happy that he was about to pop.

His soldiers loved him. He made the division. He developed its spirit and pride, he instilled the qualities that made the 104th one of the best in the army. He demonstrated why General Marshall had thought enough of him to give him command of another division after he had been relieved of command of the Big Red One.

In all of my personal encounters with Terry Allen, I cannot recall a single instance in which he complained or dwelt on any adverse aspect of his life. He lived for the moment, he lived for the future, he lived for what he could do—not to recall or even try to erase memories of instances when others, correctly or incorrectly, thought he had not measured up. When he and I sat up all night, during my several visits to Fort Bliss in later years, drinking a bottle of scotch and reminiscing, he never mentioned any unpleasant incidents in his life or career.

The knowledge I have of his being relieved of command of the 1st Infantry Division in Sicily may or may not bear some relationship to the facts of the matter. There were stories, recollections, rumors passed down over time by soldiers who might have been present when certain events occurred, and whose memories may be clear or perhaps a bit blurred. Anyway, this is what I have heard.

The 1st Infantry Division was a highly charged outfit that reflected the daring, hell-bent-for-action character of Terry Allen. Reportedly, when they had time off from the rigors of combat in North Africa, they would tear up the towns they visited—get drunk and get in fights. People complained about this, and in one instance, an inspector general investigator was sent to the 1st Division to look into these charges. Terry suggested they go into the nearest big town that night. When they did, every 1st Division soldier they met, unlike other soldiers, saluted smartly and said something like, "Good evening, General." They were model soldiers and outshone their fellow counterparts in other divisions by a large measure. Terry asked, "What do you find objectionable in the behavior of my soldiers? They look pretty good to me."

But the charges persisted, and one night Lieutenant General George Patton, senior to Terry, visited the 1st Division. Terry and Patton were both cavalrymen. They had competed throughout their careers with each other, and I do not think they really liked each other. After dinner, Patton, Terry, and Teddy Roosevelt, the assistant division commander of the 1st Division, sat around a campfire drinking and swapping war stories. At one point, Patton made some demeaning remarks about the 1st Division. Terry stood up, almost challenging Patton to do the same. Patton got up and Terry took a swing at him. Terry missed, and supposedly, he fell into the bonfire. Teddy got up and decked Patton. Terry was relieved over this incident. It appears no action was taken against Roosevelt, perhaps because his decking Patton would have revealed an incident not in keeping with Patton's reputation as being a pretty tough guy. Anyway, that was the story that circulated among soldiers at the time explaining his relief.

The more telling fact of the matter was that General Marshall had such a high regard for Terry's leadership abilities that he gave him another division command after his return to the States. While I have since read later accounts that named General Bradley as the main instigator for Allen's removal, all of the stories I heard firsthand at the time blamed Patton for the act.

Major General Terry Allen passed away nearly fifty years ago, in 1969. Jack Deane was no doubt the last soldier left alive who could personally comment on the character and leadership skills of the controversial Big Red One commander. After all, they had a standing social appointment whenever Deane's work took him to El Paso.

Deane's recollection might have been no more than an initial account explaining Allen's relief as told by 1st Division soldiers, many of whom were supporters of Terry Allen and disliked Patton. There is no evidence that the bonfire story ever happened. Deane was also correct that it appeared to be General Bradley's decision, not Patton's, to relieve Allen over what he believed was Allen's tolerance of poor discipline within the Big Red One.[7] Eisenhower and Bradley wanted cooperative team players, not go-it-alone mavericks, within their command organization. When Allen returned to the States, Marshall effectively overruled them by giving Allen another division and sending him back into combat.[8]

When we were in combat with the 104th Division in Europe, Terry visited down to the battalion level almost daily. I do not recall ever accompanying him down to any companies in my battalion. One incident that I do recall rather vividly occurred during the period after a German special ops guy parachuted in behind our lines with a force of unknown size. His mission was believed to be the assassination of General Eisenhower in particular and of any senior officers in general. *As part of the Ger-*

man Ardennes offensive in late 1944, Colonel Otto Skorzeny's English-speaking troops were charged with infiltrating American lines disguised in American uniforms in order to conduct sabotage operations and cause confusion to support the German attack. This led to a significant increase in the level of security. Passwords, signs, and countersigns took on a great importance.

Terry visited my battalion command post one night during this period of heightened security. Passwords and stuff like that were not important in Terry's scheme of things, so the guard would not let him into the command post. Terry's aide and his driver did not have the password. My guard, a new replacement, stood firm—no password, no admittance to the command post. About that time, one of my long-term sergeants came along. He said to the guard, "You had better let him in to see the colonel. That's the Chief Timberwolf." He did not say General Allen, he did not say the division commander—he just called him the Chief Timberwolf. Terry walked in with that "I am about to pop" smile and told me what had happened. He loved it.

The love for Terry was demonstrated in one of the combat actions of the division while I was still the regimental S2. The division had recently moved from operations in Belgium directed at the approaches to the port of Antwerp. We were now fighting in the industrial area around Weisweiler and Eschweiler, east of Aachen. At one point, the better part of a battalion was advancing over an area covered by slag piles, which were the remnants of the coal fuel used in the factories. These slag piles were like rock. The Germans became very stubborn in this area and were pouring fire on our troops, who could not dig in for protection. The decision was made by the regimental commander to withdraw from our positions on the slag piles and attack around them.

About that time, Lieutenant General Joe Lawton Collins, the corps commander, arrived at our command post (CP). He was known as Lightning Joe. Collins had made a great reputation for himself. He had been one of the young stars at Fort Benning in the early 1930's on Marshall's team that I mentioned earlier. Then he had been an outstanding division commander in the Pacific before being promoted to lieutenant general and assigned to command the VII Corps in Europe during the invasion and subsequent fighting. I always felt that he was motivated by a desire to build on his accomplishments.

When General Collins heard we had pulled back from the slag piles, he was furious. He was stating in very threatening terms that we, a new and young division, had to understand that once you took ground, you never gave it up. The threat was that failure to hold ground once it was taken could lead to being relieved of command. I was present. I heard the threat. I interpreted it, as did the others who were there, to mean that Collins was thinking about relieving Allen. The word of that thought swept through the division like wildfire.

At that time, the tactical plan of the VII Corps was to attack to the east with three divisions on line—the 29th Division on the north flank, our division in the center, and the 1st Division on the southern flank. Both the 29th and the 1st Divisions were considered experienced, hardened divisions. The plan was that after we reached a certain phase line, a mile or so beyond our position at the time of Collins's visit, our division would be pinched out by the 29th and the 1st and would go into corps reserve.

As I said, the threat of Terry Allen's relief swept through the division like a wildfire. We went into high gear. We attacked with such a fury that the Germans melted and ran from us. When we reached the phase line where we were supposed to be pinched out, we were so far ahead of both the 29th and the 1st Divisions that the entire VII Corps plan had to be changed to exploit the success of our attack. I attribute this entire success to the love for General Allen and his leadership.

At the conclusion of the operation, Collins took the time to write a letter to Allen to express his admiration and appreciation for the work of the 104th Division at Eschweiler. "The operation was a difficult and nasty task, and the division cleared this important area in much shorter time than I expected and with minimum loss. The speed with which this was accomplished is a tribute to the leadership, dash and sound training of the division. I regard the Timberwolf Division as one of the finest assault divisions we have ever had in the Corps."[9]

About the time that I became a battalion commander, I started to develop a philosophy regarding leadership. I had the opportunity, during both combat preparations and actual combat, to observe people pretty closely. I watched them and found some very interesting things. Some tough guys who were ready to knock people out at the first bad word folded under the stress of combat. Others who you would never expect great courage from turned out to be very courageous guys.

The S3 of my battalion was Captain James "Zeke" Grealy from Milwaukee, Wisconsin. Zeke was unimpressive looking, sort of scrawny. He had a nice personality, but he didn't give you the impression of being gung-ho or a leader. Still, he was one of the most courageous guys that I have ever run into. I remember that he and I went on a reconnaissance patrol together. We were told to take a particular village, so we went to take a look at it from a distance. There didn't seem to be any activity around, so we walked closer and closer. Finally, we went into the village. Well, it turned out that the place was full of Germans, but they were afraid we were tricking them or something. So they stayed in the basements as we walked around the village streets.

While we were coming out of that village, we heard all this artillery starting to come in. About four white phosphorus rounds landed within yards of us. Fortunately, they were duds, or we would have been fried. They just went into the ground. It scared the hell out of me, but it didn't seem to bother Grealy at all. I said, "Boy, we were sure lucky on that one." Zeke replied, "If you're not lucky, you're dead," and just walked on like nothing had happened. I couldn't believe it. When I observed people, I found that their comments and their outward appearances weren't necessarily a clue as to how they were going to react under stress.

Gerry Kelleher was a battalion commander within our division who later went to command another regiment within the 104th. Kelleher had been a battalion commander in the 1st Division in Africa with Terry Allen and had followed Terry to our division. He was a tough little Irishman from upstate New York. He later became a brigadier general in the army.[10] I was with Kelleher one night in Holland. We were going through some awful fighting. He was just walking along. There were all these sparks on the street, and he just kept stepping over them. I asked, "What are all these sparks?" He said, "They are electric wires." I couldn't see, but it was shrapnel, hitting the street and sparking off the cobblestones. He was just cooler than hell and didn't seem bothered by it one bit. I was scared to death.

Maybe a month later, we attacked, crossing a little river that was not much wider than thirty feet. The battalion that went across got into a field with some barbed wire and trenches, and surrounded by a minefield. They just stopped. Their commander was in a cellar in the building behind the troops. He wouldn't leave the cellar or answer the radio. The division commander was raising hell because the battalion was holding up the attack. By then it was midday and we hadn't made any progress since they had gotten bogged down in the trenches.

Kelleher was serving as the regimental executive officer (XO) and said, "I'm going out and take a walk." He put on his helmet liner, left the CP, and went down to the river. He grabbed some guy with a boat, went across, and walked up through the minefield. Meanwhile, there was shelling going on and machine guns firing. Kelleher walked across the field to the trenches where the battalion was bogged down and looked down at the men. Some soldier said, "Who is the jerk with the helmet liner?" And he said, "Don't call me a jerk, soldier, or I'll shoot you. Now, get your asses out of those trenches and let's go!" Well, all of those guys moved out of the trenches and went forward.

Kelleher led the troops up to the objective and then got on the radio and called the battalion commander, who still refused to answer. Kelleher said, "So and so! This is Kelleher. I'm on your objective. Get your ass up here!" Well, here is a guy who walks right out into the middle of a battle with a helmet liner on, gets the troops up, and goes on to capture the objective. About two days later, another battalion was held up and he essentially did the same thing. He went down there and personally led the attack. As the regimental executive officer, he didn't have to leave the CP. But he was a natural leader. He was also the only man I have ever known that I believed was fearless. I've seen a lot of guys who I thought were brave, but I've never seen anybody like Kelleher.

My observations led to a philosophy that applies not only to military people, but people in industry as well; this philosophy divides people into four categories. The first is people who are fearless—not just in a physical sense, but in making decisions that may jeopardize the whole corporation, or the guy's whole career or family or something. They don't fear the consequences. Gerry Kelleher was the only military guy that I feel would fall into that category.

Category 2 were the people who are leaders who are just as afraid of things that are happening around them as everybody else, but they have something that drives them on. My personal philosophy was that I wanted to do things that would be approved by my father and his friends. Several things inspire these people. For example, they have a pride in their school—guys who went to Harvard or Princeton, the Naval Academy, West Point, or Southern Cal. For other guys, it's their church, their religion, their belief in God, and so forth. Other guys, it's their family they won't let down. These are the real leaders. They can conquer their fear. This fact permits them to go on to do things that must be done.

The third category are the ones who will follow those leaders. Occasionally you can move people from this category up to the second. These people have fears that they can't quite conquer by themselves, but if somebody is there to lead, they will manage it.

Category 4 are the guys who will quit. No matter what happens, they will quit. That's a very small category, but I did see people like that in World War II—even officers—who just folded. They just couldn't stand it. The disgrace of being relieved and being sent back as a coward or something like that didn't seem to bother them; they were just so afraid of the situation that they couldn't overcome it.

Personally, I found that I looked for people in category 2, because they are the kind of people who you want to surround yourself with. They are leaders, the people who get things done. You have to look for leadership people. Train and nurture them so that they can assume important positions. The followers—you have to have some of those, too. In fact, the majority of your people are in this third category. The people you really want to look out for are the guys who are going to do the job. No matter what the odds, they have what it takes to get the job done. They make your best staff officers because they have the courage to stand up and tell you, "You're wrong, General. Here's the way it ought to be and here's why."

Before we entered combat, our training had been excellent, and we had a good idea of the necessary tactics. We had some breakdowns, but Kelleher fixed them. I could have been a battalion commander several months earlier, had I been pushy. One time, I went down to a bogged-down battalion to find out what was going on. I figured the regimental commander would like to know. The battalion leaders just didn't have the gumption to get going. So I took over one of the companies and led them to the objective.

Once I had gotten the company where it needed to be, the other companies were able to move on to their objectives. The battalion commander was wounded, so they didn't have a leader—just an XO. He was not really a competent leader; he was just sitting back at his CP. A leader has to go out and show up. When he makes an appearance, it gives the soldiers a lift. They begin to think it can't be that tough if this guy is out here.

I could have called up the regimental commander with some bold message like, "This is Deane, I'm on the objective. I have the situation well in hand and have assumed command." He might have relieved me; he might have just left me there. But I didn't do that. I just got the battalion where it was supposed to be. I just went back to the regimental CP and told my boss what had happened. He then made a guy on the staff who was senior to me the battalion commander.

Things didn't function perfectly, but in my view they functioned a lot better than they would have had we not been well trained. We could have had some real disasters. One division (the 106th Infantry Division) came right into the Battle of the Bulge. They were so poorly trained that they walked right down that road, right into death. They had no idea what they were doing, and neither did their leaders. It was a matter of poor training. They lost an awful lot of people.

When we went into combat, we were the only division that almost exclusively attacked at night. We used to attack in the dark, and we would be on our objective by the time other people were starting. We supported them with flanking fire on their objectives, and they still took more casualties than we did. Sometimes we would get on our objective without a shot ever being fired.

We had a very effective division and a great reputation because of our method of operations. When I was still the regimental S2, we attacked a town at night. Our direct-support artillery battalion commander was a guy named Gilbert. Gilbert planned this whole artillery thing and fired a preparation on positions we knew existed. He set up a band of firepower that moved as the troops moved. The artillery fire stayed in front of them as it was walked onto the objective, then he lifted part of the fire in the middle. The Germans stayed undercover because of all the shelling. Our soldiers went right through and took the position. As the enemy came out of their holes when the fire stopped, our guys were all around them. Attacking at night allowed us to do some really innovative things like that.

As a first step at desegregation, the army brought three black platoons into each division—one platoon per regiment. Previously, we had two divisions in which all of the soldiers were black. Some of the officers were black, but most of them were white. The soldiers were all segregated. In earlier days, when my father was at Fort Benning and I was a kid, the 24th Infantry, and the 25th Infantry at Fort Huachuca were all-black regiments. We also had the 10th Cavalry, where the officers were white and the soldiers and NCOs were all black. This situation persisted into World War II.

While I was commanding the 2nd Battalion of the 415th Infantry in the spring of 1945, Colonel Cochran told me a platoon of black soldiers would be integrated into each regiment. The platoon coming to our regiment would be assigned to my battalion. I was to select one of my lieutenants to be the platoon leader and he was to report to the Division Combat Training School. The 104th Division ran a training program where new soldiers would get two weeks of training before they joined their units. The school imparted "the Timberwolf spirit" of the division to the incoming soldiers.

I never knew why the platoon that came to my regiment was assigned to my battalion. Did the regimental commander think I was the best leader and therefore would handle the situation well, or did he think I should get the platoon because I was the junior battalion commander? Anyway, I got them and I was glad. We had no racial problems, which I think was the command's greatest fear. Conversely, it gave me one company that had four rifle platoons as opposed to the normal three. When we had a mission that was too small for two companies but too big for one, I would use my heavy company.

At the end of their two weeks of training, the platoon joined the battalion. I had been back to the training center to welcome these soldiers and to talk individually to as many as I could. I continued these talks after they joined us until I had met everyone. They were all super guys. I found that all of them had been at least sergeants in their former units. Some of them had been master sergeants, and one had been a first sergeant. All of these men had taken a voluntary reduction in ranks, some to the grade of private first class, in order to have the chance to represent their race in a white man's world. They were inspired to represent their people and advance the cause of the black race. They wanted to erase the myth that black soldiers could not perform as well in combat as their white counterparts.

Shortly after they arrived, I had the opportunity to give them their first taste of battle. We were on the right flank of the entire division. We had finished a night attack and were on our objectives, far ahead of the 1st Division on our right flank. They were having difficulty reaching their objectives. One of their problems was that the Germans were placing effective fire on them from a small village in front of my positions. I was ordered to capture it. My mission looked like a platoon-sized job to me.

I took the company commander, Captain Carroll, and the platoon to a point in the forest from which we could see the village. En route, I explained to the company commander and the platoon leader, Lieutenant Louis H. Trog, that all I wanted them to do was to observe the platoon sergeant and the platoon's performance. They were not to participate. I wanted to give the platoon sergeant the chance to win his spurs and gain the respect and confidence of the men. When we got to the edge of the woods, I called the platoon sergeant over and told him what I wanted him to do. Then we accompanied him to where the platoon was hunkered down. I was pleasantly surprised. He issued a flawless five-paragraph field order, one that you might expect to hear at the Infantry School. He ended up with the command, "Fix bayonets!" I looked at the company commander and he looked at me. I had never heard this command before in the war, nor did I ever hear it again. We had never used bayonets up to that point in the whole war.

The men fixed bayonets. The sergeant then yelled, "Follow me!" and charged out of the woods singing a song at the top of his lungs. The men joined him in singing "Right in the Fuhrer's Face," which was a popular song during the war. They went at full speed across the two hundred yards between the woods and the village, screaming their song.

A combination of this unusual spectacle and their first sight of black soldiers completely unnerved the Germans. They were the victims of their own propaganda that black soldiers were monsters who killed ruthlessly and then plundered and raped without regard to the rules of land warfare or the Geneva Convention. The Germans didn't want any part of this; they began to pour out of the village with their hands above their heads in surrender. The platoon numbered fewer than fifty men, yet they captured were nearly twice their number.

Things could not have worked out better. The platoon was so proud of its success that it developed an esprit and determination that made it one of the most effective platoons in my battalion, perhaps in the entire regiment. That platoon always stayed as a segregated platoon in a white company. It had a white platoon leader, but everybody else in the platoon was black. I never perceived any resentment. If the blacks resented it, they hid their resentment in a way that wasn't apparent to you. But their performance was so great that you felt that they were proud and happy with what they were doing.

We went into a town once, and one of the black guys was accused of rape. The platoon sergeant came to me and said, "That's just not true." The German people had heard so much propaganda about black soldiers that they were scared to death of them. A woman saw a black soldier coming toward her house and started screaming. The next thing you know, people were accusing him of rape. I got the soldier, talked to him, and was convinced that he hadn't done anything. I told him to forget it. The black platoon realized then that we were looking out for them. We got along very well and never had any problems.

One day, Colonel Cochrane gave me the mission of seizing and holding a village on the perimeter of the Ruhr Pocket, near Paderborn. The German forces inside the pocket had armored units with them. My plan was to use the armored platoon attached to my battalion with one rifle company to capture the village. I planned to leave both in the town to hold it. The armored unit attached to my battalion during the course of the war was not very bold. They invariably complained that the enemy tanks in the villages had holed up inside of buildings so they could not be seen. When our tanks would come into view, the Germans would fire through a hole in the side of the building before being spotted. Thus, our armored guys claimed, the Germans had the advantage of the first shot.

The tank platoon leader made this argument as we discussed the plan. I told him to hold up on the road just out of sight of the village. The infantry troops would look the town over from the forest and let him know whether we could see any enemy tanks. I also told him to listen for rifle fire. If he heard it, he was to come running.

I used F Company, which had the platoon of black Timberwolves. We started out for the village taking a route through the forest and over some hills. I was with the black Timberwolf platoon. As the village came into sight, I looked it over, saw no sign of enemy tanks, and called our tanks forward. As the black Timberwolves and I were inching our way around the side of a hill to get into a position to attack, firing broke out. We all hit the dirt—not that it did much good since there was no cover to block the bullets. It was then I realized that the fire was coming from our tanks. Three of our guys got hit and I watched bullets tearing up the grass and weeds a couple of feet down the hill from my feet. That stirred me into action.

I had a map in one hand and my carbine in the other. I jumped up, waving both of them like crazy. Lieutenant Trog jumped up and started waving and yelling as well. Fortunately, the tankers ceased their fire before we had any more casualties. One of the black Timberwolves was killed and the other two were slightly wounded. The platoon sergeant came over and thanked us for jumping up and getting the firing stopped.

After we buttoned up the village, I went back to my command post. A little after dark, I got a call from the F Company commander, Captain Carroll. He said the armored platoon leader wanted to withdraw. He put him on the phone. I asked him why he wanted to withdraw. He said he could hear tanks moving up near the village. I told him he had the Germans right where he wanted them. He was on the inside and would get the first shot! I told him to stay right where he was until he received orders to the contrary.

I was wounded while serving as the regimental S2. Some aerial photos of an objective we were going to attack had just come in. Because there wasn't much time, I took the photos and jumped in my jeep with my driver and an S2 clerk and we headed off to the company assigned the objective. The fastest way was down a road that I knew had been mined. We drove down to where you turned onto this road, and asked some people down there if the road had been cleared. They said it had. We went further and ran into a small engineer group and asked them to confirm the road had been cleared. They said, "Yes." Vehicles had been going back and forth, so we thought we were alright.

Well, we zipped on down that road and boy, did we hit a big mine! It blew one of the front wheels off, landing about fifty yards away, and flipped us over into a ditch filled with water. I was partially pinned under the jeep—hung up on my battle gear. The driver had been hit right in the forehead and died immediately. He was right there where I could see him. I was holding his head out of the water because he was more under water than I was.

My leg was crushed, but with some help I finally worked my way out from under the vehicle. There was a lot of gasoline from the destroyed jeep, which got in my bottom and burned. I thought I had been ripped apart because that's what it felt like. I said to some soldiers who pulled me out, "There's some blood in my trousers." They said, "No, I don't see any blood." I felt like I had just been split open.

The S2 clerk, who had been in the back seat and blown clear in the explosion, came running up, blood coming out of his mouth, and I asked, "How are you?" He said, "I'm fine. The explosion just broke my teeth." So he opened up his mouth and I couldn't see any teeth; "I'll say it broke them," I replied. "It broke them right off at the stumps." That was the first I knew that he had plates. He was a good athlete and had gotten all his teeth knocked out playing football and baseball.

I got hauled off to an aid station. Fortunately, we didn't get evacuated. My rations included half a bottle of scotch and a bottle of gin each month. I got in the hot tub in the aid station, got the doctor who wanted to evacuate me, and got my booze. We drank all that booze and got drunker than hell. I convinced him that I shouldn't be evacuated because I was really afraid of the replacement system. Once you left the regiment and went back to a hospital, you came back through the replacement depot. You didn't know if you were going to come back to your own unit. If you did come back, you didn't know if your job was going to be there. You felt safe and secure as long as you were with your own unit. So I talked the doctor into keeping me there.

The doctor was concerned because my leg was crushed. It got totally black and blue all the way around my thigh. They were concerned that a blood clot would break loose and go to my brain. So I had to go back every day to put heat on it and to soak it in hot water. I hobbled around on crutches for quite a while, doing my job.

We went through and captured Cologne. Then we went up the river, to the southeast, and crossed again. Then we fought up around the Ruhr, where we trapped a lot of Germans. We headed east past Paderborn, until we got to the Mulde River. This was where one of my companies was involved in a battle that later led me to another piece of personal philosophy.

We were holding a road junction that led out of the Ruhr Pocket. We spent a night or two there. There wasn't anybody near us, so we scattered around and put our antitank weapons where we thought they would do the most good. On the morning of March 31, I was awakened early. A lieutenant from the 3rd Armored Division had come through the town where I had placed my CP.

The lieutenant had gone around a bend in the road where there were a couple of little ridges. Somewhere between these ridges, some German SS infantry and armor had shot up his column. He'd lost two tanks, and the supply column he was escorting had to get through to an armored division. He described this like he pretty much knew where these enemy tanks were located. Immediately I got on the phone with Captain James A. Mauldin, who commanded my G Company, and told him, "I'll be over in five minutes. Let's take the company, go up there, and scout this thing out." My battalion was excellent with bazookas and antitank rocket launchers. They really loved to hunt tanks, so they were all gung-ho about this operation. We went through the woods, not up the road. We then went over the first two ridges, but didn't see anything in the valleys below.

Over the third ridge lay a long flat field with the village of Liesen at the end of it. There was no sign of any German tanks. But we noticed that a dozen or so villagers were leaving Liesen. This was a sign something unusual was going on, an indication that they didn't want to be involved in a potential fight. So I said to Captain Mauldin, "Why don't we just go and check out that village since we are here?"

We started crossing a field that was as flat as a billiard table. There was no place to hide or get any cover. Mauldin and I were walking ahead of the men and talking. When we were about two hundred yards from Liesen, a little movement caught my eye. It was a German soldier sitting behind a machine gun at the edge of the village. Realizing we were sitting ducks, I yelled, "There they are! Let's get 'em!" and started running as fast as I could at the machine gunner. All of us started running and yelling.

To my relief and amazement, the German got up and ran. He didn't fire a shot. We got into the village and took out six armored vehicles, killed a bunch of Germans, and captured fifty more. One armored vehicle that we didn't immediately get drove out of the village and up a small rise to the north and stopped, apparently because a bazooka shot had damaged its engine. Some of the Germans managed to escape back into the Ruhr Pocket and report what had happened to them. We later brought forward the tank platoon attached to my battalion and they finished off the enemy vehicle on the slope.

The enemy returned with a like force in the early afternoon, and we again sent them reeling, knocking out another self-propelled gun and a personnel carrier. Captain Mauldin received a Silver Star for the valor he displayed in leading his men, especially for knocking out the enemy's armored vehicles. The 3rd Armored Division's supply column moved on. All in a day's work![11]

But there is more to the story. After the war, while I was running Operation RUSTY, I lived at an estate called Luisenhof. It bordered the western side of Camp King. I lived there in relative splendor with two or three other officers for about two years. The home had belonged to a senior executive from I. G. Farben, a major German corporation headquartered in Frankfurt. It had probably seven bedrooms and servants' quarters and was comfortably furnished.

We had a "housemother," Frau Leverkus. She was an American by birth and came from a prominent Philadelphia family. She had married Herr Leverkus, the owner of a large chemical company, in 1910. Her nephew, an American intelligence officer stationed at Camp King, had brought her from her hometown of Leverkusen near Cologne to oversee the operation of Luisenhof. She was later replaced by her niece, Frau Jutta von Gruschwitz. Coming with her was her cook and a maid. The cook was marvelous. She could make a feast of the rations we were issued. The maid relieved us of the chores of making our beds and doing laundry. Every evening while I was there, we dressed for dinner, which was preceded by an hour of interesting conversation and sherry. At one point, a former German general, Lieutenant General Fritz Bayerlein, was quartered at Luisenhof while he wrote an account of his actions during the war.[12] He was a guest of the army's historians. He did not share our evening sherry nor did he eat with us. He had a back bedroom, sort of out of the way from the rest of us. One evening, I felt an urge to talk to Bayerlein. I went to his room and we chatted about the war and his role. I found out he had been a corps commander and his unit was a major part of the force trapped by the encircling movement of the US 7th Corps from the south and the British forces from the north that created the so-called Ruhr Pocket.

After several evening discussions, which I found fascinating, I mentioned that my battalion had the mission of keeping the entrapped forces from breaking out of the pocket along a major road leading from it. Bayerlein was interested and sought more detail. In the next few days, I secured maps that covered the area and took them to our evening session. I pinpointed our position on the perimeter of the pocket. As we discussed his situation, and mine at that time in the war, I told him of our encounter with an armored force just north of our defensive position, in the village of Liesen. Bayerlein told me, "I remember that quite well." He felt the corridor I was defending offered his best chance to break out of the pocket. Therefore, he had sent an armored force, which Mauldin's G Company and I encountered, to make a reconnaissance of the area. He said the few soldiers we had not captured or killed returned to him and reported that a formidable force was located at that point. In their opinion, there was no chance a breakout could succeed there, even though I had hit them with only one company!

I often think about how fortunate we were when the supply column of the 3rd Armored Division had stumbled onto Bayerlein's force and had created the opportunity in which we acted so decisively. It impressed upon me how little the other guy knows about you. He may be sitting out there scared to death that you are about to kick him in the teeth. When things seem the darkest, maybe they really aren't as bad as you think. That philosophy was further heightened when I figured that, with a battalion, I'd held off a whole corps because of bad information that the opposing commander had gotten. Maybe intelligence is not always so good. Maybe the other guy doesn't know as much as you know. If he doesn't know enough to make good decisions, that could be a great advantage to you. You have to remember that.

I read the book *Grant Goes South*, written by the famous historian Bruce Catton. Either Grant or one of his leaders said that, during a battle where both sides come to a point of sheer exhaustion, the leader who mounts one more attack will be the winner, whether he deserved it or not. That comment, along with the German battle I just mentioned, influenced my thinking over time.

My battalion was gung-ho about bazookas, because earlier we had been in a little town when a group of about five German tiger tanks attacked. They came in, turned their guns, and fired point-blank into Company F's command post, then turned again and blew up another building. A platoon sergeant named George E. Burns from Findley, Ohio, grabbed a bazooka and some rounds of ammunition, ran out of the building he was in, and fired his bazooka standing seven feet in front of the lead tank. It didn't damage the tank at all. A bazooka wouldn't go through the front of those tanks, but it scared the driver so badly that he turned the tank around and retreated. Burns hit him again in the engine compartment. That set the tank on fire. When the other tanks saw that tank on fire, they turned around and took off. So we knocked out one tank and the rest were gone. We awarded Burns the Distinguished Service Cross and promoted him to lieutenant on the battlefield, and he became a platoon leader.

At the end of the war in Europe, my battalion was on a tributary of the Elbe River southeast of Magdeburg. As I recall, my command post at one point was in Dessau. I was awakened early one morning, maybe 1:00 or 2:00 a.m., and told I had to leave immediately for Paris by order of the adjutant general of General Eisenhower's headquarters. I was given specific instructions as to where to go to pick up air transportation to get to Paris. As it turned out, I went from place to place, changing planes until I finally reached the French capital.

I found out I had been ordered to Paris by Major General Robert G. Lovett, a close friend of my dad since their Fort Benning days together. He had sent for me as a favor to my dad so I would be able to see him for a couple of days as he returned to Moscow from a conference in Washington.

I was put up at the Ritz Hotel, one of the top hotels in Paris. The Ritz was being used as a hotel for senior officials like my dad. We had a pleasant reunion, and when Dad left a few days later, I was given the option of staying on a few more days. While I was there, General Allen arrived for a short vacation. He called me, and we got together for dinner a couple of times. After dinner, he introduced me to Georges Carpentier, a heavyweight boxer of some renown when I was a boy. He fought Jack Dempsey for the world heavyweight title at one time but was defeated. I also met the owner of the Folies-Bergère and attended the show in the best seats. All of this with Terry Allen. ˙

3

Operation RUSTY

After World War II ended in Europe, my division redeployed to the United States and was stationed at Camp San Luis Obispo, where we trained for the invasion of Japan. That war obviously ended before we deployed again. As the division was demobilized, I was reassigned to Europe to work in the G3 section in the USFET (US Forces, European Theater).

The chief of staff of USFET was Lieutenant General Bedell Smith. My father had been an assistant secretary of the Army General Staff when Smith was the secretary. Dad later replaced Smith as the secretary when Smith went to London to become General Eisenhower's chief of staff. I assumed my new appointment stemmed from his association with Dad.

When I checked into headquarters, the personnel people were unavailable at the moment so, with time to kill, I decided to pay a courtesy call on Colonel Carl Fritzsche in the G2 section. Carl had been the heavyweight NCAA boxing champ while at West Point, and he had given me boxing lessons during the cruise on our trip to China. He was a contemporary of my father and we had been friends since I was a boy. I went in just to call on him. He asked me what I was going to do. I told him what my understanding was. He said, "I'm going to get you into this section. We have a job that you are ideally suited for." He couldn't describe the job in detail because of its highly classified nature. He said it had to do with espionage and that it was a very responsible position and would be an extremely interesting assignment. I agreed to accept the position.

When I later met with General Smith, I told him about my conversation with Colonel Fritzsche. He called Carl to see what he had in mind. When he heard of Carl's plans for me, he approved the assignment. The job was to establish an espionage network to gain information about the Soviet Union. The operation needed a code name. At the time, my only child was my son, Rusty. Since he was my first experience in fatherhood and this operation was my first experience in espionage, I decided to name it Operation RUSTY.

During the war, the German Army had an organization that specialized in intelligence work against the Soviets. The unit buried all its records in Bavaria and surrendered to US forces in May 1945. The top leaders in the organization went to the United States under the auspices of the US Army and had been providing intelligence from a place called Fort Hunt, just south of Washington, DC. Their organization at the General Staff level remained virtually intact. All of their records were available; they just had to be dug up from where they were buried in Bavaria.

The head of this organization was Major General Reinhard Gehlen.[1] As the end of the war neared, Gehlen directed his officers to preserve their records and surrender to the Americans. He knew that his unit had some of the most important files in the Third Reich and that possession of these records offered their best means of survival in the post-Hitler period. He believed that the Western Allies and the Soviet Union, although wartime partners, would soon become rivals. With his knowledge about the Russians combined with his former organization's collective resources, Gehlen felt he could influence relations between the East and West and help shape Germany's role in postwar Europe.

The decision was made by the army to allow this group of German officers to continue collecting intelligence on Soviet forces in Germany. This marked a radical departure from the previous concept of using former German officers only to write "lessons learned" studies based on old Wehrmacht files. Gehlen agreed to work for the Americans and try to reconstitute the espionage operation that he had previously used against the Soviets.

I was put in charge of this operation and believed the concept of the plan was a prudent one. As far as using former German soldiers to help, I viewed it like this: at the interrogation center, almost all of our people were either German-born Jews or first-generation American Jews of German descent. Some of them may have gotten some sense of satisfaction, some feeling of power out of being in a superior position vis-à-vis the Germans, but I never heard any of them complain about working with them. Here they were, Jews, those most directly affected, and they weren't complaining. They could and did make the distinction between Nazis and non-Nazis, and those people at Oberursel were not Nazis.[2]

Gehlen was sent back to Germany from Fort Hunt in August 1946. Our headquarters was set up in the vicinity of an interrogation center called Camp King at Oberursel. The location served as a cover, and because there were foreigners going in and out of the interrogation center all the time, the foreigners in my operation wouldn't be so suspect.

Just before the German party was to arrive from Fort Hunt, Captain Eric Waldman joined my staff. His wife, Jo, came with him as a Department of Army civilian and worked as our secretary and office manager. Eric was a delightful and very capable fellow. He had a great sense of humor and was fun to be around. He was a Jew who was born and raised in Vienna. He and his family fled to the United States to escape the persecution of the Nazis. Obviously, he spoke fluent German. Eric later became a history professor at Marquette University.

General Gehlen gathered a few men who had been on his staff from various places in Germany. We operated for the two years or so that I was stationed there. According to the people I knew, and all of the people in what was then called the Central Intelligence Group (CIG), we were producing some of the best intelligence on the Soviets. So our operation seemed to be successful.

Captain Waldman recalled how the Gehlen organization began to take shape. "Gradually, Gehlen's field operatives, under Lieutenant Colonel Hermann Baun, recruited and organized agents. Reestablishment of old sections of Baun's apparatus absorbed much of the effort. There was a noted tension between Gehlen and Baun. The situation facing Gehlen was a difficult one. Baun had had a year in which to install himself into the program before Gehlen's arrival from the United States, and whatever understanding Gehlen had with the US Army, Deane had bought into the arrangement of 'two horses abreast'—Baun as Chief of Collection, and Gehlen as Chief of Evaluation; the general and the lieutenant colonel as equals. A not unimportant point here is that Baun was not a general staff officer, and most important of all, Gehlen didn't trust him."[3]

Deane's quantum jump in the intelligence field from youthful regimental S-2 to building a major national intelligence apparatus led to some interesting observations from the German members of his team. Gehlen remembered that the first time he had a discussion with Deane regarding obtaining false identity cards for his organization, Deane responded with an astonished, "Why, that's against the law!" It took some time for Gehlen to convince Deane that it was not really a true violation of the law and that the use of fake identity cards was a common practice in intelligence circles. Gehlen noted that he gradually succeeded in convincing Deane of the necessity of adopting other peculiarities of the espionage trade, and soon Deane threw the full weight of his personality behind the effort.[4]

As Deane was not fluent in German, he mainly dealt with the policy aspects of the organization while Waldman handled the daily interac-

tion with the Germans. Waldman described two incidents that convinced Deane of Baun's untrustworthiness—which was abundantly proven in later years. Gustav Hilger, a former German diplomat who was part of the Gehlen team from Fort Hunt, discovered that Baun had stashed away a large trunk of US dollars, money that should have been spent on operations. In another incident Baun tried to blackmail Colonel Heinz Herre, another operative and a strong Gehlen supporter. These incidents were brought to Deane's attention, and by the end of 1946, Deane was persuaded to appoint Gehlen chief of the German element. Mounting questions regarding Baun's agents and finances resulted in his gradual removal from the organization in 1947.[5]

Hermann Baun cooked up a lot of schemes in the time before Gehlen got there. Mainly he wanted to reactivate his old net. I considered him an unsavory type, but he was very knowledgeable and had a lot of connections. I gave him the go-ahead to try to reestablish contact with his agents in the East and get the network functioning again. He caused nothing but trouble from the start. He was constantly going off somewhere, no one knew where, making contact with someone, no one knew who, and returning to Oberursel with his financial records all in a shambles. When Gehlen arrived, things changed for him.[6]

Gehlen was nervous when we first met; he wasn't sure what our relationship would be. He was very proper and correct, but it was obvious he was nervous. But as far as I was concerned, there wasn't any awkwardness. We had some discussions and it was clear we were both seeking the same goals, so the way I visualized it, he had a company and I hired his company to do a job. We had mutual respect for each other. Eric Waldman was the one who dealt directly with his people, but when it came to policy, I got involved.[7]

Three of our strongest sources of information came from ties to the intelligence people in the Vatican, the Armenians, and a group of White Russian émigrés located in Paris. The Vatican had a tremendous intelligence network through its priests scattered throughout the world. We reached into the Vatican through the religious group known as the Knights of Malta. The Armenians responded to a great Armenian hero, General Dro, who was in our organization. Finally, our ties with the Paris group were through a White Russian within our organization, Prince Kudasheff.

I had an excellent relationship with General Dro. His real name was Drastamat Kanayan.[8] He was sort of an Armenian George Washington. I saw a picture of him on horseback with a great white beard and a drawn saber. They said this picture could be found in many Armenian homes in Turkey and Russian Armenia. We found Kanayan in a displaced persons camp south of Stuttgart, Germany. At the end of World War II, the United States established these so-called displaced persons camps where people who had ended up in Germany through war or political upheaval would be safe while their futures unfolded. In these camps, they received food, medical attention, and shelter while awaiting the opportunity to return to their homelands or some other place of sanctuary.

Using my special emissary card issued to me by General Lucius Clay, I immediately had Kanayan released to my custody. I took him to an apartment I had requisitioned in Heidelberg, again with my card. Here he would remain until I arranged passage to and entry into the United States. This was no small feat in itself. Kanayan soon made it known that his wife and son, a lad of about four, were in Rome, and he wanted them with him in Heidelberg. This posed no great problem, but I felt I had to handle the matter personally. Kanayan was of such great value to us that I did not want him upset by some overzealous border guard detaining his wife and son as they made their way to Heidelberg. Kanayan and I drove in my car to Rome. I remember very clearly that, as we entered Switzerland, he asked me to stop. He went into a grocery store and bought a large bag of assorted fruit. He probably had not had fresh fruit in seven or eight years. We located his wife and son with no trouble and headed back to Heidelberg. On the return trip, Kanayan was a different man. He was overjoyed to have his family back again. He idolized his little boy. Years later, I met his son in Washington at a banquet honoring me as the Armenian of the Year for the role I had played in Kanayan's life. He was, as I recall, living in the Detroit area and was an engineer.

In December 1946, Kanayan told me he had heard that George Mardikian was visiting Major General George Horkan, the quartermaster general in Germany. Kanayan asked me to invite Mardikian to visit him. Mardikian was a prominent San Francisco restauranteur, the owner of Omar Khayyam. He was not accustomed to dealing with lieutenant colonels. Generals were more his style, so my initial attempt to reach him failed. I then told an intermediary that I was from San Francisco, the son of General Deane and the cousin of Helen Cameron. My father was a San Franciscan of some note. Helen was a one-quarter owner of the *San Francisco Chronicle,* the wife of its publisher, George Cameron, and a doyenne of San Francisco society. I asked him to pass this along to Mardikian. This brought instantaneous results.

General Horkan's aide asked me to come to the general's quarters that evening for cocktails. There I met Mardikian for the first time. I saw him many times later at his restaurant, where dinner was always on the house, but I had to endure his selections from the menu, grape leaves and things—unfortunately, no steak and potatoes.

I extended Kanayan's invitation and Mardikian's eyes almost popped out! It was not a matter of whether he would accept the invitation—it was a matter of how soon we could go. We went the next day. Kanayan and Mardikian had a long visit that led to Mardikian's visiting the displaced persons camp, Funkercaserne near Stuttgart, where Kanayan had been incarcerated.

Mardikian was so distressed with the plight of the Armenians in that camp that he started a charity to improve their conditions. Upon his return to San Francisco, he formed the Armenian National Committee for Homeless Armenians, or ANCHA. He went on radio frequently to plead for food, clothing, and money to send to the Armenians. He always mentioned me in those radio appeals as having been the person who started the whole thing.

The method used by Deane's organization to insert an agent into East Germany was virtually foolproof. Deane obtained blank official American Prisoner of War Release documents, entered the agent's operational name and fictitious background, and then signed the papers. Eric Waldman remembered, "If we wanted to get a man into Dresden, in the Eastern sector, we would release him as POW Heinz Schmidt, or whatever, from Dresden. With that piece of paper, he could get all the others he needed legitimately, so he could get back 'home.' It worked beautifully."[9]

We once had an instance of a Soviet agent who had infiltrated into the field organization of Operation RUSTY. We captured him and he was incarcerated in the jail portion of the interrogation center. He later escaped. The knowledge he had posed a great threat to the lives of those agents who were in East Germany or the Eastern Bloc. We pulled out all the stops to find him. A couple of days later we had a tip that he was holed up in a house in Hoechst. I sent a squad of military police to apprehend him. I knew most of the men on the squad quite well because I played baseball and most of the squad were on the team. I told them of the threat he posed. I said it was imperative that they capture him. I admonished them to shoot to kill him if he tried to escape. Frankly, I was so concerned about the safety of our people that I hoped he would try to escape and the police would do him in.

The squad apprehended the escapee. I asked why they had not shot him. The man who made the actual capture told me, "I got into the house quietly and was standing at the foot of the stairs. I could hear him upstairs. The second guy in must have made a slight sound because suddenly there was no movement upstairs. Then he started down the stairs. When he got to the bottom, I stuck my pistol right in his stomach. Sir, you said to shoot if he made a move. He didn't move. He didn't even breathe."

As the army's demands grew, Operation RUSTY transformed from a select cadre of German General Staff officers to a larger group of recruits that suffered from poor cohesion and mixed allegiances. In addition to covering the Soviet zone, Operation RUSTY took on new missions in Austria and other areas of Europe, as well as broadened wartime contacts with anti-Communist émigré groups in Germany and with members of the Russian Vlasov Army. The few American officers assigned to Oberursel barely knew the identities of RUSTY agents, thus making it difficult to confirm the validity of German reporting. Baun's recruiting and training of agents proved haphazard, while their motivation also raised questions because of RUSTY's black-market activities.[10]

In the fall of 1946, General Gehlen told me our White Russian group in Paris had been contacted by an Eastern European attaché in Paris. The attaché said that he would pass on to us copies of all cable traffic that came to his embassy. He did not want money or any other material things in return. He did, however, want a promise from senior American officials that he and his family would be flown to the States and granted citizenship if he were ever summoned home by his government. Such a summons would likely be the signal that his activities had been discovered.

I realized that access to the cable traffic would be a reliable source of invaluable intelligence. At the same time, I knew I could not guarantee safe passage or citizenship to the attaché and his family. General Edwin L. Sibert was the G2 at the time.[11] During World War II, he had served as the G2 for the 12th Army Group and had fallen under a lot of criticism for not detecting German preparations prior to the Battle of the Bulge in December of 1944. His deputy, Colonel Bobby Schow, on the other hand, had spent most of his career in the intelligence business, and to my mind, was a real pro.[12] When I had questions or needed a decision, I usually went to Schow. If he felt a decision was beyond his authority, he would take me to Sibert. I would make my pitch and he would recommend that Sibert approve my request or recommendation.

I went to Schow with my Eastern European dilemma. I told him the full story. I told him that I felt this operation was getting too big for the army to handle. I recommended we seek a way to get the Central Intelligence Group to take it over. They were in a position to spirit the likes of the Eastern European attaché into the United States if need be. They could arrange citizenship through the State Department. He agreed, and had me discuss the matter with General Sibert. Sibert also agreed.

Sibert sent a message to the G2 of the army in Washington. His memorandum, supported by extensive documentation, noted that the army's headquarters in Germany considered RUSTY to be "one of its most prolific and dependable sources." He laid out the situation and recommended that the War Department G2 inform General Hoyt Vandenburg, the director of the CIG, and seek an appointment for me to brief the director.[13] It was arranged, and I prepared to return to the States.

My preparations consisted of four actions taken in the following order. First, I asked for and received permission to take a few days of leave while in the States. Second, I called my wife, Betty, in Baltimore, told her I was coming home on business, and asked her to get tickets to the Army-Navy game. Those were the days of Glenn Davis and Doc Blanchard, the all-American Mr. Outside and Mr. Inside, on the Army football team. Arnold Tucker was the quarterback. I met him later in Thailand. I had never seen this great team play because I was overseas most of the time it was having its heyday. Incidentally, Betty got the tickets and we saw the game—which Army almost lost and should have lost. Tucker was hurt early on and did not play for the remainder of the game. Davis and Blanchard each had a few good runs, but nothing spectacular. The game ended with the score something like 20-19, with Navy on the Army one-foot line.

The third thing I did was ask General Gehlen to have a chart of the organization made that only someone familiar with the code to unlock it could interpret. Fourth, I began packing and arranged transportation.

When I got to Washington, I briefed the G2 and then went to my appointment with General Vandenburg. My recollection is that he had been called out of town unexpectedly. He had left word for me to go to an address in New York and arrive there at a specified hour. There I was to knock on the ground-level door, and certain unnamed people would be there to hear what I had to say.

I arrived at an old brownstone house in a nice section of the East Side. The door they had told me to go probably was the servant and delivery entrance in earlier days. Once inside, however, I found myself in a large, beautifully furnished room. It was more like a den or an office than a living room, yet it was comfortable and gave one a sense of warmth.

There were three gentlemen there. All had well-known reputations in the intelligence world. Allen Dulles headed up the meeting. He was the brother of John Foster Dulles, later secretary of state, and had been very deeply involved in intelligence during the war. He was a member of the OSS and had run its Swiss operation for some time. He was one of the senior advisors to the government during the establishment of what later became the CIA. He later became its director. The second was William Jackson, a senior and highly regarded former army intelligence officer. The third was another former member of the OSS, a gentleman of Italian ancestry whose name escapes me.

I took out the organizational chart that Gehlen's people had prepared for me. It appeared to be an electrical wiring diagram for a large home. I interpreted the chart so my audience would have an idea of how we were organized and the extent of our organization. I told them what we were doing, where we were doing it, and how we were doing it. Why we were doing it was obvious. I ended with a discussion of the Eastern European attaché and the potential source of intelligence he offered. This current situation was really beyond the capacity of my organization. It seemed to me that this was something the US government had to get involved in. I pointed out that the Department of War's inability to make the guarantees, the promises this man sought in exchange for his services had led me to the conclusion that the CIG, with its expertise and resources, was the appropriate home for Operation RUSTY. Apparently they thought the operation was at least worth a look. So they recommended that the CIG send a representative to my headquarters to live with us and examine our operation for several months.

At the end of this time, based on his recommendations, they would decide either to take over the operation or to let the army continue to run it. Sam Bossard of the London office of the CIG came to Camp King as the observer.[14] At one point, Sam informed me that his boss, the CIG station chief in London, had summoned him back to London to give an interim report. Sam asked me to accompany him, and I agreed. Sam said the CIG did not want the British to know I was coming to London, nor did they want them to know of the relationship they had with Operation RUSTY. To this end, Sam requested that I travel incognito. He stressed that I should not take large quantities of whiskey or cigarettes with me. These would attract attention if discovered as we went through British customs. He said that we should show no signs of association although we would be traveling on the same plane. Sam told me not to be alarmed if he was called out from the rest of the passengers when we arrived at the London airport. He was going to make arrangements through a friend in

MI-5, a division of the British intelligence, to get whisked through customs. He would take a cab and be at his flat when I arrived.

To comply with his incognito request, I arranged to get a new ID card. It had my picture on it, but bore the name of my brother-in-law, Douglas C. Plate. This is another item that I still wish I had kept as part of my memorabilia. In addition, I packed no liquor and only a few packages of cigarettes. I smoked in those days.

The British were aware that I had some kind of operation going on. Although we shared our intelligence reports with them, they did not know any of the details. The British intelligence liaison officer to the G2 Division at USFET was Major Hembley-Scales. He was diligent, but to the best of my knowledge unsuccessful in ferreting out the details of how we were acquiring the intelligence we were sharing with them. It was even said that he had taken to sleeping with a female captain, let's call her Sue, who was the aide to the USFET G2, General Sibert.

Sam and I proceeded to the airport at Frankfurt in separate vehicles, totally unaware of the surprise that awaited us. Sue also would be on our flight to London. She was flying over for an interlude with Hembley-Scales. Upon my arrival at the terminal, I heard this loud feminine cry, "Jack! Oh, Jack Deane!" It was Sue. I hurried to her and told her I was traveling undercover on business. I asked her to avoid further contact with me or, if contact was necessary, to call me Doug Plate.

Everything proceeded smoothly until we reached the London terminal. As expected, Sam's name was called and he was led away by a customs official. When the officials finally got around to letting the rest of us enter the customs room, there was Sam standing at one of those long counters where customs agents delight in having you spread out everything in your carefully packed luggage. You never get them back in place quite right. On the counter were eighteen bottles of assorted liquor. As I passed behind Sam, I heard the customs official say, "But sir, you said you had only two bottles of spirits." I could not suppress my laughter.

I took a cab ride to Sam's flat. Fortunately, he had given me a key because he did not arrive for quite a while. Two major gaffes in our Laurel and Hardy undercover comedy.

Even then it was too early to relax in the thought that, despite the two bumps in the road, we had made London without the Brits knowing I was there or that the two of us had traveled together. We had just settled down to a martini after Sam eventually made it when the phone rang. It was Hembley-Scales, who told Sam, "I would like to invite you and Colonel Deane to come over for cocktails tomorrow evening."

At the end of the CIG inspection time, Sam recommended that the CIG take over the operation. I left about then for reassignment to Washington and was not directly involved in the turnover. Before leaving, I had frequent conferences with a young operative in the CIG—a middle-grade manager named Dick Helms. Helms later became director of the CIA, followed by ambassador to Iran. Dick sought my advice on matters pertaining to the operation, like knowledge of the personalities involved and what to expect of them. I served as sort of a consultant, over a period of a year or two, while the CIG was taking the operation over. This operation later broke off and became the basis for the Federal Republic of Germany's intelligence setup, which was headed by Gehlen, who became, in essence, their director of German Central Intelligence.

The thing that impressed me about this operation was the amount of authority I was given at the age of twenty-seven. It amazed me and demonstrated something that I don't see frequently today: senior people giving somebody a job and having confidence that they can and will do it properly. I was given a card about the size of a credit card. It had a little message on it: "The bearer of this card is my personal representative; he is to be given anything that he asks for. If you have any question as to the validity of his request, grant the request and then call the following number to get confirmation. Signed: Lucius Clay, Supreme Commander." Incidentally, Clay was the father of two of my West Point classmates, Lu and Frank Clay. I wish I had saved that card as a memento of an interesting period in my life.

I could get anything I wanted. If I needed an automobile, I could go and requisition ten or twenty. If I wanted to requisition cigarettes for use in barter or to get agents paid, I could do that. I could get food, drugs, women's stockings, and lipstick—all the things that were very valuable for bartering in war-ravaged Europe. I was never questioned about the disposition of any of these things. I used to travel from Oberursel to the headquarters at Frankfurt, about fifteen miles, monthly and was given on the order of $500,000 to $1 million in greenbacks. Cash. We would order cigarettes by the thousands of cartons. It was unbelievable. I never had to sign a receipt; I never had to account to anybody for the disposition of that money. That was the confidence that people had in me—that I would do the job properly and wouldn't abscond with a million bucks. I just don't see that happening very much now.

This confidence let us move ahead without constantly justifying ourselves and getting decisions from higher authority. Today, justifying and getting decisions slows down everything that is done in government.

Nobody is willing to give somebody a job and let him do it. They have to have ten layers of supervision. Each layer has to make a decision as to whether you proceed, and each decision takes anywhere from a couple of weeks to a couple of months. Things get slowed down significantly. In my view, that is one of the problems we have in our government today, particularly in the army.

There was another issue with Operation RUSTY. Through the Knights of Malta, we were able to gather all the intelligence that was coming through the Catholic Church from all over the world and into the Vatican. That was a tremendous amount of intelligence. It pertained not only to the Soviet Union, our primary target; it offered other kinds of valuable information, only peripheral to us but important to people back in the United States who were looking at other countries besides the Soviet Union.

It became touchy as to whether the army could really maintain that relationship, because we weren't the kind of people to do it. It was out of our league. The operation was growing, and it was growing into fields where we didn't have the expertise. We thought it was better for somebody else to take advantage of the intelligence and take over the clandestine operation.

While at Camp King, I also had a chance meeting with Hanna Reitsch, the famous German aviatrix.[15] Hanna was a "guest" at the interrogation center, providing all the information she could on the last days of Adolf Hitler. She was in the bunker with Hitler and his close associates in Berlin just prior to his death. A small person with a face that showed the effects of at least one aircraft accident, Hanna had great energy. She spoke with animation; her eyes sparkled and held your attention as she spoke.

Hanna, unlike most Germans after the war, never denied being a Nazi. She was a strong and courageous woman. She never groveled, protesting that she now hated the Nazis and Hitler, while pointing her finger at fellow Germans and denouncing them as Nazis. I encountered many Germans who did exactly this. I believe she was a victim of the Nazi propaganda machine; she had honestly believed Hitler was good for Germany and did not hesitate to say so. I admired her for that.

She told me of her last trip to the bunker. Hitler summoned Luftwaffe General Robert Ritter von Greim to Berlin.[16] Hitler had become suspicious that Hermann Goering, head of the German air forces, was trying to sell out to the Allies to end the war. He was going to appoint von Greim as the new head of the Luftwaffe.

General von Greim asked Hanna to fly with him to Berlin. The Russians were closing in and it might be the last chance she would have to see Hitler. Hanna was not only a strong supporter of Hitler, she was an aviatrix of world fame who did much to develop the Luftwaffe's aircraft and the V-rockets that almost did in the British. She knew Hitler well and would be welcomed at the bunker.

They took off in a Storch, a small plane similar to a Piper Cub. The plane was designed to carry only a pilot. Hanna was small so she was able to fit in a space behind the pilot seat. As they flew in low over Berlin to make their landing on a major thoroughfare, they took ground fire from the Russians below. The general was hit in the foot and unable to control the aircraft. Hanna reached over his shoulders and, using only the stick and consummate skill, was able to land the plane. They proceeded to the bunker, where they met Hitler and his mistress of many years, Eva Braun.

Her account of her visit to the bunker was, in large measure, the basis of a book titled *The Last Days of Hitler,* written by Hugh Trevor-Roper, a British intelligence officer and author who had access to all of the reports our interrogators compiled. After General von Greim was treated for his wounds, Hitler charged Goering with treason and replaced him with the newly promoted Field Marshal von Greim. Hanna and von Greim then flew out in the last plane to leave Berlin.

I mentioned that Hanna contributed to the development of the V-1s and V-2s, which were so devastating in their attack on London. During the development of these bombs, the Germans did not have the instrumentation to provide accurate readings as to the aerodynamic qualities of the bombs, which in fact were the first long-range missiles in the world. The intricacies and effectiveness of the guidance systems were not fully understood.

Volunteers were called upon to fly the first missiles and collect data needed to perfect them. Hanna volunteered and flew at least one mission. None of the others who actually flew survived. She told me that they equipped the experimental missiles with miniature controls similar to those in an airplane. Because the space for the missile pilot was so limited, he had to perform his duties lying flat on his stomach inside the missile. He had to operate the controls from this awkward position, which complicated a series of tasks requiring the deftest of touches.

Once the missile was launched, the operation of the controls was critical only to the collection of the desired data. The missile had no springs or shock absorbers to handle the forces imposed on it when it touched down. The landing had to be made in a perfect tangent to the landing surface to minimize these forces, which could snap the pilot's spine or splinter the missile. Hanna's great skill and delicate touch enabled her to be the only volunteer to survive.

Largely in Germany, but to some extent in France, Belgium, and Holland, the war had caused tremendous devastation. Food distribution was practically nonexistent and people were scrimping. What food was available was going at tremendously high prices. A lot of people bartered off their treasures—carpets, figurines, furniture, whatever they had of value—for practically nothing. They would sell them on the black market for a few cartons of cigarettes. Cigarettes, in turn, became a form of barter to buy food, medical care, or whatever they needed; it was a pretty sad situation. People were reduced to pitiful conditions.

That was why in this espionage operation, we used things that were the currency of trade over there, like cigarettes. We had people in the Soviet Union, where there was a great demand for lipstick, stockings, and other things that guys would give to gals to gain their favor. We used all kinds of food. But the value of those things was established by the black market. The people who got cigarettes from us, for example, could then use the cigarettes in turn to buy food or whatever they needed.

So instead of getting a little bit of this and a little bit of that from us, they got one valuable item to buy commodities with. There were a lot of people involved in the black market—many of whom were caught and sentenced to prison terms. I think that the US government made extensive efforts to try to stamp out the black market, but the fact of the matter was that there were greedy people on one hand and needy people on the other. The two met, and one had what the other needed and wanted—which created the black market. I wouldn't say it was a bright and shining page in the history of the United States, but it was there.

4

Lessons Learned Serving as a Cold War Staff Officer

In October 1947, I was reassigned to Washington, DC, and essentially did the same type of job most of the time during the four and a half years I was stationed there. I had two different jobs because of a reorganization that I was involved in. Initially, I served in the Joint War Plans Branch. That was a fantastic experience. The people I worked with there were tremendously capable, and I learned much by being associated with them. That became the reason that going to Washington always had an appeal to me; you were dealing with such high-quality people.

For example, in that organization I was a lieutenant colonel—a very young lieutenant colonel—and others were somewhat older than I. General Goodpaster, who later became SACEUR (Supreme Allied Commander, Europe), was there.[1] Ed Rowny, who is now a retired lieutenant general, was also there.[2] Jack Norton also retired as a lieutenant general.[3] Ted Conway retired as a four-star general after commanding the Strike Command.[4] Bob Porter, who was our branch chief, later retired as a four-star general commanding United States Southern Command in Panama.[5] Almost every guy in that organization went on to at least the rank of major general. There I was, as a young officer, dealing with these guys. That closeness gave me an unbelievable mentoring opportunity.

My next proposed assignment was an interesting one; the situation is probably better now than it was after World War II, when career management got the name "career manglement"—because that's what it was. I went in one day to see the chief of infantry, the guy who assigned people to the infantry. I was trying to stay on the army staff for an extra year. I did that because I had been selected to go to the Command and General Staff College that year, but when they cut the number of guys who could go, I was so junior that I got bumped off the list. I figured I'd have a good chance next year, but if I went on some three-year assignment,

I wouldn't make it. So I wanted to stay another year. My boss, General Charles Bolte, wanted me to stay, but the career management people wouldn't agree.[6]

I had to go down to see this infantry guy. I told him, "Look, I want to go to the school." He said, "You're going to go. Don't worry; you'll go sometime." I said, "The sooner I go, the greater chance I will have to go to the Armed Forces Staff College, and then to the War College. If I don't go until late in my career, I might miss both and will probably miss at least one of them. I'm interested in getting that kind of education." He said, "You don't worry about your career. We will worry about it." I said, "I worry about it, whether you worry about it or not."

So he called a guy in—he apparently had him all primed—and said, "Take Colonel Deane over to your office and discuss some assignments with him." So we went over there and this guy said to me, "You're a lieutenant colonel and need Reserve component duty, because you have never had any." I said, "I really don't want any Reserve component duty. To me, that's a waste of time and a waste of my career, compared to other things. So I don't want that."

Then he said, "Secondly, you're due for an overseas tour. I have just the job for you; it's fantastic." I immediately envisioned the position of professor of military science and tactics at the University of Hawaii. He said, "You are going to be in charge of the Army Reserve Program in Alaska."

I said, "You have got to be out of your mind! What do you mean, 'fantastic job'? If it's so great, why don't you take it for yourself and leave me here?" He said, "Furthermore, because it's an expensive area to live in, you get an extra $60 a month while you're up there. With an extra $60, you can afford a house that's got an indoor john." "You mean I might have an outdoor john and be running through the snow every night? I can't believe you guys!"

Well, this is what they wanted to assign me. It just was a job that had to be filled at the time, and my number came up. So whether I was the best guy for the job or whether it was the best job for my career pattern had nothing to do with it, as far as I could see.

General Ridgway got me out of that assignment.[7] General Bolte or somebody had talked to him. General Ridgway had me interviewed by his executive officer, a colonel some years senior to me. He called me in and said, "Why do you feel that you're the only guy in the army who can do the job you're doing here?" I said, "I don't feel that I am. I can name fifty guys, right off hand, who can do it better than I can." Apparently, that impressed him because he said, "Well, don't do that." The next thing I knew, I was staying.

Next, these clowns from career management told me, "You've had intelligence experience a few years back and we don't want you to have any more. You had it as an S2 and, later on, in an espionage operation. So you have had plenty of intelligence experience to make you a well-rounded officer." It wasn't more than a month later that some guy there called me to say, "Come on down here. I have to talk to you about a job that we are thinking of assigning you to." I said, "Well, tell me about it." He said, "I can't tell you over the phone."

So I went down to see him. He said, "This is just the job for you; it's fantastic." I said, "What is it?" He said, "The intelligence officer of Joint Task Force Two"—some atomic test thing out in the Pacific. I said, "You guys told me a month ago that I should never have any more intelligence experience." It was a job that had come up that had to be filled at that time. Their boss was insisting on somebody with past intelligence experience. So they went through the cards. Were they interested in my career? Hell, no!

I got pretty sour about the way career management was running things, and it got to be worse. It got to be that, when you were a division commander, you couldn't pick your brigade commander. They would assign him to you. Whether the guy could command a brigade or not, it didn't matter. As a result, you had some bum brigades or had to relieve people because they couldn't handle the job. Instead of sending guys who really had a future down to get those important brigade command assignments—of all the colonels, whoever came up next got the job. Well, I don't think it was good. Industry couldn't run that way.

In the autumn of 1950, I had the good fortune to be called to brief the secretary of the army, Frank Pace, on activities that I was involved in. At the end of my briefing, unbeknownst to me, the secretary told his executive officer, Jimmy Curtis, whom I had known for many years, that he was much impressed with my briefing and my knowledge of the subject.[8] The secretary told Curtis that he felt it was a very important field and should be pursued very actively. Jimmy knew of my plight, because he had an intelligence background and I had talked to him about an opportunity I had to go into the CIA.

After learning of career management's plans for me, I asked him, "Do you think I should go to the Central Intelligence Agency to beat this rap of going to Alaska?" So when the secretary made this comment, he said, "Well, Lieutenant Colonel Deane is about to be ordered out of

Washington, and this thing is going to fall on its face until somebody else takes it over and gets up to speed."

The secretary asked, "Why is he being ordered out of Washington?" Jimmy said, "Well, that's just the way the army works when the time comes and there is a hole someplace. They grab somebody to stick in that hole, and that's what they are doing." The secretary said, "Well, you send word to the personnel people that Colonel Deane will not be transferred out of Washington without my personal approval." None of those guys in personnel management wanted to get that approval, so I was put on hold.

That had some advantages. I did get to go to the Command and General Staff College. But because I worked for Secretary Pace, I went a year later than I hoped; it wasn't as bad as it might have been otherwise. There was one disadvantage. In 1951, unbeknownst to me, I had been recommended to take over a regiment in Korea, and that request was turned down because of this freeze on me. To take over a regiment in combat would have been fantastic. Had I known that I was being recommended for a combat regimental command, I would have worked hard to get that freeze taken off.[9]

I continued in my old job for a while, and then there was an opening for an executive assistant to the secretary of the army. I had a friend working in the office at that time, Jack Norton. Jack apparently recommended to the secretary that I be interviewed for the job. So I went up to see the secretary. The title of the job was aide to the secretary of the army. I never had any desire to be an aide, so I was not too enthusiastic.

When he finally finished asking me questions about myself, my background, and my experience, he asked me if I would like to come there to work. I said, "I wouldn't." He said, "Why?" I said, "In the first place, I have never wanted to be an aide, so I don't want to be one now." He said, "Well, that can be taken care of because you're not going to be functioning in the role of an aide. You're going to be functioning in the role of one of my principal assistants. I expect you to review everything that comes into this office and recommend what I should do about it. You have a lot of experience on the General Staff, and that's what I need. If there is something wrong with whatever is being proposed, you know enough people on the staff that you can go and find out why they proposed what they did and what the pros and cons are. That's what I need to make decisions. We will change the title to executive assistant, so that knocks down your first objection. What is your second one?"

I said, "Well, I'm doing this job that a few months ago you thought was so important that I ought to be frozen here in Washington. Now you are pulling me out; if it's as important as it was, then there is no one available right now to take over. So there is going to be a period in which it's not going to be properly covered, because it is going to take somebody some time to get up to speed on it." He said, "Well, that's just a risk we are going to have to take." So I got assigned there in February, I think, and stayed for just over a year.

Jack Norton and I worked there together. I took everything that came out of certain offices in the staff. Other offices Jack was responsible for. Any papers that came in recommending action by the secretary or just information papers, we reviewed. We had little cards already made up that read, "Sign"; "Send to chief of staff with the following message" and space to add the message; "Information only"; "Review if you have time"; and those kind of things. You just had to put a check in the box. So if the secretary didn't have time to review each paper himself, he could simply act on our instructions. If we felt that there were some critical issues in a given paper, we would say, "Read it and then sign it" or something like that. Other papers that we thought he shouldn't see at all, we just didn't send in; he was under a tremendous burden anyway. He had sufficient confidence in our judgment that, when we said "Sign," he generally didn't spend a lot of time reading the thing. He just signed it.

He had such confidence in us that if we said, "Ask the chief of staff these questions"—despite the fact the chief of staff had approved the paper—he would send it back with the questions. Frequently, because the staff had not done its job well and the chief had not seen the problems in the paper, the whole thing would be changed around. This caused some resentment on occasion, but when they changed it around, they did it because they thought they should.

Figuring out the informal power structure within the Pentagon helped. I'm not sure how much is accomplished without eventually being approved by some branch chief, but an informal system—knowing people—helps. Say that you're working in operations and you have a policy paper that you have to get a lot of concurrences on. If you know a guy in logistics, you go over and explain your paper as you're writing it. Then he tells you what's going to be the problem when you come to logistics. If there is a problem and you can accommodate it, you do it in the paper in the beginning. You convince him the paper is something that the logistics people should sign off on. So when the time comes to get a concurrence, the skids are greased.

There were occasions when I was working for the secretary's office that we would not feel that a paper really rang true, even if we couldn't put our finger on the reason. Jack and I had to go down and see the action officer involved, talk to him, and see if he could answer the questions that were bothering us. Sometimes he couldn't. He realized that he hadn't thought the thing through very well and made an erroneous recommendation as it went up. On occasion we could then go to somebody higher up and say, "Look, we have these kinds of questions." Then they would say, "Maybe we had better withdraw the paper and work it over a little more."

Then, rather than presenting it to the secretary at all, we would just send it back. Then they would have to worry about how they would get back through the chief again. You know, we could talk to the guy in the chief's office. Our counterpart was a guy named "Swede" Larsen, the exec to General Collins when he was chief of staff.[10] Swede, who was an outstanding soldier, had served in General Collins's division during World War II. General Collins looked upon him as almost a son. You could get a lot of things accomplished through Swede that you couldn't otherwise. Swede subsequently retired as a lieutenant general commanding 6th Army.

He was succeeded by Johnny Throckmorton. With the two of them, Jack and I had a relationship that let us accomplish things informally, without causing a confrontation between the chief and the secretary. That was one of the things you wanted to avoid. In our government, everything is controlled by civilians, not people in uniform, and you don't want a fight between the people in uniform and the people in civilian clothes.

Many times, we had to take the brunt of it. I remember one time a paper was sent to the secretary that didn't ring true at all. I said, "Here are some questions you should ask the chief." Well, the questions actually went to the vice chief, who was Ham Haislip at the time.[11] His answer to these questions was that the secretary should get a briefing. It turned out that it was a very sensitive subject. Really, the Army Staff was doing something that they didn't want the secretary to know. My questions, which were logical ones, revealed this. It was just happenstance, but the Army Staff and Ham Haislip were very nervous.

I walked down to the secretary of the army's conference room. The secretary hadn't entered the room yet. As I walked through the door, I heard somebody say, "There he is." I felt like I had walked into a lion's den. Haislip got hold of me and gave me almighty hell for butting in, asking questions, and causing problems. The situation got so bad and everybody in the room was so tense that when the secretary walked in, he could sense the tension. Everybody was so upset at this point that they told the secretary that they didn't think it was appropriate to give the briefing. There were some other things that had to be examined, and they had not had time to do it.

When we got back up to the office, the secretary called me in and said, "What the hell is going on down there?" I said, "I don't know; they are a little upset." I didn't say much about it because I didn't want to tell him that the vice chief of staff had just raked me over the coals. Later, Haislip sort of apologized. He said, "You know, you are a soldier. You expect these things. You are a good infantryman and are used to getting beat on."

We avoided a confrontation there. If I had told the secretary that the vice had laced me out because I asked good questions and revealed that they were doing something wrong, he would have come down on Haislip like a ton of bricks. That would have been a problem, and we didn't need that kind of problem. So I didn't make anything out of it. Later, we got the thing all squared away and everyone was happy.

You're in a ticklish situation when you work with senior people. You are trying to be sure that they get the information they need to make appropriate, sound decisions. At the same time, in doing that, you are uncovering the weaknesses of guys down the line who don't have the competence to do the job properly in the first place. There is always some resentment of that. Or maybe somebody has an ax to grind, so he is not being totally honest in his recommendations. You have to weed that out. How do you keep from getting everybody mad at you? It's not easy.

When you're working on a high-level staff, you have high-quality people, yet you run the risk of making enemies by doing your job well and uncovering problems. But by and large, Jack Norton and I handled this pretty well. I don't think we made any real enemies. We had little problems from time to time. By contrast, I've seen guys who I felt were not making an honest effort to do a good job. They really were trying to get people. If they could find something wrong in a paper, instead of trying to get it smoothed over and straightened away, they tried to make a cause célèbre out of it. They would try to make themselves look good because they discovered this terrible flaw, while those dummies down there were giving bad information.

Then you get a situation where people really start to hate these guys who are higher up. I've seen officers like that, where they were so bad that other officers would spend the rest of their career trying to get them.

There was a guy on the staff of the commandant of Fort Leavenworth who used to sit in on classes and observe the instructors. He could have gone to the instructor and said, "I have a job to look at your class. Here are some deficiencies that I have noted; let's see if we can get those things corrected, and I'll come back next week." Instead, he would go running back to the general and say, "Gee, I went down to this class and the instructor was terrible," that kind of stuff.

I've been told by people who were present that when this guy came up for promotion, the guys on that promotion board said, "Screw that son of a bitch! He'll never get promoted as long as I'm on the board." He was hated because of the way he handled his Leavenworth position. You should keep in mind that your objective is to do what's good for the organization—not what is going to make you or your boss look good, or make other people look bad. What is the objective of the organization? How does it go forward in harmony and effectiveness? If you keep those things in mind, I don't think people can fault you very much. When you begin to get personal about it, you're treading on shaky ground.

In 1956 I was a colonel working for Major General Andrew P. O'Meara, who retired as a four-star commander of US Army, Europe.[12] As a major general, he was the deputy director, deputy chief of research and development under Lieutenant General Gavin.[13] One of my tasks was to produce and update a small four-by-seven-inch black leather notebook that contained data on all of the army's research and development programs. It contained a brief description of each item of equipment, its capabilities and limitations, status of development, status of funding, expected completion date, the contractor's name and address, and the army project manager in charge. The notebook contained secret information and was clearly marked SECRET in gold letters at the top and bottom of the front and back covers. Each page was marked with the appropriate security stamp based on the classification of the material contained on that page. It was a very valuable document for those few who had access to it because at a moment's notice at any meeting the bearer could describe whatever program might be under discussion.

We recently had gone through a bunch of security violations and O'Meara wanted them stopped. To emphasize how strongly he felt on the matter, he had called a meeting of all the division chiefs. He said, "There has been a rash of security violations. The next violator is going to get fined $150." This was a huge sum of money for junior army officers in the 1950s. Well, the next violation was his. He left the little book that was marked SECRET out on his desk overnight. His executive officer found it on his desk when he came in the following morning before O'Meara arrived.

Well, on the surface, it appeared to have been a security violation. I got appointed as the investigating officer. Here I was, a colonel investigating this general. I didn't like that one damn bit. So, somewhat nervous about the task at hand, I went to see the IG (inspector general) and JA (judge advocate) to get all the advice I could about how to handle this situation. I probably should have gone to the chief of chaplains to see whether he could provide me with a little divine guidance as well. The one thing that impressed me was: if you don't have a case that you could put to a court-martial, don't recommend any judicial action. With that in mind, I went about my investigation. I investigated everybody—not just army officers who worked there, but security guards and secretaries.

Nobody had seen this secret book on O'Meara's desk, either overnight or during the period when there were people in the office. So there was no definite proof that this book had, in fact, been left there overnight. Somebody could have borrowed it the day before and returned it before the general came in and put it on his desk. So there was a question. Although it seemed fairly obvious, it was not conclusive that General O'Meara had left the book on his desk. The evidence of his guilt was only circumstantial. I went back to the JA and the IG and told them what my findings were. They said, "You can only recommend some kind of an administrative action or reprimand." So I wrote in my report all the things I found and the corrective measures I thought should be taken. Then I recommended that General Gavin, who was the chief of research and development, administer an oral administrative reprimand to General O'Meara.

I took my report to General O'Meara and said, "General O'Meara, I have completed my investigation of this alleged security violation. Since it involves you and I have made recommendations adverse to you, I'd like you to read it. If you have any comments, we can talk about them."

He read through the report and his face got red as a beet. He turned to me, looked like he would have liked to kill me, and said, "Why didn't you recommend that I get fined $150?" I said, "Sir, if I had the evidence, I would have recommended you be court-martialed." He stared at me with fierce eyes for what was probably only three or four seconds, but for me seemed like an eternity. Then he smiled and said, "Okay, Jack." God, he could have chewed me up, but the experience, although nerve-wracking, engendered confidence.

From then on, I could do no wrong as far as General O'Meara was concerned. He had the confidence that when I told him something, it was on the level and not some wishy-washy recommendation made in the hopes of pleasing him. After that, I received excellent efficiency reports from him.

One of Jack Deane's close colleagues in the Office of Research and Development was Major Howard Cooksey. Through the course of their careers, Deane's and Cooksey's paths would cross many times. Cooksey, who would retire from the service as a lieutenant general, commented on the working conditions in their office.

> General O'Meara was the meanest man in the Army. He qualified hands down for that distinction until he introduced me to a friend of his, General Willie Palmer, who was even more terrible than General O'Meara.
>
> All of this was very frustrating because I would come home at night and complain about O'Meara and Palmer to my wife, and she would say, "How can you say those nasty things about these nice men?" Both of them had an uncanny ability to charm the wives something terrible.
>
> Once, we had a change of command and a big reception following the ceremony. I remember we were all going through the receiving line and I was right behind the Headquarters Commandant, a full colonel who carried a big load for Willie. As he went through, he must have said something to Willie like, "good luck to you on your new assignment, or sorry to see you go," and Willie replied, "Well, you are not as sorry as you will be, because I am relieving you, as of now." So he was relieved on the spot and sent to another assignment. To do that in a receiving line, at a reception, I felt was a novel approach to command and leadership.[14]

We used to have to make a quarterly presentation to the vice chief of staff on the status of the programs. You picked five or six that you would discuss. I got assigned this duty because my boss didn't like to make this briefing, for reasons that I didn't know about at that time.

Well, I had heard so much about Vice Chief Williston Palmer being a real bear.[15] He just chewed people up and spit them out. So I prepared myself meticulously. Major Jim Shanahan prepared my presentation. He went out, got all the information, and put it together for me. I studied it and formulated many questions for Jim to get the answers to. I read it again with the answers that were provided, and thought of more questions. After these were answered, I felt confident that I had a solid grasp of my subject.

By this time, I had gone over this thing in every way I thought possible. I went in to give the briefing. There was a little room around the side where the briefers stayed. You approached the podium in the secretary of the army's conference room through a curtain. As I was about to go in to give my briefing, this sergeant in the room said, "Good luck, sir." His tone made it sound like he felt I was about to face the Grim Reaper. I said, "You sound pretty dismal about this, like the world is about to cave in." He said, "Well, the last briefer from your organization fainted in the middle of it because General Palmer was right on top of him. I'm just hoping that won't happen to you." On this reassuring note, I entered the lion's den and took a good toehold on the carpet.

I had gotten out about ten or twelve sentences when Willie Palmer said, "That's not right. I don't know what you are talking about." The testing had begun. I said, "General, I cannot attest, from personal knowledge, to the accuracy of what I have just said. I can assure you, sir, I have spoken personally to the project manager on this specific matter and I have reported to you exactly what he told me to be the facts." He said, "Okay, go on."

A moment later, he challenged me again. I told him who I had talked to and what they had said specifically. I then cited, in some detail, what the facts were, the source of my facts, and why his understanding of the matter was incorrect. It was obvious that I knew what I talking about. There were a couple of minor skirmishes but I finished without any mortal wounds.

The briefing I had given really should have been given by my boss, Colonel Fred E. Ressegieu. He may have been the one who fainted; I never knew. Fred, a self-effacing, modest person, was a brilliant guy but very quiet. I learned a lot from him. After he retired, he joined Bechtel, one of the country's leading engineering firms. They put him in charge of a major project in Canada. On one of his trips to the project site in a small airplane, the plane crashed and Fred perished.

A couple of quarters later, General O'Meara and I were discussing the subjects to be discussed at the forthcoming review. I protested that Fred should really be giving the briefing. Preparing for Willie Palmer was no small task and jousting with him was no fun. O'Meara then told me, "As we left the room after your first briefing, General Palmer told me, 'That man knows what he is talking about.' I knew I had a winner and when I get a winner, I stick with him. You will be giving this briefing as long as I am in this job, so let's get back to work." Well, Willie Palmer had confidence in me because I had spoken up to him; I didn't weasel and waffle around, as so many people did in his presence.

One time, I had to go up to his office with General Gavin. We were recommending approval of a study I had made that called for the establishment of a field office in the Washington area, at Fort Belvoir or someplace, to take some of the overflow work off our shoulders, because the Army General Staff was limited in numbers by Congress. We had more work than we could handle and were working terrible hours. I called the action officer in the Secretary of the General Staff (SGS) office because I had never been in the vice chief's office. Some guys have a table in front of their desk. You sit at the table and have your papers spread out. Other guys have a podium. Sometimes you sit in a chair. The situations are all different. I asked the officer what to expect in Palmer's office. "What is the format when you go in there? Do you sit down at a table in front of his desk?" He said, "Are you out of your mind? You never sit down in Willie Palmer's office!" So I said, "Fine."

Well, we went up to Palmer's office and went in. Willie Palmer was talking on the squawk box to somebody and waved us to these chairs. General Gavin sat down beside the desk there. I went to the front of his desk and took a toehold on the carpet, so I was ready to charge. The SGS guy was standing in the corner. Willie got off the squawk box, looked at me standing in front of the desk, and said, "What are you being so damned formal about, Jack? Sit down, for Christ's sake!" I looked around at the SGS guy and his eyes were just about popping out of his head. So I sat down and made my presentation in a comfortable manner. I handed him a couple of charts. He said, "Looks good, fine," and it was approved. The SGS guy came out of there muttering to himself.

The point in all these stories is: I'm sure I was as lucky as hell that I had people who were sufficiently broad gauged to take what I had to say. By and large, though, you do better if you know what you are talking about. I don't mean fighting the system. A lot of guys just fight the system. That doesn't do you any good; it gets you in trouble. When you know what you are talking about, have the courage of your convictions, you probably will come out better if you present your case not in a bitter way, but in a firm, straightforward, factual way. There are just too few people who really do that.

Willie Palmer had a great reputation for putting people in stressful situations, but not with people who knew what they were talking about. If you answered that challenge, you didn't have to be disrespect-ful or fight the system. You just tell the Palmers you deal with what the facts are, as you see them. You should research the facts, obviously. If you know what you are talking about, by and large, that establishes you as a person who has what they think it takes. From then on, you are in great shape. You are more effective when you say something; they accept it. You don't have to spend an hour justifying everything you say. I think there are too few people who really feel that that's a good thing to do, but I think it is. That's something that I think young officers should take to heart: if they know what they are talking about, they should stand up and say it.

I was lucky in my superiors. If you deal with a guy who is so small that crossing him would mean your last promotion, then you would have to be more careful. But I don't think guys who are that small generally get to those positions. They are discovered long before that. Still, there are some, and you have to recognize that and measure your words. You have to make a determination. If you have a sense that they can't stand to be criticized, or to be told something that's not consistent with what they happen to be thinking at the moment, or that they are not big enough people to accept or even consider anybody else's view, then you try to get transferred.

In August 1952, I left Washington for Fort Leavenworth, Kansas. I really don't remember much of my time as a student at the Command and General Staff College. Basically the curriculum, our studies, and exams had to do with division exercises—in attack, defense, river cross-ing, and so on. The commandant at the Command and General Staff College at the time was Major General Lionel McGarr. We called him Splithead McGarr for the wide part in his hair right down the middle of his head. The deputy commandant also had the same hair style. The stu-dents at the college had a saying: "To solve the promotion riddle, part your hair down the middle."

5

Korea

After graduating from the course in 1953, I was assigned as the chief of the Plans Division of the Armistice Commission in Korea. The war had just ended, and the Armistice Commission had just been set up. It was my job to oversee the development of position papers on issues the head of the United Nations Command part of the commission would wish to raise with his North Korean and Chinese counterparts during meetings at Panmunjom. I should note that the Chinese representative claimed to be an observer, not a member of the commission. We saw, however, that the North Koreans never said anything that the Chinese had not obviously approved. We also noted that the time it took from when an issue was brought up by us until the issue was resolved was about the same time it took to get the North Koreans' position developed and approved by Beijing.

Incidentally, when I was there and participated at Panmunjom, the senior Chinese official was a Harvard graduate who spoke fluent English. We learned this through intelligence channels because he never spoke in English during the meetings.

The protocol for each meeting of the commission allowed the side that had asked for the meeting the right to make the opening statement. The North Korean delegation usually called the meetings and would use the opportunity to accuse us of all sorts of dastardly deeds. It was the policy of the senior people on our side to respond with an innocuous statement like, "Your statement has been noted." Well, I didn't think that was very good; it was totally defensive in nature. The press was reporting the things that were being said about our violations of the armistice and nothing about what the North Koreans were doing. I began to seek ways of turning that around, opportunities for us to go on the offensive.

Then I had a really good break. At one meeting the allegations the North Koreans were making rang a bell with me, as though I had heard them before. I just couldn't figure out where; I certainly couldn't have dreamt them. Suddenly it dawned on me that, in reviewing the propaganda broadcasts from Beijing, which we had copies of every day, I had read these same allegations. So I went back and looked them up. Sure enough, there they were.

I began to compare the minutes of prior meetings at Panmunjom with the propaganda broadcasts. There was almost a direct correlation, about two weeks apart. So I said, "Why don't we study the propaganda broadcasts and prepare positions in response to them, presenting the real facts? Let us call the meetings with the North Koreans and, before they make these allegations, attack them on the same subjects." In other words, through "preemptive" strikes we would blunt the thrust of their charges.

I presented this idea to Major General Julius Lacey, who was an air force general and the senior member of the Armistice Commission on the United Nations' side.[1] He thought about it for a while and didn't say much. Then he called me one night and said, "I want you to go to Tokyo. Present your plan and see if we can get approval to do this."

He wanted that approval because my idea was such a departure from the way the situation had been handled in the past. I had already made up a book of how we would attack—essentially, the position statements—and all the backup material to go with them. I grabbed my book and took it with me on the flight to Japan. As soon as we landed, I jumped in a jeep and tore off, arriving at the Far East Headquarters building at 5:00 in the morning. I used the men's room to shave and wash up. I had an appointment with the commander in chief of the US forces in the Far East, General John E. Hull, a good friend of my father, at 8:00.[2]

As a lieutenant colonel, I was a little apprehensive about my meeting with this four-star general. But General Hull put me at ease. He greeted me very warmly and spoke glowingly of his admiration and fondness for my father. I presented my thoughts to General Hull, gave him my book, and said, "This is an example. Here are the things that came up in these various broadcasts. Here are the minutes of the meetings." I showed him the correlation, then said, "Now, we have these broadcasts from the past few days. Here are the position statements that I would take. What I would suggest is that we now call a meeting with the North Koreans. Furthermore, I think we should have a big press turnout. We should inform *Time, Newsweek,* and all those guys that there is going to be something new."

He said, "I think that's a pretty good idea. Let's try it." So I jumped on the airplane, went back, and told General Lacey that my plan had been approved. We got the PAO (Public Affairs Office) people to lay it all on and we scheduled this meeting. Sure enough, when we made our charges it took the words right out of the North Koreans' mouths. They weren't prepared. They didn't have the flexibility to come back with answers because their answers hadn't been preapproved by the Chinese.

We had them reeling. They were sitting there looking at each other and didn't know what to do. Our people were greatly heartened by this and the press covered it well. There was an article in *Time*, I remember, about how we laced into them and showed them the things they were doing in violation of the armistice.

That became our modus operandi from then on. I don't think the North Koreans ever figured out how we were moving inside their decision cycle so fast. If they had, they probably would have turned the propaganda broadcast off or done something new themselves. In essence, we had very good intelligence on what was going to be coming and therefore were able to get in the punch before they did. That was an interesting assignment and one in which I thought I'd made a good contribution to the intelligence and public affairs effort.

After my tour on the Armistice Commission was complete, I was given the opportunity to command the 2nd Battalion, 17th Infantry Regiment, 7th Infantry Division in April 1954, even though I had already commanded a battalion during World War II. I had a number of experiences there that might be of interest to potential battalion commanders. Throughout my career, I've had the experience of dealing largely with high-caliber people. Major General Lionel C. McGarr, my division commander, was one of those.[3] He used to eat one meal a day, and that was supper. The talk in the division was that he survived the rest of the day on lieutenant colonels' assholes. He used to relieve people right and left.

I joined the division on a Sunday and immediately went down to the battalion I was to command. I don't know why—just my nature, I guess—but I got ahold of my S3 (operations officer) and asked, "What's the battalion doing?" They were training at the time. So I said, "Let me look at the training schedule." It looked like lousy training, as far as I was concerned; a lot of time was being spent on useless subjects. We were going to a reception at the regimental headquarters that evening at which the division commander was going to be present. I said to the guy, "Look, we have to redo this schedule; it's unsatisfactory. As soon as we come back from that reception, we are going to start it. You can be working on it while I'm gone. Does this bear any resemblance to the division's master training schedule?" He said, "The division doesn't have a master training schedule." I said, "I can't believe it! Every division has a master training schedule." He said, "Not this one."

When I went to this reception, I had been in command for maybe three hours. General McGarr grabbed me and said, "Deane, you have wasted two or three weeks of training. The last time I was down there, the place was just a mess." He laced into me like I was responsible for all this, when I had only been there for three hours.

I said to him, "General, I took command this afternoon. I've already reviewed the training schedule and I agree with you that it is lousy. I'm going to redo the training schedule, and I already have my staff working on it. It will probably be Tuesday before we get the new one rolling, but we are going to have a new one. I'm in command of the battalion and I'm going to train the battalion the way I think it should be trained. If you have ideas as to how it should be trained that differ from mine, I suggest you put it in the division program. You don't have one in your division, and this is the first organization I have belonged to that didn't have one."

He said, "What are you talking about?" I said, "I just told you that you do not have a master training plan in this division." He called over his G3 (division operations officer), John Acuff, and told him, "John Deane here tells me that we don't have a master training schedule. What happened to that schedule I approved?" Acuff said, "Well, it's in the AG (adjutant general) office being printed." So I looked at John and said, "That's what I'm telling you, General. Until I get that, I'm going to train my battalion the way I think it should be trained." I didn't have any further problems with him; he just shut up. He was really testing me, wondering if I had the guts to stand up to him. I passed the test.

Everybody told me that McGarr visited every battalion in his division daily, and that you were in danger of being relieved every day. Well, he didn't come to see me for about a week. He gave me a chance to get my feet on the ground. When he did come by, we had an exercise going on with a platoon in the defense. I took him down to the company just as one of the young corporals had put his squad in a defensive position. It was not as far down the slope of this hill as McGarr thought it should be. So he said to this young corporal, who was a pretty good soldier, by the way, "Why don't you put your men farther down the hill?" The corporal said, "Because there is a minefield down there from the war, and we don't know exactly where the boundary is. I'm just reluctant to get my men blown up for a little training."

McGarr turned to me and said, "Deane, if you don't train your men properly, when combat comes, you'll find yourself standing all alone at the top of the hill. They will all be gone." I said, "General, I've seen just as much combat as you have. No soldier under my command ever ran from battle, and I don't expect it will ever happen." He put his arm around my shoulder and said, "I didn't mean to get personal about this." He never visited my battalion again while he was in command. He had total confidence that I was going to run that battalion and run it right. He was out after the guys he didn't think could handle it. Now, I was fortunate in that McGarr was a big enough man to accept straightforward talk. You get some guys who are not that way, but I was fortunate.

Another interesting experience I had was with my regimental commander, Sid Wooten, who later retired as a major general.[4] He was a very nice, competent guy with a good record, but he had a tendency to get a little excited about things. There were certain things that really got him going. One was vehicle accidents. Fires were another. If there was a fire anyplace, it used to drive him out of his gourd.

Anyway, one night I got a call from Wooten that one of my trucks had run off the road and wrecked. He gave me almighty hell about this truck running off the road. He said that my drivers weren't properly trained, that they weren't disciplined. I hadn't known about the accident, so I got all my commanders together and said, "Look, if anything goes wrong in this battalion from now on, I want to know about it before the colonel knows it. If I don't know it before the colonel, you guys are going to have a problem. I recognize that I'm asking you to squeal on yourself when something goes wrong, but I'm going to find out anyway. If you're straightforward, that will be taken into consideration when I judge what happened."

From then on, they would report to me, and I would immediately call the colonel and inform him of what happened. I'd catch him before he found out anything about it, and that would take the sting out of the whole thing.

In one instance, there was a fire in a bunker and my battalion had to run a special court-martial. The kid who was in the bunker when the fire started was a Mexican from Los Angeles. He'd lived with oil heat or space heaters, exactly the kind we were using. The one in the bunker was defective. He had reported it as defective and warned that it was going to catch on fire at some point, but nobody had done anything about it. The fire wasn't his fault. I knew that Wooten thought the kid should be convicted because he was the only guy in the bunker when the fire started.

Well, we couldn't find this kid guilty; he didn't start the fire, and it wasn't his fault. We found him not guilty. I said to the members of the court and everyone present, "Everybody stay in your chairs, and don't move until I come back." I went out, called Wooten, and said, "Colonel, I want to tell you that your staff has just wasted the entire afternoon for me and my company commanders. We have sat on this case and heard the damn thing from beginning to end and there was no case to begin with. Your staff screwed this up and wasted all of our time."

Wooten replied, "Don't get excited, don't get excited." I wasn't excited, but I knew if I didn't call him first, he'd be roasting me. If I attacked him first, he would always say, "Don't get excited."

He had a command inspection team come down and inspect my motor pool. Some clown, one of his guys, was trying to help out. He took a torch to weld a bracket in my jeep while there were still some gas fumes around. The jeep caught on fire. My guys immediately called me, and I called Wooten and said, "Colonel, you sent this inspection team down here to try and do some good. I'd really welcome them if they did us any good, but they are not trained properly; they burned up my jeep!" He said, "Don't get excited! Don't get excited!"

I found out that, if I got to Sid Wooten first, everything was all right; if I didn't, my fat was in the fire. Wooten really respected me because he thought I was on top of everything. It was sort of a big game. I don't think he really realized how much of a game it was with us. With Wooten, you had to go after him like it was his or his staff's fault. You couldn't accept any of the blame yourself; it had to be all his fault. I used to do that and I really enjoyed that gentleman. He and I haven't seen each other since, but we always enjoyed each other.

Another thing we did in the battalion was not, in itself, a model but sort of an idea. I didn't think the unit morale was all that great when I got there; I didn't think we really had a gung-ho spirit. I was sitting there with my S3 and XO one evening, I said, "You know, we have to think of some idea to make this an individual battalion. There are other 2nd Battalions in the army, but this is the only 2nd Battalion of the 17th Infantry. We should identify it as different, a unique unit. We need a slogan. We are the White Buffalos."

That was our call sign on the radio. The buffalo was the regiment and we were the white battalion, so we were the White Buffalos. My S3 was a black guy with a lot of rhythm. He said, "Man, how about, 'Go, Go, White Buffalos,' or something like that?" I said, "That sounds pretty good." So we made up all these stencils with GGWB (Go, Go, White Buffalos) and painted the letters on rocks. We painted them throughout the regimental headquarters. We painted them on the sides of tents. We painted GGWB all over the damn place. Nobody knew what it meant and nobody knew who was doing it.

It became a big thing in the whole regiment and the regimental staff tried to ferret it out. They acted like they already knew what was going on, trying to get us to slip and give them a little information that would point the finger at us. We kept doing this for a while—it got bigger and bigger. Of course, our soldiers began to know who was doing it and were taking great glee and pride in this thing. Finally, it was discovered who we were.

I'd sort of borrowed this idea in part from Terry Allen and the Timberwolves. We didn't have printed stationery, so you had to type the heading in. I started making the heading "Headquarters, White Buffalo Battalion" and signing "Chief White Buffalo"—all that stuff. Well, all the guys in the battalion saw those things, and it was new and different. It went on for a while until finally, of course, some AG guy said it was against regulations to do this on your official papers. So we had to quit it.

But by that time, what I had sought had been accomplished. The battalion slogan was GGWB; we were the White Buffalos. The whole battalion then became a group of people who were different from everybody else. We had a great spirit, and it was terrific.

The fundamental thought behind these examples is that people like to be identified as some kind of a group, not just a part of the masses. They like to be identified in some way. Just saying you're in G Company of the 17th Infantry or something like that is not enough of an identification. There are a lot of G Companies, so you would like to have a more unique identification. Even the Boy Scouts wear the Silver Beaver Patrol or Red Fox Patrol badge. People take pride in that.

Serving in the 7th Division at this time were half a dozen other officers who had all graduated together from the same Command and General Staff course and received the same follow-on assignment to Korea. Willis D. "Crit" Crittenberger Jr., Jack Deane's old childhood friend, was one of them. Crit recalled,

Jack was a happy soldier and liked to pull jokes on his friends, as he had done with me in China years before. There were five or six of us classmates in the same division, with different jobs, of course. We would gather together periodically to commiserate with each other and, during one meeting, one from our class noted that Jack had received an award because his unit had a lower amount of garbage than other units within the division. The classmate asked him how he was able to do it.

With a straight face, Jack related how he rides around in the garbage truck on its daily run to all of his companies and takes notes on which units produce more garbage than others. When he offered this suggestion to the interested classmate, he also passed the word to the rest of his friends to meet for breakfast at one of the division kitchens. All of his friends got a laugh when they saw this battalion commander ride up in the garbage truck the next morning.[5]

I'd like to relate a story that might be useful to somebody. It's about how maybe you shouldn't do things. We got a new regimental commander in the 17th Infantry following Colonel Wooten named Hank Nielson. Hank came to us from another division. He had the impression that the 17th Infantry was totally incompetent and the division he had come from was the greatest in the world. That in itself was bad. There is an old saying in the army that the unit you join is the best unit in the army. You don't talk about the old one being better. You don't get anywhere that way. He was constantly criticizing the regiment he was now commanding.

He went with me one day to look at our defensive positions and said they were just unacceptable, would not withstand attack, and so forth. I explained that we were doing everything we could to improve, but we were having difficulty getting materials from the engineers. He said, "You guys just don't know how to get them. You submit your requirements to me and I will get you what you need." So I said, "Fine." He told all the other battalion commanders to do the same thing.

I went back to my headquarters and sat down with the blueprints that had been dictated by the 8th Army Engineers as the way to build these various kinds of bunkers. I then calculated how many bunkers we had of each type, how many board feet of what kind of lumber had to go into them, the timbers that held the top up, the sandbags on top, and the certain kinds of nails that were eight to a pound or whatever. I had a young sergeant, studying to be an engineer, who had an engineer manual. We calculated right down to the last nail what we needed. It was an awesome amount of stuff. The nails alone were something like 3.98 tons. When we sent the figures in, my request, which had been calculated with great care, exceeded the total for the rest of the regiment. The other battalions hadn't personally calculated it as I had. Those guys just sat down and did a rough estimate.

A little later Colonel Nielson called me on the phone and said, "Get in your jeep and bring the knothead who figured out this lumber and nail request up to my headquarters." Well, I took my S3, because he had helped me calculate everything. I wanted him to appear to be the goat, so this colonel would really lay it on the line. Then I was going to step in and say, "I'm the knothead."

Well, we got up there and the colonel said, "You know, I have this request from you and it's just totally asinine. It just shows the incompetence I've been talking about. I'd like my S3 here to address some of these issues." His S3 was a young major. By this time I was feeling like a grizzled old lieutenant colonel; I'd been a lieutenant colonel for ten years or so by then.

This major said to me, "You have this request for four tons of nails. Do you know what four tons of nail are?" I said, "Major, to the best of my recollection, I've never seen four tons of nails in one place at one time. So I really can't say that I know what it looks like." He said, "That's a lot of nails." I said, "I think it probably is." And let him go on with all this smartass stuff.

Finally, I said to him, "Major, do you know how many nails go into the juncture of these timbers?" He said, "No." I said, "I'll tell you. 8th Army Engineer prescribes three," or whatever it was. "Do you know how many nails there are in a pound?" He said, "No." I said, "I do," and told him how many. "Do you know how many junctures there are?" He said, "No." I said, "I do," and told him again. "Now, if you multiply the number of nails at each juncture by the number of junctures, you get the total requirement for nails. Do you follow that?" He said, "Yes, sir."

He could see now that he was in deep yogurt. I said, "Then you know that you divide that number by (whatever it was) and that tells you how many pounds there are. Do you follow that calculation?" He said, "Yes." Then I said, "I'm sure you know that there are two thousand pounds to the ton." He said, "Yes." I said, "So you divide it by two thousand and that gives you tons. I want to tell you, Major, you probably did a lot of calculations and found me out. There are 3.98 tons, actually; I just rounded it off to four. I'm sure you found that little error in my calculation, but if you want to call it four, go ahead."

The colonel was sitting there just gasping at this point. He said to me, "Well, I can't make a request for all this material." I said, "I didn't ask you. You're the one who said, 'Let's do this.' I told you we were going to have difficulty getting this stuff. I did what you told me." Then he said, "I want you to withdraw this request." I said, "Colonel, I want to tell you something. You told me that my positions would not stand an assault. I have now officially requested the material necessary to make them withstand an assault. If you want to accept responsibility for turning it down, do it; but that request is in your lap and will stay there until you do something about it officially." I got up and walked out. He was just steaming, but he had made everybody in the regiment feel like I felt toward him—he was a damn asshole.

He once told Jack Wright, who later retired as a lieutenant general, that Jack didn't know his butt from first base.[6] Jack Wright was a very proud, smart guy, the G4 (chief logistician) of the division. Jack went down and inspected the place where we dumped all the garbage. There had been terrible pollution problems because the dump had so much liquid in it that the sump holes would fill up. You had to keep digging new holes, and there was a big drive on to strain all the liquid out of the garbage that you could. Well, he went right down there and started taking notes on how bad the garbage from our regiment was—not how bad it was from everybody else's, but just how bad ours was. Within a week he had poisoned the division commander against this regimental commander. Then the engineer and G3 did the same. The guy was relieved from his command, and that kept me from getting in trouble because I had to deal with him.

The point is that here was a guy who thought he was too good for the system. He antagonized everybody in it, got relieved, and retired as a colonel. That was the end of Hank Nielson. Nielson had capabilities; he could have been a very good officer, a very effective officer. He served with me in the Pentagon and was an effective staff officer there, but he didn't know how to handle people. He didn't know how to handle himself; he didn't know how to handle his responsibilities. That ended him.

You have to recognize that you have a lot of people around. Some of them are good, and some of them are bad. You've just got to do the best you can with the ones you have. It doesn't do you any good to tell the ones who are bad that they are bad; that doesn't make them any better. If you keep making them feel like they are dummies, they are going to resent you; they'll get you if they can. They got Nielson. He deserved it, as far as I was concerned. When I finally left the regiment, all the lumber was starting to come in.

Even though you are in a position of high responsibility and stress, I think you have to treat it with a sense of humor or it will really get you down. There is pressure there all the time. You do the best you can and try to have a little levity, so that everybody doesn't get uptight.

The guy who replaced Hank Nielson was not a very competent guy and was having problems. He was hoping that this was his stepping-stone to something greater, getting command of the regiment. He was nervous and thought everything was going down the tubes because we would have a few DRs (deficiency reports) here and an accident there. So he started a "zero defect" policy. At a meeting one night with all of the battalion commanders, of which I was one, he told us how we were making all these mistakes that were reflecting on the regiment. He said, "I'm going to bring Colonel Deane in here as my exec to straighten out these mistakes." He was blaming a lot of it on his staff, who were pretty good. They were doing the best they could and weren't getting much help from him. I felt for them.

So I said, "Look, I don't want to be the exec of this regiment. I'm just like the other guys; I make a lot of mistakes and you don't like mistakes." He said, "I don't care if you like it or not. That's what you are going to be." So I went up as the exec. I served as the regimental executive officer for the 17th Infantry Regiment only a short time. Really, I got the operation calmed down a bit and things began to roll a little smoother because he wasn't wound up so tight. I didn't have much time there. I was sent home because my tour was up.

En route, I went to Japan for about three months to work on some deception plans. The guy who was in charge of planning there knew I had that background. They didn't have any deception plans in their war plans, so he wanted that done. So I spent about three months working on some cover and deception plans for the Far East Command. Then I went back, picked up my gear, and went on to the Armed Forces Staff College, which was interesting but not terribly useful.

6

James Gavin and Research and Development

It used to be that if you went to the Armed Forces Staff College, you would go there in lieu of going to the War College. When they first started it, they tried to elevate it to that level. It was a joint school, as opposed to the Command and General Staff College, which was basically army. One-third of the class came from each of the services in round numbers, but the school was not particularly useful.

The navy guys who came there, by and large, were very capable young men but seldom had any high-level staff experience. They didn't know how to write a staff study; they didn't even know what a staff study was. They didn't know how to write orders or anything. So they were really starting from scratch. Most of the army guys had spent three or maybe six years or so on the general staff level, so it was a piece of cake for them.

We weren't learning much and the navy guys were learning from us. The air force guys were a mixture. Half of them were happy-go-lucky fighter pilots who didn't care what happened anyway. They were great guys and competent air force officers, but they didn't get uptight about anything. They lived the creed of the old fighter pilots, "Here today and gone tomorrow."

You didn't learn a lot from either. I wanted to go there because I didn't know that it wasn't going to be very useful. I thought it was important to get as much schooling as you could as you went through your career. It did help in later service because it gave you some contacts. Otherwise, it wasn't all that great.

From there I moved back to Washington in July 1955 as the chief of programs and budgeting in the Deputy Chief of Staff for Research, Development, and Acquisition. That was my first assignment in R&D. I just fell into it. The office at that time was the Chief for Research and

Development and retained that title until I became the chief of research and development. Then there were several title changes. It changed to the Deputy Chief of Staff for Research and Development. Finally it became the Deputy Chief of Staff for Research, Development, and Acquisition. I held all three titles. I was there throughout the transition.

Lieutenant General Gavin was the first chief of research and development. I came there just as the department was being formed. Among the several men I have known and considered to be great leaders in peace or in war, James M. Gavin was clearly the greatest.

I did not serve with or observe General Gavin in combat situations. I first met him in 1941. He was a member of the Tactical Department at West Point while I was a first classman in the Corps of Cadets. At the time, I was the chairman of the Camp Illumination Committee. He was the officer in charge of this cadet activity.

Camp Illumination was an annual event. It was a big, informal, fun kind of an event, somewhat like a county fair. Our committee decided the site for the event should be the new Field House, a very large structure that would easily provide adequate space and, at the same time, afford cover from the elements in the event of a summer rainstorm. In addition to the honky-tonk games, rides, and food concessions usually found at a typical county fair, we planned a gigantic slide from the rafters to the floor of the Field House. The rafters, as I recall, were probably the height of a four- or five-story building above the floor. Obviously, there was a little danger involved. It would be a long fall if someone did something foolish and fell out of the bed of the slide, but we didn't give it much thought.

When I presented the plan for the event to Captain Gavin for approval, he asked several questions about the slide, some of which the committee had not considered in its deliberations. It became clear to me right away that Captain Gavin had some serious concerns and was not likely to approve the slide idea. My insight proved correct in short order. This was probably only the second meeting I had with him but, impetuous youth that I was, I jumped to the extraordinarily erroneous conclusion that Captain Gavin tended to be timid.

As most people are aware, General Gavin became one of the best known and most highly decorated and respected combat leaders of World War II. He commanded the 82nd Airborne Division at age thirty-seven. My good friend Lieutenant General Jack Norton was General Gavin's G3 in the 82nd Airborne. He told me countless stories of General Gavin's leadership in battle, something I never had the good fortune to observe.

Gavin was an inspirational leader who brought out the best in everybody but, at least in my experience, he never really said, "Here is what I want you to do" or "Here is what I want you to accomplish" in very concrete terms. Being his exec was a think-type job. You had to be producing whatever he wanted, and I didn't know what he wanted half the time. I'd write him notes to try to find out. I would go around to see Jack Norton and say, "Jack, how do you understand what this guy is trying to tell you? I can't communicate with him." Jack said, "It was the same way when I was in the 82nd. I used to write him notes and he would write me notes. I never could understand what he wanted. I just guessed." Jack was a good guesser, I guess. He was highly respected by Gavin.

At the end of a week, on a Saturday afternoon, we were in the office. Gavin was getting ready to go home and I asked, "Are you going to be in the office tomorrow?" He said, "Well, I don't know yet. I'll call you if I'm going to come in." I said, "Well, I don't have a telephone because I've just arrived in Washington. If you think you're going to come in, I'll come in at whatever time you want. Then, if you decide not to come in, you can call me and I'll go home."

He said, "How come they made you the executive officer, if you haven't been here for a while and know what's going on?" I said, "I don't know, sir." Gavin said, "What were you doing before?" I said, "I worked over in the Plans, Programs, and Budget office." He said, "Did you like it?" I said, "Yes, sir, I'd like to go back there; I really don't know what's going on up here. Frankly, I just don't feel like I can give you the kind of support that you need." So he said, "Okay, let's look around and see who has been around here long enough to move in and have some background."

So they moved in somebody who had been around a while and I got out of there. I went back to this job where we did all the planning, programming, and budgeting for R&D. That's how I happened to work on the Army Program Advisory Committee. The deputy to Gavin was the member who was the representative for R&D and I was his backup. I prepared all the position papers and so forth for him. Then I would go to the meetings with him. When he was not present, I would sit in at those meetings on the Program Advisory Committee and the Budget Advisory Committee.

That was a very interesting and useful experience because the guys on that committee were all pretty smart. Creighton Abrams, who was on that committee, later became the chief of staff of the army. I had known Abe only by his World War II reputation: that of a fearless battlefield leader who led his tank battalion with success and distinction in many battles against the superior armor of the German panzer formations. He was a brigadier general at the time, and all the rest of the committee members were major generals. He didn't say much, but whenever he talked, the room would fall into dead silence. They all would listen to what he had to say. They obviously respected him and his judgment. It was during these budget battles that Abe did two things that endeared him to me, maybe made him my hero.

One of the things that went on at those meetings was to divide up sort of a fixed total budget for the army among various accounts. Procurement and R&D were the two capital accounts. The personnel account was fairly fixed. The O&M (Operations and Maintenance) account was relatively fixed. So getting within the budget generally depended upon how much money Procurement or R&D would give up, and there was always a fight between these two.

One day they were looking for another $10 or $20 million, and the whole damn committee landed on me. "You guys in research and development always want all the money. You're always talking about what you are going to send to the field, and never deliver. You always just keep experimenting." They were giving me a hard time. Then the conversation slowed down and General Abrams spoke up.

"You know I share your views. The people in research and development don't do all the things they should do about getting equipment out in the field when they should." I thought, "Gee, I'm really sunk now. When he starts talking everybody listens." Suddenly he said, "But in this instance, I believe Colonel Deane is right, and I would like to express my view to this committee that I support his position." Those comments turned the whole thing around. Suddenly, I was in like Flynn.

On another occasion about a year later, in 1956, the Army Budget Committee was deadlocked on a major issue, an issue that had nothing to do with R&D. I had very little knowledge of the factors involved and had not intended to take a position on the matter. But as it turned out, my vote became the deciding vote. The deputy comptroller, a very senior civil servant called Herman the German, demanded that I vote. The committee chairman was the army budget director and Herman was the number two guy on the committee. I refused. He said I was out of order and again demanded that I vote.

I explained that I would not vote because my vote, cast by the least knowledgeable person in the room, would decide the issue. I went on to say that the chief of staff would not know how the issue was decided, just that one position or the other was being recommended by the committee. I said I, and the committee for that matter, would be doing the army and the chief an inexcusable disservice.

This quieted Herman for a moment, but he began another attack on me. Then Abe interrupted, saying, "Colonel Deane is right. I find his position not only the correct one, but an admirable one." Again, the clouds parted and the sun shone through.

He was that highly respected, even when he was a brigadier general. These other guys, who were older than he was and senior in rank, spotted him right away as a guy who knew what he was talking about. He assimilated his experience on that committee much better than I did mine.

A major part of my work was that program and budget stuff. Another major part was preparing all the testimony for Congress on the Hill. Any documentation we had to submit to the Hill was my responsibility and I used to go with Gavin any time he testified there.

When General Gavin had ideas he wanted the staff to develop, he would have the appropriate division chiefs meet in his office. I was always included because whatever came out of the meeting would impact Plans and Programs. When we were all seated, he would tell us what he had in mind. His voice was so quiet, you could scarcely hear him; everyone strained to hear. We became inspired; we were mesmerized.

As we left his office, we would be walking three feet off the floor in la-la land. Then, as his door closed behind us, we would come back to earth, and we would wonder, "What did he say?" We would go back to our respective offices and work like hell to develop something that we felt approximated what he had asked for. When we went to see him again, he knew immediately whether we had succeeded or failed miserably. If the latter, he would pump us up again and we would go through the same routine until we finally got it right.

This was a daunting exercise. He never told me his purpose. I concluded that it consisted of three elements. One, he was not sure himself of precisely what he wanted and hoped our views would help him put meat on the bones of his thoughts. Two, he did not want to constrain our thinking by setting forth specific goals or ideas. Three, he wanted us to develop our abilities to think beyond the current capabilities of man and technology in setting goals and objectives.

In retrospect, I would guess it was a combination of all three elements with special emphasis on the last two. I can say this, however; the officers who served with him in research and development came away better equipped for future service than the officers in any other part of the Army General Staff. I am firmly convinced that R&D produced, during General Gavin's period of leadership, more officers who later became three- and four-star generals than any other part of the General Staff. I am, equally certain that this style of leadership, his manner of inspiring people to outdo themselves, was the basis for the success of those he touched.

I had quite a bit of contact with congressional staffers. There, again, if you grease the skids a bit, or find out what their hangups are and have your boss prepared to address those hangups, you get things accomplished better. It was a distasteful job in some respects because I didn't have a lot of respect for either congressmen or the staffers. They had a myopic outlook on life—and, I figured, were not always out for the best interest of the country. It was distasteful to me to have to go up there and plead with them to do this or that. Later, that was one reason I was glad to retire. I had just gotten fed up. Be that as it may, that was what I had to do. One of my duties was to accompany Gavin when he went to testify on the Hill.

At the time he retired from the army, there was a controversy about what the R&D budget should be. He had been told to cut back. As I recall the situation, he thought it should be increased. Gavin had a great vision of the future. He might not be able to articulate what his vision was, but he visualized where we should be going. You know, even then, when we had an annual budget of maybe $400 million, he was talking about a $2 billion budget. He used to have me make it up, so that he had it in his hip pocket all the time. Well, trying to go from $400 million to $2 billion and spend the money wisely was not easy. It used to keep me awake at night trying to figure that one out. He had the vision that you needed these monies to make the army what it is today.

The secretary of the army at that time was Wilbur Bruckner, a very political guy. Every time we came back from the Hill, Gavin would have honestly answered the questions he was asked. Bruckner would say, "I've read your testimony and it's not in accordance with my policies. I don't think you should be talking about that much money." Gavin would say, "They asked me a question; I had to answer." Bruckner would say, "Yes, but there are other ways of answering. You don't have to be so forthright."

Gavin did tell me that the secretary warned him not to tell the congressional committee members that he, General Gavin, did not believe the funds requested in President Eisenhower's budget were adequate to modernize the army. The secretary, in General Gavin's judgment, was not asking him to outright lie but to choose his language carefully so that the committee members would believe he considered the funds adequate. This disturbed General Gavin greatly because he was determined to tell the truth and would not attempt to mislead the Congress if they asked his opinion. General Gavin told the secretary that he would not lie about the matter. He would not bring the matter up on his own initiative, but would not lie if he was asked by the committee members.

Gavin felt very strongly about being forthright, and that led to his decision to retire. There were rumors that he had expected to become commander of the army field forces. I guess people believed that because he was not going to get that command, he was bitter. Therefore, he was retiring. Well, I was very close to Gavin at that time and went to the Hill with him during this entire period, and it was a very trying time for him.

To me the most impressive example of his leadership, which I have always embraced, but certainly espoused since I worked for General Gavin, came as we drove to the Hill the day he was going to testify before Senator Lyndon Johnson's Preparedness Subcommittee. This was to be his second committee appearance at the request of Senator Johnson. The first appearance was sort of a last-minute, informal event at which he was to appear alone. I did not accompany him, nor did any of his staff. The events that transpired at this first meeting eventually led to General Gavin's decision to retire. During this hearing, he was asked his opinion as to the adequacy of the funds being requested and, true to his statement to the secretary, he said that he did not consider them adequate.

Upon his return to the Pentagon, he was summoned by the secretary, who was furious. I was not present at the meeting, nor do I believe anyone else was there, with the possible exception of the chief of staff. As a result of the position taken by the secretary at this meeting, General Gavin made the decision to retire after the second meeting with the Senate Preparedness Subcommittee. He did not make this decision known to me. He did make it known to others, perhaps the chief of staff, the secretary, and some old friends.

He was getting all these accusations because his budget stance went against the administration and the press was riding him. I remember going up to the hearing of the Senate Preparedness Subcommittee of the Senate Armed Services Committee, where he was finally going to lay it on the line and tell them he was retiring. In the car on the way up to the Hill, Gavin said, "Now, when the hearings are over, I'll have some classified material in there, but because of the nature of this event, the press is going to be in there too. There will be a lot of people from the press, and

I'm just not going to have the time to think about getting all this classi-fied material together. So I want you to come into the room immediately and gather it all up."

I was astounded and said, "Won't I be in the room with you?" He said, "No." I said, "Well, I'm always there when you testify. I have all the backup material for you and everything. Why won't I be there?" He said, "You're not going to be in the room for this reason: There are a lot of people who don't like me, or what I stand for, or are jealous of my success, or whatever. I don't want you to be tainted by that. I don't want people to associate you with me and wreck your career. While I would like to have you with me because you would be a big help to me, I think it would be better for you to stay outside."

I was so touched that I almost wept. Here was a man who was an orphan. He had no family until he joined the army. The army became his family and he loved it as much as anyone had ever loved his family. When he was a young enlisted man, his officers observed his dedication and constant study to improve his stature. They encouraged him to apply to West Point. Now he was facing the darkest moment of his career, facing the possible destruction of the relationship that had been the most impor-tant part of his life, his relationship to the army. Yet he was thinking of me, thinking of how I might be harmed by loyalty to him. That, in my humble opinion, is the greatest trait of leadership a man can have—con-sideration of the well-being of those he is honored to command.

I said, "Look, I work for you, I admire you, and this is all immaterial, as far as I'm concerned. I'm going to be in the room." So Senator John-son permitted me to be in there. I was the only person there outside of the committee and Gavin. He was testifying about what was going on, what he was doing, and so forth. Then one of the senators asked a question that, with its phrasing and his tone of voice, was really asking, "General, aren't you really quitting in the face of fire?"

Well, that got his hackles up, but Gavin was a very calm guy who had complete control of himself at all times. He was very articulate, and had a good command of the language. He said, "I'd like to address that question." He started with his background as an orphan—how he never had a family, how tough life had been as a kid, and how he had always yearned for a family. Then he joined the army as an enlisted man, and the army became his family, the first family he had ever had.

He spoke of his experience at West Point: what that had meant to him and the ideals he picked up. Then he went through his career—what he had done, how he had always marched to the sound of the guns. He pointed out that he had been under fire many times during World War II, and how on one occasion his aide, standing next to him, had been wounded by rifle fire, but he had never quit the battlefield.

During his oration there was not a sound in the hearing room. It was a terribly moving experience. Every one of those senators—grizzled old politicians who would wring a baby's neck if it meant a vote—were crying. Tears just rolling down their faces. It was a spectacle that was hard to believe.

When the hearing ended, as I gathered up the papers we had brought, I noticed Bill Ryder, General Gavin's friend of many years. Bill Ryder commanded the first airborne unit in the army, the Airborne Experimental Platoon established to determine whether it would be practical to activate larger airborne units in the army. He later retired as a brigadier general. Bill was there at General Gavin's request. If Gavin announced his decision to retire, Bill was to go immediately to the general's quarters to retrieve the letter requesting retirement that Bill and other close friends had been framing over the preceding days. Upon his return to the Pentagon, Gavin met with the chief of staff, General Maxwell Taylor, and submitted his resignation.

My admiration and respect for General Gavin, and our friendship, continued until his death. He visited me at Fort Bragg once when I was commanding the 82nd Airborne Division. He marveled at the changes time had wrought in the training and equipment of the soldiers. He warmly recalled that the airborne spirit, the esprit of the division, in whose development he had played such a major role, was still alive and kicking.

General Gavin's vision did much to shape the army we have today. His was a success of extraordinary proportions as an army officer and leader. He was equally successful in civilian life after his retirement. He became the president and CEO of Arthur D. Little, Inc., a consulting company he took from a $10 million domestic concern to a $70 million international corporation based in Boston.

Once, at a meeting we had while he was CEO of Arthur D. Little, he asked if I might be considering retirement, and if so, would I consider joining Arthur D. Little with the idea of replacing him when he retired. I was greatly honored, but I had no intention of retiring at the time and was not enthusiastic about living in Boston, a town about which I knew little other than the fact that it was the home of the Red Sox. Had I joined him, though, I would have had the opportunity of seeing firsthand more of his superb leadership ability.

After Gavin's retirement, General Trudeau came in and took over. I continued there for about three or four months until my tour was up, and then went to the National War College. One thing about the Office of the Chief of Research and Development in those days—the talent within that organization was exceptional. I don't know how they did it. We had a civilian executive officer for personnel who was a GS-15, I think; he had a lot of pull with the personnel people. When we needed to get people into R&D, he would go down and screen the records in career management. In those days, they had a numerical rating on your efficiency report. The max was 140, as I remember. Guys who scored 135 to 140 were the "water walkers." Our executive officer never came back with a record that was lower than 135. We got these guys, and those colonels and lieutenant colonels who were in R&D while I was there later became three- and four-star generals.

Bill Fulton, who later retired as a lieutenant general, was there when he was a major, as director of the General Staff, or whatever the title is now. Bob Coffin, who later retired with three stars, was a colonel, like I was. Jack Sutherland, Jack Norton, Phip Seneff, and Tom Dolvin retired with three stars. Mike Davison, who was commander of USAREUR (US Army, Europe) later, retired with four stars. We were all division chiefs. That indicates the quality of people they had there. I can't begin to recall them all.

We were the guys running that place, and we had tremendous power in the general staff. Whatever we prepared for Gavin was so far superior to what was prepared for other general staff officers that he always prevailed at the Army Policy Council or General Staff Council. This illustrates the importance, to you as an individual, of getting the best possible people you can at any time. You really should fight for that.

Anyway, I then went off to the National War College. The National War College was really a great experience. Unlike the Army War College then—and, I guess, even the National War College now—it was what they called a gentleman's course. We went there and had a lecture almost every morning by some prominent senior guy on the army or air force staff. After the lecture, there would be a brief break. Then we would get into assigned groups and kick around what we had just heard, what we thought about it, and have a general discussion.

You were associated with just terrific people. They were the cream of all the services, the State Department, the CIA, and other government agencies. The National War College provided great contacts for you later in the service. When you get to that level, you get into more and more joint operations. Right after we graduated, a guy in the State Department called a civilian member of my class who worked in OSD (Office of the Secretary of Defense), who, in turn, called me up. He said, "We are going to establish a military college, like the War College, in Indonesia." I was getting ready to go to Europe at the time. I called another guy in the class and said, "I know you don't have a follow-on assignment yet, and this sounds like an important mission. Would you be interested?" He was. So, because all these people had known each other from the War College, within a matter of a week, we had this guy assigned to the job. If it had gone over formally to OSD in the form of a letter and a request, it would have been months before they assigned somebody. So those contacts were important, and one of the major benefits of the War College, as far as I was concerned.

Jack Deane's father, Major General John R. Deane (*seated center*) served as General Marshall's chief assistant from the start of World War II and accompanied President Roosevelt to the Casablanca Conference. In 1943, he was ordered to Moscow for the remainder of the war to serve as US ambassador William A. Harriman's chief military assistant. (US Army)

On his first day at West Point, July 1, 1938, Cadet Deane receives guidance from Cadet Harmon "Jack" Lampley, class of 1939. (Carolyn Deane)

John Deane (*left*) and his West Point roommate James E. "Josy" Josendale pose for a picture during a break in yearling field training during the summer of 1939. (Carolyn Deane)

Senior Cadet John R. Deane Jr. was captain of the West Point Polo Team in 1942. He is pictured here atop his favorite horse, Blue Hour. (Carolyn Deane)

Jack Deane's graduation photo as a member of the West Point class of 1942, the first class to graduate during World War II. Of the 374 officers who made up the class, seventy (19 percent) were killed in action during the war. (Carolyn Deane)

Lieutenant Colonel Deane, twenty-five-year-old commander of the 2nd Battalion, 415th Infantry Regiment, 104th Infantry Division with his S-4, First Lieutenant Joseph Giglio. The photo was taken in Germany in May 1945, just before the division redeployed to the United States to prepare for the upcoming invasion of Japan. (Marilyn Shinavar)

New York governor Hugh L. Carey pays off a World War II bet to retired brigadier general Gerald C. Kelleher at the Executive Mansion in Albany in 1978. Carey and Jack Deane served under then Colonel Kelleher in the 415th Infantry Regiment, 104th Infantry Division during the war. In 1945, the two men made a wager on who would reach Nazi-occupied Cologne first. Carey paid the winner with eleven cases of beer, calling Kelleher "the finest soldier I ever met in the uniform of the U.S. Army." Kelleher would go on to serve in Korea and Vietnam, earning two Distinguished Service Crosses, seven Silver Stars, and a Purple Heart over the course of his career. (New York State Archives)

Major General Terry Allen led the 1st Infantry Division on campaigns in North Africa and Sicily before being relieved by Lieutenant General Bradley in 1943 for perceived disciplinary problems. Upon his return to the United States, General Marshall immediately gave Allen command of the 104th Infantry Division, which he finished training and led into combat in 1944. Allen became an important mentor to Deane throughout their time together during the 104th Division European campaign. (US Army)

During Deane's tour in occupied Germany managing Operation RUSTY, he met several intriguing personalities, including General Fritz Bayerlein *(left)*, Rommel's assistant in North Africa and later commander of German forces in the Ruhr Valley at the end of the war, and Hanna Reitsch *(below)*, famed pilot and one of the last people to see Hitler alive. (Bundesarchiv, Bild 183-B02092 / Schwahn / CC-BY-SA 3.0); Bundesarchiv, Bild 146-1978-033-02 / Dinstühler / CC-BY-SA 3.0)

West German economics minister Dr. Ludwig Erhard and West Berlin mayor Willy Brandt meet Colonel Deane at Friedrichstrasse in August 1961. (US Army)

Lieutenant Colonel Howard Cooksey, deputy commander of the 2nd Battle Group, 6th Infantry in Berlin in 1961. Cooksey and Deane served together as staff officers at the Pentagon and in Berlin, and were together again at the end of their careers, General Deane as commander of DARCOM and Lieutenant General Cooksey as deputy chief of staff for research, development, and acquisition. (Carolyn Deane)

General Charles D. Palmer, deputy commander, US European Command, visits West Berlin in the fall of 1961 to confer with local leaders and is briefed on unit border positions by Brigadier General Frederick O. Hartel, commanding general, Berlin Brigade, and Colonel John R. Deane Jr., commander of the 2nd Battle Group. (US Army)

Colonel Deane participated in an interview with television personality Jack Paar at the Berlin Wall on September 6, 1961. UPI print media ran a critical news story of the interview before the television episode ran and the ensuing political fallout led the army command group in Berlin into an ill-advised damage-control operation. (Hal Gurnee)

A photo given to Colonel Deane by a West German reporter shows the aftermath of a confrontation that occurred in 1961 at the Berlin Wall. Deane stood his ground in front of a rock-throwing crowd of West Germans protestors while an East German riot-control water cannon shot out bursts on each side of him, forming a perfect V. The situation was defused as Deane refused to retreat and the East Germans backed down. (Carolyn Deane)

Deane was fortunate to serve under another mentor while a staff officer in the Pentagon. He had a close relationship with Lieutenant General James Gavin, describing him as an inspirational leader who brought out the best in everybody. (Record Group 13, Office of the Governor, Governor Robert P. Casey, Proclamations [series #13.99], courtesy of Pennsylvania Historical and Museum Commission, Pennsylvania State Archives)

While Deane was serving as 1st Infantry Division assistant division commander, his helicopter crashed during a combat operation in October 1966. Deane suffered a broken leg, but continued to go into combat in a leg cast and on crutches after his release from the hospital. (Carolyn Deane)

The command and staff team of the 1st Infantry Division in Vietnam during 1966 was exceptional. *Seated, left to right:* assistant division commander Brigadier General John R. Deane Jr. (note the cast on his left leg), division commander Major General William E. DePuy, and assistant division commander Brigadier General James F. Hollingsworth. Lieutenant Colonel Alexander M. Haig Jr., division G-3, is pictured standing second from left. (US Army)

Brigadier General Deane confers with the 1st Infantry Division G3 Lieutenant Colonel Sam S. Walker in Vietnam early in 1966. Both men were graduates of West Point and the sons of army generals. They would both rise to four-star rank. (US Army)

Brigadier General John R. Deane Jr., commanding general, 173rd Airborne Brigade, Vietnam, 1967. (US Army)

While in command of the 173rd Airborne Brigade, Deane spent many hours of the day coordinating or observing operations unfolding below. (US Army)

French photojournalist Catherine Leroy accompanied the 173rd Airborne Brigade on their combat parachute jump on February 22, 1967, during Operation JUNCTION CITY. (US Army)

Members of West Point class of 1942 at Headquarters, Brigadier General Willis D. Crittenberger's II Field Force Vietnam Artillery (II FFV, known as 2nd Field Force Vietnam), Long Binh, Vietnam, spring 1967. *Left to right:* Colonel Bob Offley, deputy chief of staff, II FFV; Colonel Don Bolton, assistant division commander, 25th Infantry Division; Colonel George Allin, deputy commander, II FFV Artillery; Colonel Ted Marks, commanding officer, 1st Brigade, 25th Division; Brigadier General Jack Deane, commanding general, 173rd Airborne Brigade; Colonel Charlie Mizell, commanding officer, 54th Field Artillery Group; Brigadier General Bud Ryder, assistant division commander, 4th Infantry Division; Colonel George Rehkopf, commanding officer, 199th Light Infantry Brigade; Brigadier General Crit Crittenberger, commanding general, II FFV Artillery. (Carolyn Deane)

Deane commanded the 82nd Airborne Division during difficult times for the army, 1968–1970. He worked hard to maintain readiness while at the same time combating drug and racial problems that plagued a military fighting an increasingly unpopular war in Vietnam. (US Army)

Army Vice Chief of Staff General Bruce Palmer pays a visit to Fort Bragg in 1970. Palmer (*far right*) greets Jack Deane, Hank Emerson, and John H. Hay. These three warriors, with their service in World War II, Korea, and Vietnam, had between them been awarded five Distinguished Service Crosses, twelve Silver Stars, and three Purple Hearts. (Courtesy of Henry E. Emerson)

As part of his duties as DARCOM commander, Jack Deane meets with his counterpart in the British Army, General Sir John N. Gibbon, master general of the ordnance, on April 21, 1975. (US Army)

Still serving on behalf of the army at the age of ninety-two, General Deane returned to the new Army Materiel Command headquarters at Redstone Arsenal, Alabama, to participate in the Former Commanders Conference held there in 2011. (US Army)

7

2nd Battle Group, 6th Infantry Regiment, and the Berlin Wall

By the fall of 1959, I was a colonel and knew that I wanted to have a command. When I went to Europe, I was supposed to go to a command job. When US Army, Europe told the career management people that they were going to put me in programming and budgeting, the career management people said, "No, he should get a command, so we will send him someplace else." That's when Europe said they'd guarantee me the command. The career management people asked me if that was all right with me. I said, "Sure, fine." So I went over on that basis.

As a commander, I made it a practice to eat breakfast with the troops a lot. I'd just go over and show up at a mess. I didn't tell anyone I was coming. Sometimes you would find that the company commander or the first sergeant wasn't there. Nobody was with the troops. Then you would say to people, "Somebody should be around to see that things are going right—that they are getting their breakfast." I'd talk to a guy at breakfast and find out that he didn't get any eggs that day or he didn't get very much bacon.

I would find out there were enough eggs being issued for each soldier to have two for breakfast, but the mess sergeants were using a large amount of them when they baked cakes. They could have used powdered eggs for that, but they were using fresh eggs instead. So I put out a directive that from now on, no fresh eggs would be used in cakes. It was a soldier's right to have two fresh eggs for breakfast. I also found out that the bacon ration wasn't really adequate, so I arranged to get an extra strip of bacon per man.

When I was in charge of the 82nd Airborne, I used to call the division together once a month or so in the stadium and talk to them. I'd say, "Here is a problem I saw last month about the eggs," and I'd tell them about it. If it was a problem I couldn't or wouldn't handle, I'd tell them so and why. So I was eating breakfast with the troops to learn things, but I also enjoyed talking to the kids.

When I was the commander of the battle group in Berlin, once every two or three weeks, I'd take an evening off and hit about five or six bars where 99 percent of the soldiers went. I'd sit down and have a beer with a guy and start talking to him. You would learn a lot about how they felt about the outfit, what motivated them, how they thought things ought to be happening.

Also, you find that some kid has had too much to drink, and he is about to get himself in trouble. So you call an NCO and say, "Hey, take this kid home." Your DR rate goes down like crazy. When the company commanders see you're doing that, they begin to do it. Then they are looking out for soldiers. It wasn't command presence, but I was learning things.

I liked to go sit with a soldier when he was at an outpost in the middle of the night, because he is nervous. He is by himself and hears sounds in the night. He is so happy that you are there, he just blurts out everything he has on his mind. Then you find out some things that you otherwise wouldn't. You find out about some things that are not going so well in your outfit and you can correct them.

I went to Europe initially to set up a programming system. After serving on the staff for about a year and a half, in February 1961 I was assigned to Berlin, where I commanded the 2nd Battle Group, 6th Infantry Regiment. Lieutenant Colonel Howard Cooksey, who I had worked with closely before in Washington, was assigned as the deputy commander of the battle group. *Cooksey later recalled, "During this period of time, I learned a lot about good leadership watching Jack Deane, and a lot about bad leadership watching some of the others; how they reacted under the pressures that existed at the time."*[1]

The 2nd Battle Group was rather a routine command. The only difference from the command in Berlin and a command the US zone of Germany was that we didn't have many places to maneuver and do field exercises. We had a forest in our maneuver area, but it was pretty small. Everybody got to know the place like the back of their hand, so there wasn't anything strange about the training. That was a disadvantage. We came down into the major training areas only once a year. Even then, we went with only a couple of companies at a time because the rest of the battle group had to remain in Berlin.

I did something similar to the GGWB stencil from my Korean days while I commanded the battle group. I was talking to Bruce Clarke, who was the commanding general of US Army, Europe at the time.[2] Bruce had a tremendous reputation as an expert in training. I admired the old gentleman very much. He was very kind and supportive. I was in Heidelberg for some kind of meeting, so I dropped by his headquarters to pay a courtesy call on him.

During our conversation, General Clarke said, "You know, there is too much emphasis today in the army on the best squad, the best soldier, the best this and that. There is only one guy who can be the best. So the guys that can't quite make it are discouraged. They don't want to compete. They know they are never going to be the best squad, or best mess, or whatever. I think we lose something by that. When I was a young officer, we had in the army what they called the Chief of Infantry's Rifle Squad. Any rifle squad in the army that passed certain tests could be a Chief of Infantry's Rifle Squad. You know, like an Expert Infantryman's Badge or an Expert Medic's Badge. Some tests are physical; some are mental. Everybody could strive toward meeting those standards, so there could be a lot of those squads. The standards were sufficiently high that you didn't have them all make it, but people who really set their minds to getting there could get there. We don't do enough of that today."

I said, "Boy, that's a great idea." I went back to Berlin, sat down some people, and started thinking about how we could do this thing. It was against regulations, I guess, but we did it anyway. On the blue cord that the combat infantry unit wears—like the thing an aide wears, but it's a blue cord, a fourragère—we used to wear our little battle group crest. Our battle group was called the Guardians.

Howard Cooksey, who was my deputy and later retired as a lieutenant general, was probably the guy who had the idea.[3] At least, he was the guy who really implemented it. He took one of these little crests, tore off the wreath that goes around the cross in the middle of the Expert Rifleman's Badge, and had a jeweler mount the wreath around the little battle group crest. It was a very nice-looking thing.

We took this and said that guys could become "Outstanding Guardians" and be permitted to wear this badge. We would present these things at appropriate ceremonies, once a month or so. If any squad leader got his squad up to certain level, they could all wear them. Any mess sergeant who got his mess up to a certain standard could wear one. Then we didn't have one best mess in the battle group; we had five messes. You might have all five of them, if they made the standard. We really wanted to have a standard so that maybe only three could make it, but at least they could all strive for it.

Well, it went over like gangbusters. Everybody wanted to wear that badge. They all wanted to know, "How do I win this thing?" Boy, everybody wanted to win one of those things and it was a great thing for the battle group. It was unbelievable.

Sensing the efficiency of a unit is very difficult and a matter of experience. In the 2nd Battle Group in Berlin, for example, we used to have alerts. We had to have one once a month. SHAPE (Supreme Headquarters Allied Powers, Europe) dictated one was to be held every quarter or something like that. Other commands in between would call alerts from time to time. When you had an alert, troops had to assemble and load on trucks or be someplace in a certain time.

When I took over this battle group, I found that the prior alerts had been a farce. The S3 would say to the commander, "We haven't had our alert this month; why don't we call one tonight?" And the commander would say, "All right. Let's make it 3:00 in the morning." Everyone would be home and sleeping in their battle gear. The minute the buzzer would go off they would fall out of bed fully clothed, run out, jump in their car, and drive to the battle group assembly area. The truck drivers were sleeping in their trucks. I said, "This is no way to train. I'm going to call alerts from now on and I'll call them from home. I'll call the duty officer up and say, 'Alert.'"

The S3 was unhappy with me; he said that I didn't trust him and didn't have confidence in him. I said, "You go home and your car pool says to you, 'What time should we pick you up in the morning?' You mumble about 'I think I'll go in on my own tomorrow.' Then they know there's going to be an alert. I don't think you deliberately tell anybody, but it leaks."

Well, the first alert we had, instead of making it in an hour or whatever you're supposed to make it in, it took three hours. I said, "This demonstrates how well trained we are." I called the next one the next night and we did a little better. Within a short time we did very well. If you are going to screw around, go through the motions of training and say you're training—you're crazy. Reports can be dummied up, or they are the perception of some guy who is not as good as he thinks he is. You have to go out, see it, sense it, and feel it.

"We were in the Berlin area at the time the Berlin Wall was put up," Lieutenant Colonel Cooksey recalled. "We went to the Wall and so did the Russians, and we thought we were going to war, really. We thought this was World War III." But Deane thought otherwise.

The Berlin Wall going up on August 13, 1961, gave me an opportunity to flesh out some of the confrontation philosophies I'd developed, both from my own experiences with the Communists while serving on the military armistice commission at Panmunjom in 1954 and my father's experiences in the Soviet Union during World War II. I came to believe that all Communists would push you right up against the wall, but would give and look for another weak point the minute you started to push back. Until they really wanted a battle, they were not going to push too far.

When they put the wall up in Berlin, I got word of it early on a Sunday morning as they were just starting. I went to the headquarters and requested permission to tear it down. The people at the headquarters began to shake in their boots at the suggestion. I was convinced that if we did tear it down, they would build another wall, maybe a couple of hundred yards further back. Then we would tear it down again, because we had the right through the agreements with the Soviet Union to be in any part of Berlin.

We weren't confined to our little sector, nor were the British or the French. As an occupying power, we had a right to be anyplace, without restriction. I believed in exercising that right. If we tore the wall down, after they tried it about three times, they would lose face and quit. That was my belief. The people in headquarters didn't believe that. They were scared to death that they would start a war or that they would be taken over the coals by the political authorities at home.

I went down myself, walked through the openings, and walked around in East Berlin. When I determined that there was no danger, I took my family and drove in and out of every entrance and exit point they had left. I drove through the wall at least once during the day with my family in an American-marked official sedan. I was in uniform and nothing happened.

One day I was visiting with the commanding general of the Berlin Brigade, Brigadier General Frederick "Fritz" Hartel.[4] Hartel was my immediate superior. While I was in his office, word came in that the East German government had announced on their public radio that anybody who approached within one hundred meters of the wall would be shot. Simultaneously with receiving this word, Hartel received orders to test the East German resolve. I was told to be on the wall within an hour and a half.

I was wearing my class A uniform on this visit to Hartel—shirt and tie, blouse and trousers—the usual uniform if I were not going to be in the field on an exercise or inspecting field training. I called my battle group and started it on its way to Tempelhof. There I wanted my unit to assemble a squad of riflemen from Captain Jack Davis's company to meet me at what later became known as Checkpoint Charlie. I also directed my driver to bring my jeep and battle gear to a point one block short of Checkpoint Charlie. I wanted my own jeep because it had all the communications gear that I needed to control the battle group and direct operations. We would initiate a patrol from there.

I left Headquarters, Berlin Brigade, and proceeded by sedan to the designated point in the vicinity of Checkpoint Charlie. Shortly after I got there, my jeep arrived. I stepped into a doorway and changed uniforms as modestly as the situation permitted.

The travel time from my battle group headquarters to the wall was about half an hour. The battle group immediately went into an alert condition. The troops, who were out training and doing such details as hauling trash and picking up rations, were assembled. They got into their battle gear and were down at Tempelhof in under an hour. The squad that was deployed to the wall met me there in less than the hour and a half that we were allocated.

We were so much ahead of schedule that a company of tanks, which were supposed to come down and support us, didn't show up until after we had completed our patrol. The German police, who were supposed to make the patrol with us, never showed. The press, who had been alerted, didn't get there on time. These young men who went on this first mission with me never got any publicity.

I told the squad of the East German threat and the orders I had been given to put out a patrol on the wall. I told them they were not to fire unless fired upon. If fired upon, they were to return fire and kill as many of the sons of bitches as they could. I said the battle group and the tank company would be called into action if a firefight started. I told them there was always the possibility that the East Germans would carry out their threat, but I did not believe they would. I said, "Just to show you how strongly I believe this, I am going to lead the patrol. Follow me— let's go." I called the Berlin Brigade on the radio and announced the patrol was moving out to accomplish the assigned mission. Well, at this point we were all alone.

The mission entailed little risk, in my view. From the men's viewpoint, they didn't know whether they were going to get shot or not. We walked along the wall for two or three miles, so close you could reach out and touch it. The East German soldiers who were on the wall didn't know what to do. They weren't expecting this confrontation, and were apparently stunned. They had not received specific orders to shoot, so they were afraid to shoot. They had heard something but didn't know what to make of our actions.

At the end of the two miles, I called Berlin Brigade on the radio carried by my radio operator. I told them where we were, that we had patrolled for about two miles, and felt we had made our point. I received permission to discontinue the patrol. I called for my jeep and truck to come pick us up.

It was another confrontation in which they backed off after making a specific threat. When challenged, they refused to carry through. We stayed on the wall for some months, I guess. There were various confrontations along the wall, some of which my battle group and others were involved with.

This story tends to corroborate the firm conviction that my father had regarding the Soviets. He spent two years with them during World War II and developed this conviction during his dealings with their military people at many levels. He believed that regardless of what the United States and its Allies did, the Soviets would not go to war until it suited their purposes. When they perceived that going to war was in their best interest, they would do so regardless of what the West was doing. If necessary, they would trump up an incident to use as a justification of their actions.

Although the Communists of East Germany uttered a public threat, our calling their bluff did not precipitate action. It was simply not in their interest to act. Numerous other events during my tour of duty in Berlin produced the same results. The withdrawal of the Soviet Union during the Cuban Missile Crisis after President Kennedy's threat of action by the United States also demonstrated the validity of this theory.

Later on, in September 1961, public affairs people briefed me that a television talk show personality, Jack Paar was coming to Berlin. Paar was the host of the *Tonight Show;* he was incredibly witty, and the show was amusing and very popular. He had asked to interview me. I was supposed to do the interview and make whatever arrangements were necessary. Jack Paar was not popular with the press at that time. He frequently ridiculed them on his show. He was liked even less by members of Congress and the Senate. He made a point on his show to take every opportunity to portray these people as a group of dolts, interested only in votes and devoid of consideration of what was good for the nation.

Personally, I was not pleased with this assignment because the actual filming was scheduled for the day I was supposed to drive from Berlin to

Wiesbaden to meet my parents and my aunt and uncle, John and Eleanor McDonald. They were to arrive in Wiesbaden on a Rhine River cruise, spend a couple of nights at a marvelous old hotel between Wiesbaden and Rüdesheim, then pick up a car and driver and proceed to Switzerland. I was to meet there with my car and go with them for at least a part of their trip. I knew the area well because I had become a friend of a vintner in Rüdesheim and visited him from time to time to buy wine.

I had lunch with Paar and he asked me if we could do the show down at Checkpoint Charlie. I said, "Fine with me." My battle group was not on duty on the wall, another battle group was. Still, I felt that this was an opportunity to take the original squad of men who had made that first Berlin Wall patrol with me, the first guys to meet the challenge, and to let them appear on TV. I would explain to him during the course of the interview that these were the men who had been on the first patrol. We went down to the wall.

I was supposed to go on leave that morning but delayed it because Paar couldn't do the show at any other time. The squad and I, the television crews, and Paar arrived at Checkpoint Charlie as planned. Paar asked the soldiers their names and hometowns. He asked about the patrol and what they thought of the experience and the time they'd spent on the wall now that it was over. Paar asked me what I thought about the current situation. I told him that I didn't expect any trouble here. He then asked what my family thought about living in Berlin. I told him they were happy and wouldn't leave Germany for all the tea in China. The interview went fine; Paar was pleased and so was I.

Then Paar asked a few questions about the rifle we had, the new M-14. We had been one of the first units to receive the new rifle, about which there was some controversy. Many people contended it did not present sufficient improvement over its predecessor to warrant its procurement. Some in the scientific community, people who would never have to use it, pressed for a lightweight rifle, which we in the army knew would not withstand the rigors of combat use.

In any event, I had been the chief of programs for Lieutenant General Gavin when he was the army's chief of research and development. I was with him when he wrestled with the naysayers on the Army Staff and the scientists. We were at a point in time when there had to be a major procurement of rifles and, more significantly, the appropriate ammunition. He knew the lightweight rifle would come along sometime and we would want it. He contended that, if we broke the mold of the M-1 rifle and its caliber 30 ammunition and went with the M-14 and its 7.62 ammunition, we would have half the battle won when the new lightweight rifle was perfected. Far more than half the investment in a new weapon system lies in the ammunition.

I decided to give the M-14 a publicity boost, probably because I idolized Jim Gavin. I took one of the rifles in hand and described as succinctly as possible why it was an excellent weapon and why my soldiers liked it. In describing the weapon, I inadvertently pointed it in the direction of East Berlin. I did not aim it or anything like that; it was just pointed in that direction as I discussed it. This became the basis of a cause célèbre.

We did the show and finished it up about midafternoon. There was a United Press guy there who kept asking me if my troops were supposed to be on the wall at this time. I said, "No. The 3rd Battle Group is here now." He asked me if I would normally bring my troops down there. I was answering him factually because I had a pretty good rapport with the press. I didn't know that the reporter was trying to get ammunition to sink Jack Paar. I left to go on leave that night and drove down to Wiesbaden, where I was going to meet my parents and my aunt and uncle.

Jack Paar related the Berlin episode in his book My Saber Is Bent, *published in 1961.*

> *Our request in Berlin was very simple, I wanted to interview Col. John R. Deane, Jr., a much decorated officer, and asked him to bring along one or two soldiers so that Peggy Cass and I could talk to them. As it turned out, he brought a squad of twelve men, explaining that he didn't want to single out some and leave others behind. I asked for a jeep, in order to have something to sit on during the interview. That was the extent of it.*
>
> *There happened to be an operational changeover of units while we were preparing to shoot, which accounted for more military personnel being at the border than normal. Also, a few off-duty officers had drifted up out of curiosity to watch the goings-on. The blown up UPI story made it sound as if the Army had restaged Pickett's Charge for my benefit.*
>
> *All that took place was that Peggy Cass and I chatted with Col. Deane and a private, and Col. Deane briefly showed us the new army rifle. Our interviews with a handful of soldiers consisted mostly of talk about their wives and babies. The conversation was about as provocative as the small talk at a PTA meeting. It was all decidedly unwarlike. When the program finally aired,*

showing on film what had really taken place, it was generally admitted the whole thing had been a tempest in a TV pot.[5]

All hell broke loose that night. Of course, I didn't know about it. I was in a hotel and nobody knew where I was. I met my parents the next day, and we took a look around Wiesbaden before we left to go on to Switzerland. In the course of looking around, I saw a copy of the *Stars and Stripes* newspaper and picked it up. There was all of this furor about the Paar interview on the wall. They seized upon my pointing the rifle toward East Berlin as an action that could have thrown the world into World War III.

In the course of that portion of the interview, Paar was looking at the rifle. Guys were looking at the rifle and showing it to him. The press made it appear that we were threatening the East Germans by pointing our rifles at them, as though Jack Paar was stirring up World War III. This hit the press like wildfire. People in the Senate, led by Mike Mansfield, demanded that immediate action be taken against this irresponsible commander in the field who was trying to start World War III.

Well, the Department of Defense didn't react very well to this unfavorable publicity. They didn't look into the facts before they took action. Arthur Sylvester, a lightweight who was the assistant secretary of defense for public affairs, demanded action. Anyway, I was down in the main part of Germany en route to Switzerland when all this happened. My mother and father saw the article and were concerned. I wasn't concerned because I didn't think I had done anything wrong.

I was acting in accordance with the directives of the higher headquarters and had not been starting World War III or pointing rifles at anybody. When I got to Switzerland, my deputy commander, Howard Cooksey, reached me at the hotel where I was staying and said that things were really going badly. The other battle group commander, my deputy, and others had an all-night meeting with the major commander, Major General Watson, whom I had known for quite some time, and with General Hartel, the Berlin Brigade commander.[6]

They decided that the only way they were going to cool off this firestorm was to issue an official reprimand to me. It was in the press that I had been officially reprimanded, when I hadn't even talked to these guys. My deputy told me how people reacted at this meeting. He said there he was, trying to fight off all the guys who were worried about their rank. He wasn't successful. It was finally General Watson's decision that I be reprimanded and it was announced that this action had taken place although I was in Switzerland. My deputy, Howard Cooksey, was not permitted to attend this meeting.

Cooksey recalled, *"I spent the whole day trying to track down Jack in West Germany so that he could at least get his day in court. But Hartel said there was no need for Deane to present his side of the case. The pressures brought on as soon as Jack Paar aired this program were intense. The Pentagon hit the command in Berlin with questions like, "what is going on over there?" and those sorts of things, and the commander in Berlin's solution to the problem was to relieve Deane."*[7]

I called General Hartel and said, "I understand you have issued me a reprimand." He said, "Yes. We were just trying to protect you." I said, "I don't call that protection, and don't see how you can issue me a reprimand without speaking to me. I haven't seen any reprimand. How can you put it in the press that I've been reprimanded? That's a bald-faced lie, General. I'm on my way back now; and as I drive back, I am contemplating stopping by Heidelberg and talking to General Clarke." General Bruce C. Clarke was the CINCUSAREUR (Commander in Chief, US Army, Europe) then.

He said, "God, you don't want to do that!" I said, "Well, I don't have any real reason for talking to General Clarke about this incident. I'm not seeking his help; but from all I hear, I've been painted in a totally false light. General Clarke had sufficient confidence in me to make me the commander of the battle group. I like and admire him, and I don't want to let him down. I'd like to have him hear my side of the case, so I'm going to think about it."

Hartel, visibly shaken, insofar as you can sense these things over the phone, said, "Oh, you don't want to do that." In shaky tones he said that the reprimand had been issued in my best interest. The people in Washington were screaming for blood, and Watson's action had warded off something more drastic. I said, "If I want to, I'll do it! I have access to the command and I'll do it if I want to!" I was really contemplating going and having a press conference and blasting this thing wide open.

I was upset because the reprimand was so unjust. I decided as I drove back up there I wouldn't go to General Clarke. Instead, I drove back to Berlin, went to see the people who had reprimanded me, and said, "You know, I think, first, that this is cruel and unjust punishment. More importantly, I was tried and sentenced without my day in court. That's not the American way and I don't see how you guys can do things like that." "Well," they said, "let's just keep this quiet now. Let's not get excited." So I cooled it.

Then Hanson Baldwin, a great military writer for the *New York Times,* came to Berlin. Watson and Hartel told me that I would not be permitted to be interviewed by him. But Baldwin came to Paris, SHAPE headquarters. General Lauris Norstad was the commander. General Norstad's public affairs officer (PAO), Brigadier General Bill Rider, was a close friend of mine.

Hanson Baldwin approached him about getting this interview and Bill directed that it be done. Hanson Baldwin came to my home in Berlin and we talked. He said, "I think I have some good news for you. It's something that hasn't been released yet, but people have really seen through what happened to you here. This is all going to be cleared up." Bill Rider didn't tell me, but he knew it, because on the phone he had been kidding me. If the situation had been as serious as it appeared to me at the time, he wouldn't have been kidding.

While Hanson Baldwin was there, General Clarke called me and said, "I've looked into this matter and know that you did not act improperly. I had confidence all along that you didn't. That's why I looked into it." He had gotten some of the staffers to find out what had really happened. He said, "I've directed General Watson to withdraw the reprimand. If you wish to really rub his nose in it, I have also directed that he, at your request, read the withdrawal in front of your entire command."

The Associated Press broke the following story, which ran in national media outlets on September 28, 1961:

The Army has rescinded as unjustified actions taken against two staff officers following the controversial filming of a Jack Paar TV show on the border between East and West Berlin. General Bruce C. Clarke, commander of the U. S. Army in Europe, issued a statement on September 28, 1961 saying no one did anything wrong enough to warrant criticism, although in hindsight what was done might have been done a bit differently. The two officers are Colonel John R. Deane Jr. of San Francisco, who was admonished; and Lieutenant Colonel Dallas W. Hoadley of Baltimore, removed as information officer of the Berlin command and transferred to Heidelberg.

Deane, with a squad of 13 enlisted men diverted for the purpose, was on hand Sept. 7 for the filming of the show at the Friedrichstrasse checkpoint. So were numerous other officers and soldiers. The Army participation caused a storm of criticism in the United States. The original disciplinary action was announced in Washington Sept. 9. Clarke said he concluded after seeing the film of the show and reinvestigating the matter that an injustice had been done to the two officers.

"Therefore," he said, "in order to right an injustice, I have directed Major General Albert Watson in Berlin to withdraw orally the admonition given to Colonel John R. Deane Jr., and to remove from the files anything pertaining to this incident which is adverse or derogatory to him, and I will similarly remove from the files anything pertaining to Lieutenant Colonel Dallas W. Hoadley." Deane, he added, will continue to command the 2nd Battle Group, 6th Infantry, in Berlin; and Hoadley will keep his new assignment in the information division of Army headquarters. Clarke said he considered Hoadley's position here as of equal importance to the assignment he had in Berlin.[8]

Meanwhile, Fats Waller and his band had come over to West Berlin to entertain the troops. This Berlin Brigade PAO guy was there telling one of my companies that he wanted them to get in their personnel carriers and roar into the company area in time for lunch. The guys would charge out of the personnel carriers and gather around Fats Waller, playing with his band. This was to be a staged thing.

About the same time, General Watson called me up to his office, but he could hardly bring himself to read the withdrawal of the reprimand. It really gagged him. He read it, but he couldn't resist saying after he had finished reading it, "I still think you exercised poor judgment." I said, "General, I was acting on instructions from your headquarters. I assume, when instructions come from your headquarters and your staff, they reflect what you want done. I can't check everything, but I will in the future. I'll call you every time I get a directive from your headquarters. Then you'll get some idea of what I go through. Furthermore, I have a directive now." I described this thing about Fats Waller and the personnel carriers.

"After you got so upset about the wall, do you want to do this totally unusual action? Your staff has directed that I do it. I've issued an order not to allow it because I was prepared to defend myself in light of what has happened in the past." He said, "Oh, my God!"

Well, I lost what little confidence I had in him. I figured if the balloon went up, Watson would not be our leader. He would be cowering down in a bunker someplace. I figured both he and Hartel would fold. I began to walk all the defensive positions in Berlin so that I'd be in position to assume command. I wanted to know where the other battle groups and tanks would be, what their positions would be, and what avenues of approach they would use. I had all the information down pat, and certain members of my staff knew what I was doing. We had all the facts lined up so we would be able to take charge when these guys folded.

Further evidence of General Watson's lack of stability came at a dinner party at the home of the 3rd Battle Group commander, Wayne Hinder. General Watson and his wife, Wayne and his wife, and my wife and myself were there with a San Francisco opera singer, who was an acquaintance of Wayne and his wife. The singer was aware of something having happened in Berlin concerning me, but didn't really understand the situation. She kept asking questions during the course of the dinner. This was just killing Watson, who finally broke down in tears at the dinner table. He said what he had done to me was the worst thing that he had ever done in his life and he was ashamed of himself. My respect for him went even further down. Anyway, we got over that. I was exonerated and we finished up our tour.

There was another instance with the Soviets that pointed out what I was saying about confrontation: if you have the gumption to stand up to them, the Soviets are going to back away until they are ready to go to war. When they are ready to go to war, it doesn't matter if you stand up to them or not; they are going to war.

We had to send patrols into East Berlin every day just to show our presence. I used to periodically go on these patrols because I wanted the soldiers to know that it was something that had to be done but wasn't dangerous.

Once when my battle group had duty on the wall, I was touring and saw this mob of West Berliners collecting down a little side street by the wall. I went down and found they were hurling insults at the East Germans. The East Germans wheeled up a water cannon, a big truck with a water tank and some kind of pump that sends out a high-velocity spray of water. It will knock you down if it hits you; it's for riot control. They wheeled it up and pointed the gun across the wall at the gathering. The West Germans happened to be fixing a sidewalk in the area, and there were little cobblestones all around that were almost the size of a tennis ball. The West Germans picked these up, and soon the air became black with these cobblestones being thrown across the wall. Several stones bounced off the water cannon, which didn't seem damaged. The East German soldiers backed away, so they weren't in range of the rocks, and began using the water cannon on the rock throwers.

I was standing in the front rank of the group of Germans and I was in uniform—clearly an American officer. All the West Germans fell back out of range of the cannon. Well, I felt that I couldn't retreat. I had to stand there, all alone. This happened right next to the building in which a newspaper had its headquarters, and one of their photographers took a picture from above. I have a picture of where the water shot across to the left of me; then they pointed the gun at me and dribbled a little out. Finally, they decided they weren't going to shoot at me. They didn't dare shoot at me. You can see a perfect "V" right where I was standing. This was another confrontation in which they backed off.

The morale of our soldiers in Berlin was very high. I mentioned earlier the badge we created to set them apart. In the first place, the troops who went to Berlin were carefully selected. They had to be mentally stable. The Soviets' concern about sending their people to Berlin was that a guy might defect. It would be easy to defect up there, and they didn't want that to happen. That brings to mind another incident.

Our policy makers in the State and Defense Departments had a great fear that some member of our services in Europe would defect to the Soviet Union, much to the embarrassment of our government and to the joy of the Soviet propagandists. Accordingly, soldiers assigned to Berlin were carefully screened. The thought was that if a soldier were going to defect, the easiest place to do so would be Berlin. Until the East Germans built the Berlin Wall, there was complete freedom of movement from the western sectors to East Berlin.

I had a black first sergeant who was, without a doubt, the best first sergeant in the battle group. First Sergeant Adams had my headquarters and headquarters company. He was a quiet, serious, determined man—a real professional, a super soldier. One day, I was surprised by a call from General Hartel, who said there had been an investigation of Sergeant Adams that indicated he had some association with Communists. Hartel said, "I want you to order him out of Berlin immediately. Have him pack his bags, keep him under surveillance, and have him out of Berlin within twenty-four hours."

I said, "General, I haven't seen this investigation, and I am not going to act on it until I do see it." He said, "You don't have to see it. I'm telling you to do it." I answered, "Well, put your order in writing and send it to me. I'm not taking any orders like this over the telephone. Sergeant Adams is by far the best first sergeant I have. I am responsible for his welfare and for seeing that he is treated fairly. I have no reason to suspect him of anything but complete loyalty to our country. I'm not going to destroy his career the way you are suggesting. Unless I know the basis for this action, I cannot see my way clear to do it." He said, "I'll send the investigation report down to you and let you take a look at it."

I did not look forward to the forthcoming visit. I did not have a high regard for people in the Counterintelligence Corps (CIC). I had had a number of bad experiences with them on an earlier tour in Germany. They were an arrogant group, more intent upon demonstrating their power than what was good for the country. Within an hour, an agent from the CIC came to my office and produced the report. He was a pompous jackass. He produced the report and I went through the damn thing. Sergeant Adams's sister had gotten involved with some pro-Communist youth group in Pennsylvania when she was perhaps ten years old, and she took him to a picnic with the group. Because of that, they were branding him a Communist. I couldn't believe it. As I finished reading, I glanced up into the gloating face of the agent. He made some comment about the effectiveness of the CIC in uncovering this news, which he viewed as earth shattering. I asked why it had taken them so long. After all, First Sergeant Adams had been in the army for over twenty years.

The agent then opined that I would have to act on the recommendation contained in the report. He apparently had convinced Hartel that the recommendation was sound. I believe he might have convinced Hartel that if he did not take action when he had knowledge of the contents of the report, he would be subject to severe criticism and possible relief from command for the exercise of poor judgment if Adams defected. He then tried this line of reasoning with me.

Without responding to his comments, I picked up the phone and called Hartel. I said, "I have read the report you sent. The recommendation is one of the most asinine I have read, although it is probably not the worst the CIC has made over the years. I'm not going to order Adams out of Berlin unless you direct me to do so in writing. I feel so strongly about this that I am willing to put my career on the line. I don't think Sergeant Adams is going to defect and I don't think he is a Communist. If anything goes wrong, you can relieve me for cause. That will be fine, but I just don't believe that will happen."

Hartel muttered words to the effect that my career would be over if Adams defected and that he hoped I clearly understood that. I told him I did. I said, "It is just one of the perils of being a commander and supporting your troops." I called Sergeant Adams in and told him what this was all about and what I had done. He said, "You don't have to worry about me." I said, "I didn't worry about you." And that took care of that.

I can relate one other incident that might be interesting. At Checkpoint Charlie, as you faced into East Germany, there was a drugstore just on the left side of the street. There was nothing in between it and the wall for a distance of fifteen or twenty yards. We had a little guard shack in the middle of the road at Checkpoint Charlie for people to check in or out of our zone.

The Germans had put up a maze so nobody could make a high-speed run at the entrance or exit. We had a bus go over again to test the Germans, and they had demanded we produce IDs. They were just trying to irritate us and establish their control or whatever. We refused to show the IDs and had this whole busload of guys in uniform. They didn't know what to do, so they let them through into East Berlin.

When the bus was coming out, they stopped and held it. Here was the bus, stopped in the German maze. Thirty yards or so away are our guys at Checkpoint Charlie. This went on for several hours. We had snipers up on the roofs by this time. When I arrived down there, events were already under way. I stood on the windowsill, because the bottom of the window was blacked out, and looked over the top part of the window to view the situation.

I had a telephone and I reported to General Watson, who was on the other end of the line, "They're now trying to get on the bus." Watson, I guess, had two phones in his hand. He would talk to General Clarke at the end of the other line and say, "They are now trying to get on the bus." Clarke, who apparently had two phones, too, would say the same thing to General Norstad in Paris. General Norstad would call back, I guess, to the chairman of the Joint Chiefs or someplace. Eventually, it would get to the president.

The communication was something else! Here I was, standing on this windowsill, reporting blow-by-blow what was happening over all these channels. Eventually the information was getting to the White House. Finally the East German police released the bus and let it return to West Berlin. That was a pretty antiquated command and control system. Even so, it was better than when McNamara was the secretary of defense and could talk directly to the field commander, so that he could run the war from his office.

8

Office of the Director of Defense Research and Engineering

After I left Berlin in July 1962, I was assigned to the Office of the Secretary of Defense in the Office of the Director of Defense Research and Engineering. I was the executive officer to the principal deputy director of Defense Research and Engineering. There were a few interesting aspects to it from a historical point of view. The army was at that time trying to do several things. They were trying to develop a computerized artillery fire control system, to develop the Redeye missile, and to lay the ground work for a future tank.

One day I was meeting with Harold Brown, then the director of Defense Research and Engineering; he later became secretary of defense. Harold Brown, seeing a computer for the field artillery in the budget, flew into a mild rage. He said that the army wanted a computer just for a status symbol; they didn't need a computer in the field artillery. I didn't say anything at the moment; but right away, I took my boss, Brown's principal deputy, out into the field. We went to the headquarters of Harry Crites, an old artilleryman who commanded the 7th Army Artillery.

I told Harry, "You know, we have to show this guy how a fire direction center works." Harry said, "We have a battalion out in the field right now firing a howitzer. Let's hop in a helicopter and go on over there." We did so and showed him what went on in a fire direction center. Then I told Harry, "Now you have to show him how they compute the firing data."

We went into this shelter and here was this young kid with a slide rule. He was figuring out the firing data, making circles on the overlay, and plotting the concentrations he'd figured out. The staff came in and put a meteorological message on his desk; he pushed it aside and went on with his slide rule. My boss asked him, "Doesn't this new message change things?" He said, "Yes, sir, but I haven't finished with the last one yet." So he went on with his slide rule.

When we got back to Washington, behind the scenes, I got the computer back into the budget so it would come up again in Harold Brown's office. Brown said, "I said to take this computer out last time." My boss said, "Wait a minute now. I went out in the field and looked at the artillery. You can't believe how antiquated they are. A little computer could make all the difference in the world." So Brown said, "It would?" And he said, "It sure would." And that's part of the reason we now have the TACFIRE (Tactical Fire Direction System) and the BCS (Battery Computer System).

These greatly increased the effectiveness of the artillery. We would have gotten computers anyway, at some point, but nobody on the staff that should have been defending this program was prepared to do it then. They just let this guy, who was very bright but who didn't know about the situation, take the money for something very important out of the budget.

Similarly, we had some money in the budget for tank suspension research. Some civil servant was supposed to be defending that money. Harold Brown said, "Oh, the army doesn't need that money." So the guy, instead of defending the need, said, "Well, we could defer it for a year, I guess." I said, "Now wait a minute. Let's look at this thing. You're saying the army doesn't need it. Why do you say that?" He said, "The tanks go fine." I said, "They don't go fast enough. They need a better suspension for them to go faster." He said, "I've seen tanks going forty-five miles an hour." I said, "Sure, they go forty-five miles an hour down a road. Do you know that the maximum across-country speed of our current tank is about six to eight miles an hour? That speed is dictated by the tank's suspension. If you go any faster than six to eight miles an hour, the crew inside is dead or knocked out after about a hundred meters. Now you, as a brilliant physicist and mathematician, know that if you go from point A to point B twice as fast, the enemy can only shoot half of their shots at you." He said, "That's right." I said, "Well, that's the idea we have in mind, to be less exposed in the tank." He said, "You mean to tell me that it will only go six to eight miles an hour across country?" I said, "I not only mean to tell you; I'll be glad to take you out and demonstrate. I'll let you go ten or twelve miles per hour across country by yourself, but don't expect me to go with you." He said, "Gee, I never thought of that."

We then approved the tank suspension budget, and that research information was incorporated into the new M-1 tank. Finally, we had the Redeye missile, a forerunner of the Stinger. I had been deeply involved with the Redeye over the years and had been one of its staunchest defenders from my staff days under Gavin.

Having been strafed in World War II, and knowing what an airplane could do to you, I was convinced that a soldier would be a lot better off if he had something to knock that enemy plane out. There has never been enough artillery in the air defense to knock down all the enemy planes in our forward areas. I was very much impressed with the potential capabilities of this weapon and its importance to infantry operations.

Years after I'd worked under Gavin, they were having technical problems with the damn thing. One day at a meeting my boss said, "We are going to put that weapon back into advanced development," which meant putting it back into a more basic stage of development. Doing that would add two or three years to the program, at least. I said, "Don't make a hasty decision like that. It's a terribly important weapon." I explained to him why and cited my experiences when I could have used it. I told him about how we were getting strafed one day and I had a driver shot and killed, sitting right next to me. He said, "Okay. I'll give you six months."

I hightailed it down to the office of the chief of research and development, Lieutenant General William W. Dick. I told him what had happened and said, "The army has six months to get this thing straightened out. If you don't, it's going to go back into advanced development. Then we are going to be in deep kimchee. I can't get any more time. That means you have to put a lot of personal emphasis behind this thing." He did. The technical problems were solved, and the Redeye went into production.

There's a basic point here. In offices like the Defense Department, where you have all civilians, you have to have people with the gumption to speak up and who also know what they are talking about. If not, the office is going to be ineffective. We had a lot of people like that in the army. The air force had outstanding people and was very good at using them. Arbitrary decisions—made on the basis of no knowledge—are going to be made. These are going to be detrimental in most cases.

In addition, the people up there have to be supported in those jobs. I often had a really hard time getting the information I needed to present a case to the Department of the Army staff. It finally got to the point where I would just go to the bosses and say, "Either get your guys to give me the information or screw it. You're going to lose your program." It would boil down to that. Programs could go out the window if I didn't have the information to defend them, because nobody else up there was defending the army.

There should be an effort by senior people in the army staff, even including the chief of staff, to invite civilian leaders into the field to see how the army operates. Many of these people came from the aerospace industry. They know what airplanes and missiles do, and what limitations they have. So they know the air force's problems, and understand why there should be research for this or that. But they just don't have any idea what a tank, or armored personnel carrier, an artillery piece, or anything like that does. I used to make it a point to take my boss into the field every time we could get an opportunity. I used to keep on him all the time, just urging him to come out and see this or that maneuver.

Fortunately, the two bosses I had while I was there liked to go to the field. They liked exercise, liked to walk, and liked to play touch football on the weekends. So they enjoyed going out to the field; they learned a lot and it was helpful to the army. The guys who had been there ahead of me hadn't taken people out or hadn't urged them to get out. I saw that occur after I left also.

I used to invite them out in the field, but I didn't do it enough, as I look back on it now. All the senior guys on the staff should have taken the opportunity to get these guys educated. We spend a lot of time educating members of Congress so that they understand what the army's all about. The legislative liaison people are focusing on that: that's one of their missions.

The secretary of the army has them over for breakfast now in groups of five or ten. He has a briefing for them, has a lot of movies, shows them pictures of what goes on in the field and then invites them into the field. That sort of thing should also go on with officials at the secretary of defense's level because they are making decisions that affect the army directly.

Another thing I learned was that most of these people are pretty bright and come from senior positions in universities or industry. They are bright engineers and a lot of them have a PhD. They are interested in getting the facts. They are using what they believe to be good judgment. It used to be in the services, particularly in the army, that you said, "If the general does the briefing, that's going to carry a lot of weight because he's a general." They don't care about that; they want somebody who knows what he is talking about. If the general knows the words in his briefing but nothing beyond them, and can't answer any questions, he is pretty unimpressive.

One day when I came in, there was a general about to go brief my boss about buying a computer for some intelligence purposes. This was a controversial program that my boss didn't feel the army should have. Three young guys were sitting on the couch. I asked my secretary, "Who are they?" She said, "They are with the general." The general came over and said, "Do you have some question about my group?" I said, "I just wondered who they were." He said, "They are backup people who can answer any detailed questions that may come up. I'm not going to take them into the office while I'm briefing. I'll have them out here."

I said, "General, you do whatever you wish, but let me give you a piece of advice from having been here for a while. If they have to answer any questions, they had better be there when the questions are asked. Otherwise, they will never answer them. By the time you go out to get them into the office, you'll be out for good." He very reluctantly took these people in there.

The general had hardly started when my boss challenged him and said, "This computer doesn't do that." One of these young guys spoke up and said, "Dr. Fubini, I'm afraid you don't know what you are talking about. This computer was designed to do exactly that."[1] Gene Fubini said, "It was?" And the young guy says, "Yes, it was. You're probably thinking of such and such computer." Dr. Fubini said, "I guess you're right." Another couple of sentences, the same thing happened. Soon the program was approved, but it never would have been without those kids in there.

If you're a senior officer, you have to recognize that in today's environment it's not so much form that people want, as it used to be, but substance. Don't have so much pride that you can't take some guys in to fill in the details or let them do the briefing. If it takes a PFC to tell the story, put the PFC on the stand—even if you need to put a bar on his shoulder.

In 1963 I attended the Advanced Management Program at Harvard, a thirteen-week course. At the time the course came up, I was reluctant to go, because I was not sure I wanted to stay in the service. There were some things going on that I just didn't like very much. I didn't like the politics and the way they handled things.

McNamara's regime didn't thrill me. All these systems analysis guys were making decisions that bore no resemblance to the realities of the world. I was thinking maybe I just didn't want to pursue this line of work any longer. I didn't want to commit for another two or three years of service, which would be required if I went to school. I thought about it more and more. I finally said I'd go and I never regretted it. It was a very good course and I thought I got a lot out of it. Later, I went for my MBA at George Washington University. It was earned by studying at night. We had a work day from 7 in the morning until 7 at night. So it wasn't easy to do an MBA.

I used to come into the office early and study for a couple of hours, when it was quiet, before we started working. Then I'd study in the evenings sometimes. George Washington wasn't too demanding. If I had been going to Harvard Business School, I might not have made it. In fact, I'm not sure they would let you be a candidate if you weren't doing it full-time.

With the promotion board coming up, I wanted that MBA. I felt that this was a discriminator. If I had an MBA, I'd beat out some guy who was essentially the same quality but didn't have one. To finish in time, I had to pass comprehensive exams. They only gave them twice a year, in August and January. I wasn't going to complete my course work until after the August comprehensive exams were given and would have to wait until the following January. I went to the school and asked to take the comprehensive before I finished my course work. They said they would let me do that under the circumstances.

I took one or two weeks' leave and studied like hell on all the books that went with these courses. At George Washington, they weren't interested in independent thought. They were interested in your parroting back all the writings of Peter Drucker and other famous guys in the business management world. I memorized all these books and took the comprehensives. I could have spent two weeks writing down all I knew about the questions. The only problem I had was getting down all the major things before the time ran out. It wasn't a matter of not knowing enough. I passed, got the MBA, and was selected for promotion. Whether that was a discriminator or not, I didn't really know.

When the promotion board was meeting for brigadier general selections, I wasn't confident at all, really, because my boss, Gene Fubini, was the kind of guy who takes a great personal interest in you if he likes you. I was on vacation in New Hampshire and I got a call from him. He said, "The chief of staff wants to see you." That was Harold K. Johnson, whom I'd known for many years. I asked, "Gee, you mean I have to come back from my vacation? He said, "Oh, no, whenever you come back, go in and see him." I questioned, "What does he want to see me about?" He said, "Well, I told him that I thought you were going to be a general officer. So he said he would look through your record and talk to you about it." I said, "Jesus Christ, what did you do a thing like that for?" He said, "Well, I think you should be." Boy, that's like the kiss of death, telling the chief of staff you should make general.

I went back to see General Johnson and he had read my record—very thoroughly, apparently. He said, "You are going to be a general officer, there's no question about that. But this is the first year you're coming up for consideration. You're not going to make it this year. You may make it next year or the year after. You're going to make it, but not this year."

As I said, I wasn't very confident. As a matter of fact, in that conversation we got into a discussion of how general officers were selected. I pointed out that there were some things about the selection system that I, and a lot of other people, didn't like. The selection system at that time required so many years of service or age, I'm not sure which. I was not eligible for consideration that year.

I told him that Bernie Rogers, who was later chief of staff, and George Blanchard, who later commanded USAREUR, were a class or two behind me and weren't going to get considered the year I was. I said, "General, I used to have a guy who worked for me named George Fogle. He was a lieutenant colonel when I was a colonel. He subsequently made colonel but I ranked him. I carried the responsibilities as the chief of that branch all the time. Yet because he is older than I am, or has been in the service longer, he is now a brigadier general and has passed me. I just find that difficult to accept. Why is he better than me now, when he couldn't prove that he was better than me before? I was his boss and the guy who took the rap when something went wrong. The front office didn't call George; they called me, the boss. I think that is a bad promotion system."

I went on, "I don't want to change the system, particularly this year, because I don't want to compete with Bernie Rogers, George Blanchard, Allen Burdett, and a bunch of guys who are a class or two behind me. They are outstanding guys. They should be general officers." They all later became three- or four-star generals.

Johnson said, "Well, if you had gotten to be a general officer as early as possible, forgetting about age or length of service, you could have been a general officer for fifteen years. Do you think that is a good idea?" I said, "Well, in my case, it's probably not a good idea. But take a guy like Andy Goodpaster, who is a brilliant soldier. I think it would be a great idea for him to be a general officer for fifteen years. You would be getting the maximum contribution from that type of guy for a long time. Or take someone like MacArthur or Marshall. They should have been general officers for the last thirty years of their service. They made a major contribution to this country. Maybe a guy like me shouldn't make it, but I think your rules would have prevented the army from taking maximum advantage of those people."

He said, "I hadn't thought about it like that." The next year he changed the way things worked. If you had been in grade as a colonel for so many years or you had so much service, you could be considered. I think George Blanchard made it the next year and Bernie Rogers the following year. They wouldn't have even been considered before. Allen Burdett, I think, made it and was even further behind.

It's just interesting that a comment got the chief of staff to think in a different vein than he had thought before. Anyway, I wasn't at all confident, but you always go for the gold. That's why I wanted the MBA at that point. I got promoted to brigadier general in August 1965, joined the 82nd Airborne Division, and went to the Dominican Republic.

9

82nd Airborne Division and the Dominican Republic

I had very little time at Bragg with the division before being sent to the Dominican Republic to command a task force during the civil war down there. The task force, from the 82nd Division and corps support command, was under the XVIII Airborne Corps commander, Lieutenant General Bruce Palmer Jr., a really great leader. He ran the show very well. He let me do my thing and didn't interfere. He was an outstanding guy to work for.

As a matter of fact, we had such good rapport, and he held me in sufficiently high regard that, although I didn't get along with Joe Lawrie, the 82nd Division commander, Lawrie was reluctant to really slam me on my efficiency report when I left the division because Bruce Palmer had to endorse it.[1] Lawrie probably would have got his tail in a crack if he went overboard to stick a knife in my back.

During the initial insertion of the 82nd into the Dominican Republic, our soldiers came under fire from a small Dominican Army French tank, made by Citroën. Of course, it was immediately put out of action. This miniature tank, scarcely the size of an automobile, stood in the streets abandoned for weeks. It occurred to me at one point that it might make a nice exhibit for the division museum back at Fort Bragg, a memento of this latest chapter in the division's history.

I ordered it picked up and transported to the United States and arranged with division headquarters to deliver it to the museum. Everything went smoothly. Having accomplished this, I immediately forgot about the incident. I subsequently received orders for Vietnam, and about eight months later received word that General Palmer wished to see me. He was now in Saigon, serving as the deputy commanding general, United States Army, Vietnam.

When I entered his office, he was his normal friendly self. We discussed the progress of the war for a while, how I liked my duties with the Big Red One, and such things as how the division was doing. Finally, we got to the real purpose of the meeting. He told me that the government of the Dominican Republic had approached the State Department complaining that the American forces had stolen a Dominican Army tank in 1965. They wished to have it returned.

Palmer asked if I could shed any light on this situation. I confessed that I had, indeed, sent the tank to the 82nd Airborne Division Museum. He thanked me for the information and told me he would take it from there, a fortunate break for me because the army might have sacrificed a mere brigadier general while there was no question they would ever consider action against a full general. The tank was returned.

The first time I saw a tarantula was in the Dominican Republic. I don't like spiders in general, so I really did not care for big venomous ones. I used to see a lot of them at night while driving from Santo Domingo to my headquarters near the international airport. They would come out of the sugarcane fields onto the road.

When we did our proficiency parachute jumps down there, our drop zone was in a sugarcane field. When you land, you are supposed to roll up your parachute and put it in an aviator kit bag you carry in your parachute harness. After these jumps, local kids would always run out to the drop zone. They would roll up your parachute for you and carry it in the aviator kit bag to the parachute collection point. They did this for tips, usually 50 cents. Because I did not like the idea of tangling with a tarantula and I was really afraid of being bitten, I would get up on my feet as quickly as possible after the landing, get out of my chute, toss a kid my aviator kit bag and 50 cents and tear out of the sugarcane field as fast as I could.

In the Dominican Republic, events reaffirmed my philosophy that the other guy doesn't always know from what level of strength you come from. He wonders about you. If you are bold, you can get away with actions that you might not be able to otherwise.

The event Deane referred to was later described by his commander, Lieutenant General Bruce Palmer. If the new Dominican government was to survive, in order to defuse the extreme Right, General Elias Wessin y Wessin, the most feared of the Dominican military chiefs, had to be removed from power. After meeting with Palmer, Wessin initially agreed to resign, but then asked for time to travel to his headquarters in order to say farewell. As an afterthought, Palmer sent Deane on a mission to Wessin's headquarters to bring him back to Palmer's location.

About an hour later, Deane arrived back with Wessin and his deputy, Colonel Vicente Perdom. Deane had entered Wessin's headquarters accompanied only by his G3, Lieutenant Colonel Gene Forrester, and a Spanish-speaking US Army lieutenant who was Cuban and a Bay of Pigs survivor. Through a mixture of luck and audacity, they were able to persuade the reluctant Wessin to leave with them, despite the large group of Dominican rebel soldiers who had gathered around their jeep at the last moment attempting to dissuade him.[2]

Also while we were there, I recommended to General Palmer, and through him, to the Brazilian general commanding the overall force from the Organization of American States, that we eliminate the so-called rebel zone. All the rebels were penned up in a relatively square zone. It was bordered on one side by a river and on another by the ocean. The Brazilians and other South American forces bounded the west side. The 82nd task force bordered on the north. We had the rebels penned up in there. They weren't allowed in or out except under special circumstances. I felt that Colonel Caamaño, the rebel leader, was getting undue support and publicity because of this zone. It stood as a symbol that the rebellion still existed and that Caamaño still enjoyed authority.

If we eliminated that zone, spread out his forces, told them to go home, there would no longer be any symbol of the revolution. This idea was mulled over for a while. The army talked to the foreign ministries of various countries, and they decided to do what I recommended. The Brazilian general was very much concerned that this was going to be a major operation. He wanted to have the Marine Corps, then stationed offshore in ships, to be disembarked and come across the beaches. The 82nd would then do its thing, coming out from every direction.

I told him that if you turned the 82nd loose, we would be down on the beach before the Marines ever got down their landing nets into their boats. So just forget about the Marines. He finally figured we could handle it. We went down and started our operation about 2:30 or 3:00 in the morning. Everybody was asleep and we swept down through there without any resistance except a few sniper shots. We took Caamaño, his staff, and some of his principal supporters, and put them up temporarily in a military compound on the opposite side of the river from where they had been.

We had troops outside the compound watching it. Caamaño's people were supposed to be able to come and go as they wished, but carry no weapons. When they tried to carry weapons out, my guys stopped them. They were complaining about this. Finally they set up a machine gun on top of a gate over the portico that you went through to get to their camp and pointed it at my soldiers.

I went down to the camp, to the guard at the gate. I told him who I was and that I wanted to speak to someone in authority. A colonel came out who had a reputation of being one of the real tough guys in this revolution. I knew him by name but had never met him before. He came strutting out, very pompous and full of authority.

I asked him through an interpreter what his name was. He gave his name and I said, "I've never heard of you. Do you have any authority?" I asked this right in front of all his men. That really deflated the guy. He just shriveled up. He could see he wasn't making much of an impression. I said, "I want to see Colonel Caamaño. Do you have the authority to bring me in through the gate to see him?" He said, "Yes." I radioed the division that I was going into Caamaño's compound. If I didn't call back within thirty minutes, they were to come down and blow the place apart.

I went in. I had a badly sprained ankle at the time and was on crutches, as I recall. I went clumping in on my crutches to Colonel Caamaño's office and told him, "You have a machine gun outside pointing at my soldiers, who are stationed there to protect you and your people. That's not very nice at all. I don't like it, and I want you to take that machine gun down. Furthermore, your people are continually trying to get out of here carrying their weapons with them. This is contrary to the agreements that were arranged. I don't want you to do that anymore."

He said, "I will call my president! You can't talk to me like this!" I said, "Sit down. By the time I'm through, you're going to have about ten things to talk to your president about. So you might as well wait to make just one phone call." Then I really laced into him, and he became a mass of quivering jelly. These guys were just putting up a front. They were scared to death of what was going on. Here I was, right in the middle of his camp with no friends around except my driver and my aide, but they were afraid. Being firm with them blew their bravado and made the situation easier.

There was another incident in which having some knowledge, with the other guy not knowing what you know, helped. We had a couple of the AN/MPQ-4, a counter-mortar radars, trained on the area around the rebel zone. One night about eight or ten rounds of mortar fire were fired into the rebel zone from outside. This radar would allow us to get two points under trajectory of the fired mortar round. This enabled us to plot back a line to where the mortars were located.

I went to see the chief of staff of the Dominican Army. I told him that these rounds had been fired, that he and I had certain responsibilities, and that I wanted to make sure that he was going to honor his responsibilities. He said, "Well, I'm discharging mine. I wouldn't fire at these people." I said, "Alright. It's over and done, and there is nothing we can do about it. But I don't want it to happen again. You're responsible for what happens in your area, just as I'm responsible for what happens in mine."

He said, "Well, it didn't happen in my area." I said, "Come over to the map, I want to show you something. We have a radar unit that picks up the flight of these rounds. We can project them back exactly to where they are fired from. That area is right here, this little X on the map. Three rounds were fired here; one round was fired here; and two rounds were fired from here." He knew exactly where the mortars had been and folded. He said, "It will never happen again."

While we were in the Dominican Republic, our morale and discipline were excellent. In some instances when we were standing on the border at the rebel zone, people would shoot over our heads or something like that. Our guys never responded with fire. If somebody fired at the Brazilians, those guys would return a basic load of fire on them. Occasionally some irate Dominican would come up and spit on our soldiers. Our guys never reacted to that. They maintained their cool. Unless they were in danger, they were not supposed to fire their weapons. You heard shots all the time down there. The rebels were just drinking and shooting off their guns; they weren't shooting anybody.

During the time of our deployment in the Dominican Republic it was not clear what was going to happen with our troops or how long we were going to be down there. There were a lot of rumors that one of the brigades would stay down there for a protracted period. The wives at home didn't know what was going to happen to their husbands. The guys didn't know what was going to happen to their wives. Were they going to be permitted to continue to live in quarters on the post or were they going to be forced to move off the post?

So I said to Joe Lawrie when I was on a trip back to Bragg, "You know, I have a problem down here. These officers and noncommissioned officers who have families up here are concerned about what's going to happen to them. I think you should get the wives together in the auditorium and tell them what's going on." He said, "I don't know what is going to happen to them, and I don't know what's going on." I said, "At least you know more than they know; if they knew that, they would be a lot happier. They would feel a lot happier if they had your views as to what you would recommend and what you would fight for." He said,

"That's the dumbest idea I've ever heard of, to call all the wives together and tell them a bunch of stuff."

A week later, I was back down in the Dominican Republic and a newspaper from Fayetteville arrived. Here is a big picture of Joe Lawrie with the caption, "Great Leader Talks to Wives, Allays Fears." Every time I tried to make a suggestion to Joe Lawrie, he tried to make me feel like a nincompoop. Then he would go ahead and do it; and there would be these headlines: "Great Leader."

The guy was a fathead, so when I came back to the division from the Dominican Republic, I immediately went to Washington, to the General Officers Branch, and said, "If you have any vacancies in Vietnam, that's where I'd like to go." They said, "Great! We don't have many volunteers." So I got assigned to Vietnam. Lawrie was notified about my new assignment and stopped by my quarters one evening about 5:30 and said, "Could I talk to you privately?" I said, "Sure. Let's go out on the sun porch; we can be alone out there."

Well, we were hosting a dinner party that night, so the place was all set up for this big party. He hadn't been invited and that probably ticked him off. Then he said to me, "I've just received word that you're being ordered to Vietnam as chief of staff and deputy commander of the 1st Field Force." I said, "Outstanding!" He got mad because he thought I was going to break down and say, "Please, General, keep me here with you." He wouldn't talk to me from that day on.

When I was ready to leave, I tried to make an appointment to have a departure call with him. He didn't want to talk to me and wouldn't grant me an appointment. Finally, when I was packing to go and was in a pair of fatigues, hot, sweaty, lifting boxes, and all, I got a phone call. "The general wants to see you in fifteen minutes." I think he waited until he could get me in those dirty clothes. I sponged off, threw on some clothes, marched over to his office, and had my exit interview.

Now, he was a small guy, but of course I was sufficiently senior at that time that it didn't make a whole lot of difference. I recognized that. He wasn't going to change, so I didn't want to be around him. That's why I sought to get out of the division and volunteered to go to Vietnam. You run into small guys from time to time, and you have to be careful of them.

10

Vietnam

1st Field Force, 1st Infantry Division, and 173rd Airborne Brigade

I went over to Vietnam where I was assigned as the chief of staff and deputy commander of the 1st Field Force. "Swede" Larsen was the commander. Swede, a brigadier general, was a very intense guy, a wonderful soldier, a tremendous combat leader—a guy I admired and was very fond of.

I was really surprised to find out that he had asked for me. Swede and I had met one time when I was a colonel. I was working for Gavin in research and development; Swede was the deputy commandant at the infantry school. The armor force at that time was getting a lot of research accomplished and the infantry was playing second fiddle. At the AUSA (Association of the United States Army) Convention, I ran into him in the hallway. He backed me up against the wall, poked his finger at my chest, and said, "I thought you were an infantryman. You're not doing anything for the infantry. General Gavin is supposed to be an infantryman, and he has sold out. The armor branch is the only people who are getting any support out of you guys. Why are they getting it?"

I said, "Listen, Swede, we don't make all the determinations where the money goes. We put the money where the requirements appear to be. The fact of the matter is that the Infantry School, for which you are responsible, are the ones who are responsible for generating infantry requirements. Nothing has come out of Fort Benning in the last ten years, as far as I can see. The infantry is dead on its butt. The armor branch has put together a bunch of bright young colonels—Art West and Tom Dolvin, and all these bright guys who were the armor heroes of World War II—and figured out where their branch should be going over the next ten years.[1] They have a very coherent plan and it's getting them the money. I can't give you money when you don't come up with anything that makes sense."

We had an argument, and I thought he was pretty bitter about it, because I was really telling him that he wasn't doing his job. So I was surprised that he asked for me to be his chief of staff. But the fact of the matter is, as I've said in other instances, when a guy knows that you lay it on the line like it is, you're the kind of guy he wants with him. He asked for me because he knew he could depend on me to tell him the way it was. I went there and we had a very good relationship.

I think we operated more effectively and with fewer resources in our area than they did in III Corps or I Corps, where the Marine Corps was. We were more effective because Swede was a brilliant tactician. I knew something about intelligence and helped him in that respect.

For example, we used to get an intelligence briefing every morning from the stuff that had been picked up by direction-finding equipment. It was not too meaningful; you just heard stories. I got these intelligence guys to do a daily plot on a map, where everything was picked up from direction finding—where it was yesterday, where it was the day before, and where it was a week ago. Then you would begin to see patterns of enemy units moving toward a town and be able to determine their next target.

We would wait until they got fairly close, then go out and zap them. That would knock out their plans for a month or two. As a result, we weren't having any towns overrun. Swede used his forces very well. He knew how to conserve the force, use it where it had to be used, then get it back so it was ready to move someplace else. I really enjoyed my service with him.

In the 1st Field Force, when I first got there, we had the 1st Cavalry Division plus a brigade of the 101st Airborne Division. Eventually, they had the 1st Cavalry Division, 101st Airborne Division, 4th Infantry Division, and the 173rd Airborne Brigade, plus special units.

When I was assigned to the 1st Division as the assistant division commander (ADC) in the summer of 1966, I was delighted for two reasons. First and foremost, it gave me the opportunity to get back into a combat leadership role. Second, when I joined in the army in 1937, I enlisted in G Company, 16th Infantry Regiment, 1st Infantry Division. This provided the rare opportunity to serve in what I consider to be the most famous and prestigious division in the army at both the lowest and highest levels.

General William E. DePuy was the division commander.[2] Jim Hollingsworth was the other ADC.[3] Jim was a flamboyant troop leader who had been a star football player and graduate of Texas A&M. The three of us had a lot of respect for and were really fond of one another, so we operated very effectively as a team. *The feeling was mutual with Hollingsworth; he later described Deane to a reporter: "Deane is a brilliant tactician. He is a great general because he doesn't let his brilliance get in the way of communicating with the troops. He knows his men. They know him."*[4]

Bill DePuy became one of my closest friends in the army. He was a man I respected as a leader in both combat and staff assignments. I knew him slightly when we were both very junior staff officers in the Pentagon after World War II. I came to know him best and we became close personal friends when he was the commanding general of the 1st Infantry Division, the Big Red One.

When Bill was running the 1st Division, it faced a situation unlike a division in garrison. In garrison, one ADC looks at the division support command, the logistics functions, the administrative functions, and things like that. The other ADC is responsible for training and operations. Nor was it like the deployment of a division in World War II, where you had two regiments on the line and one in reserve.

With the 1st Division in Vietnam, brigades were off fighting in different areas, not necessarily in support of each other. Frequently, there were a lot of separate little operations going on—a brigade here, there, someplace else. DePuy would tell me that he wanted me to watch a certain area. I would then take charge of that area, monitor the fighting that was going on in that area, and get support necessary to accomplish the mission.

Jim Hollingsworth would watch another area, and Bill would watch a third area. We might switch around. When I first joined the division, one of the brigades was, I guess, forty or fifty kilometers north of the brigade base where most of the division stayed when it wasn't in the field. Actually, it was in the field most of the time but not too far from the base camp. We were in the north and were supposed to protect plantations and so on. Occasionally, they would open the roads in that area to bring up rice to feed the people and to take out the rubber to be sold.

I was in charge of that northern front, as they called it, when I first joined the division. Sam Walker was the brigade commander—later a four-star general and a very outstanding guy.[5] Later, he served as my ADC in the 82nd for a while. Sam was commanding the brigade as a lieutenant colonel. He had been the division G3. When Al Haig became the division G3, Sam took over the 2nd Brigade.[6] Sam was an outstanding officer, a man of great personal courage, superb values and principles, and impeccable integrity. He and I hit it off right from the start.

Subsequently, we moved back down south and operated there. I was in charge of one area and Hollingsworth would be in charge of another. Our distinctions were not those you normally would find in ADCs. One of the independent infantry brigades, the 196th, was working in our area, commanded by a guy named Ted deSaussure. I had roomed with Ted in prep school.

In the beginning of November 1966, deSaussure led his brigade into what was to become Operation ATTLEBORO. His maneuver plans were unduly complicated and in a matter of days chaos reigned. DePuy visited his command post at Dau Tieng, and after being briefed by Ted, he feared the operation was a disaster waiting to happen. At the same time that ATTLEBORO was under way, a Special Forces Delta Force operation a few miles north had encountered a major enemy force and had taken heavy casualties. It looked like it was more than they could handle, and we were alerted that we might have to go in with the 1st Division and help out. As soon as we were alerted, the three of us jumped into our individual helicopters and flew over the area to look at the land where the units were engaged on the ground, so that we would be prepared to deploy the 1st Division in there if need be.

At this time, Fred Weyand, who would later become chief of staff of the army, commanded the 25th Infantry Division, but currently he was acting corps commander while the 2nd Field Force commander was home on leave.[7] Fred assigned Bill DePuy to take charge of these two fights. The reasons were unknown to me, other than that he might not have had sufficient confidence in his own people in the 25th Division to take over. He could have used his own force if he wanted, but thought it wasn't necessary. We had all the force in there that was needed.

Bill said to me, "I want you to take charge of the fight that is going on with the 25th Division." The 25th Division had two battalions in the fight; the 196th Brigade had one battalion engaged and two in the area ready to support. So there were five battalions there and I was put in charge of that fight. Hollingsworth was put in charge of the Special Forces fight further north of us.

I got an early start the next morning and arrived at the headquarters of the 25th Division at first light. Those guys were sitting around like they were back in garrison. I couldn't believe it. I went into the operations room and there wasn't anybody there. I went to the acting division commander's office. A soldier told me that the acting division commander, Brigadier General George G. "GG" O'Connor, was at breakfast. A few minutes later, GG showed up. I must say I was a bit astounded that he seemed unconcerned about what was happening in ATTLEBORO. Here we had a big fight going on! They started to give me a briefing as they wiped the crumbs off their pressed fatigues; it was pretty poor. They didn't know what the hell was going on. The only thing I really found out while I was there was that one of the battalions involved in the fight was commanded by William C. Barott, who had served with me as a company commander in my battle group in Berlin. He was an outstanding young officer. I was very fond of him.

The word was that Barott had been killed the night before. This greatly disturbed me. When we were in Berlin, his wife, who was sensitive to the confinement of being surrounded all the time, had a nervous breakdown. As was the case with quite a number of people, she became almost claustrophobic since we were like a little island of people surrounded by the vast horde of Soviet and East German forces in East Germany. I was concerned about her reaction to Bill's death, if he had been killed. So I was anxious to establish what the facts were. I flew up to the battle area, where Ted deSaussure, the brigade commander, had a little headquarters at Dau Tieng, a village on the edge of the Michelin Plantation.

Ted was not happy to see me. He knew I had been sent because Weyand and Westmoreland were not happy with his conduct of the battle and obviously did not have confidence in him. This was a bitter pill for Ted. It would have been for anybody, but it was particularly so for Ted. He was a proud man and a fierce competitor.

He filled me in on the situation and I said I would like to see what was going on. One of the battalions engaged was commanded by a major named Sandy Meloy, who later commanded the 82nd Airborne Division.[8] We flew to his position in Ted's helicopter. When I climbed into his helicopter, it became immediately apparent that one of his problems was his communications system. In my command copter, I had a rack of several radios—one to talk to the air force forward air controller and supporting aircraft pilots, one on the division net, one on the artillery net, and one for communication with any of the division units I wanted to talk to— plus I had a spare. Ted just had two PRC-77s, tactical FM radios, sliding around on the floor. That was his command and control helicopter! It was totally useless. Unbelievable!

Bill DePuy had stopped there previously and told Ted that I was in charge now. We had been roommates at prep school, but he was a class ahead of me at West Point because I had failed the physical and was forced to start the next year. At West Point, we had played on the polo team together for the three years we overlapped. We made BG on the same list, but he was senior to me. Now I was to take charge of his battle. It was awkward, but something that we just had to do.

DeSaussure dropped me off in a clearing where the helicopters were bringing in soldiers and supplies and evacuating the wounded. He went back to his headquarters. I asked him to send my helicopter up to me when he got back. I went in and saw Sandy Meloy, who had been hit in the elbow. He was right where his battalion was pinned down the night before by a strong force that was later determined to be a regiment of experienced North Vietnamese regulars.

He had been up all the day before, and all night fighting. He was tired and his morale was low. Things weren't progressing. His troops were in this perimeter shaped like a missile nose cone: wide at the base and narrow where the front was. We were in that pocket up in the front. What you might call the front lines were just fifteen yards away. Behind, there was just open space in the jungle.

Meloy would later remark that had he raised strenuous objections to the plan of attack with General deSaussure. "The plan was ludicrous. Command and control of the separate attacks was impossible. There was no linkup plan whatsoever. There was no appreciation of either the terrain or the enemy. I had a rather heated discussion with deSaussure before the operation began. But since I was a major and he was a brigadier general, obviously I lost."

As the attack unfolded Meloy, watching the situation deteriorate rapidly from his helicopter, knew he had to get on the ground. He ordered his command and control helicopter to fly low over the landing zone (LZ), and the entire battalion command group jumped out. The sergeant major was hit, and the helicopter took several rounds but was able to stay in the air.

Meloy crawled to the location of the wounded commander and first sergeant of the initial company on the ground. Both were severely wounded and sinking fast. Meloy decided the only hope for Captain Frederick L. Henderson and First Sergeant Sam Solomon was to get a medical evacuation helicopter to the LZ. As the helicopter flew in through a hail of automatic weapons fire, Meloy watched it flare to land and witnessed a huge explosion as it fell to the ground like a rock. One of the crewmen was killed and another had a broken leg, but the two pilots climbed out of the wreckage without injury.

Meloy recalled, "Henderson saw it happen, he looked at me as if to say, 'Thanks for trying,' and died. Solomon painfully raised himself up on his elbow, shook his head at the bravery of the pilots, and sank down, dead."[9]

I spent the better part of the day with Sandy. By this time he had eleven companies under his command, as opposed to the normal three. He had a daunting task before him. He had to rescue a company from a sister battalion that had been sent to reinforce him the night before. He simultaneously had to extricate his force from the North Vietnamese occupying the fortified position less than fifty yards in front of his position. I decided my presence would buoy him up a little.

We were talking when all of a sudden the enemy attacked. There were bullets zinging all around us. We shot off a lot of rounds and they backed off. In that small perimeter, we fought off seven attacks during the day. I was there for six of them, but left before the last one started. I think my presence buoyed Sandy Meloy's spirits. He began to get excited about the fight and get charged up again. For my actions, General Westmoreland awarded me the Distinguished Service Cross. I was humbled to be recognized for my mundane actions that day.

When I saw that Meloy was in a good frame of mind, I determined that somebody had to be in charge of what was happening on the ground to coordinate this thing. His battalion was situated, as I described, in this nose cone. A couple hundred meters to his left front was Bill Barott's battalion, in disarray. As Bill landed with one of his companies, almost immediately they came into contact with the North Vietnamese. He and his company commander were both killed as they sought a way to link up with Meloy.

On November 4, 1966, Lieutenant Colonel William Barott landed with his command, the 2nd Battalion, 27th Infantry, in order to aid a sister battalion that was under heavy attack by the enemy. While he maneuvered his men to hit the enemy flank, several well-concealed machine gun bunkers opened up, killing or wounding a number of his unit. Barott quickly organized an attack force and personally led the assault to knock out the bunkers. During this assault he was hit and killed instantly.[10]

Now we were trying to get that unit out. There was a battalion that belonged to Ted deSaussure, supposedly fighting toward us, clear over on the other side of this forest. Meloy's and Barott's two infantry battalions belonged to the 25th Division. I was concerned about how we were going to coordinate their linkup with us.

Somebody had to call the shots. I called the battalion commander, a lieutenant colonel named Lynch, and told him that I was placing his unit under operational control of Sandy Meloy, who was a major. He didn't like this at all. Over the radio he expressed some doubts about my authority and some comments that he was commanding the battalion, and had not received any orders that jived with what I was saying.

I said, "Look, I'm in charge here. If you don't like what I told you to do, get in your helicopter and go back to Saigon, because you are going to be relieved of your command right away." He decided the better part of valor was to do as he was told. We finally got all these troops together and got that battle cleaned up.

In the meantime, Hollingsworth got the Special Forces—Delta Force or whatever they called it—all squared away. That was typical of the way DePuy assigned jobs to us. Hollingsworth did one job and I did the other. It could have been the other way around. That's just the way he happened to deal with it, and that's the way we operated as the ADCs. After we got ATTLEBORO and the Delta Force operation under control, DePuy met with Fred Weyand and General Westmoreland at Fred's command post. Bill told Holly and me that when he finished reporting on the situation and telling Westy what Holly and I had done, Westy commented, "We need more fighting generals like Jack and Holly."

I've told the following story regarding women in combat units many times to provide an understanding of the basis of my personal opposition to this policy. The incident took place a few days after ATTLEBORO late one afternoon, I remember the date because it appears on an inscription by then Colonel Harry B. Summers on the flyleaf of a book he authored, *On Strategy: The Vietnam War in Context*. His inscription reads, "General Deane, who, by saving my life in November 1966, made possible this book—with heartfelt thanks and with great respect for his example and his advice."

That afternoon, Harry was the S3, or operations officer, of one of our battalions operating in War Zone C. As the Battalion Command Group moved through dense jungle, Harry and the Battalion Command sergeant major (CSM) became separated from the rest of the group. Word of this situation came to me on the radio and I directed my pilot to proceed to the area where the battalion was operating.

We hovered over openings in the jungle and other open areas, where the vegetation consisted of elephant grass, a thick-bladed grass about eight to ten feet tall, hoping to catch a glimpse of these two warriors. I knew if I could locate them, I could direct a patrol from the battalion to their location.

Fortunately, Harry and the CSM had wandered out of the jungle and into one of these elephant grass–covered openings. We were searching one of these areas, hovering just a few feet above the elephant grass, when, as luck would have it, we passed directly over them just twenty feet or so below us. The down wash from our rotor blades parted the grass just as the fur on a cat's back parts when you blow on it. There they were, waving frantically to us.

I knew we would be able to pick up only one at a time, take him to a safe place, drop him off, and return for the other. My command helicopter was loaded down with two pilots, two door gunners, my aide-de-camp, myself, and hundreds of pounds of communications equipment. We did not have the lift to take on two additional people.

We made a turn to come back to them to pull one into the helicopter. As we hovered over them and began our descent, a message came over my radio that immediately changed our plans. The voice was that of the division G2, the intelligence officer. He said a long-range reconnaissance patrol, which was operating nearby, was in contact with an enemy force. He went on to say that the patrol had a French photo-journalist with them. It was Cathy Leroy, a courageous young lady who spent much time with the 1st Division. When she was with us, she was always in the field where the action was, not in our rear headquarters where you only heard of the action.

My father was a product of the modern age of chivalry. Men protected women. He instilled these values, among others, in me. My decision was instinctive and instantaneous. Go rescue Cathy. I will never forget the panic in the faces of those two soldiers on the ground as we lifted back up away from them. They had no idea what was happening. They did not know whether we were going to abandon them or what. They did not know, with the noise of the helicopter, whether we had received ground fire that would mean there were enemy forces in the immediate vicinity.

We located Cathy and picked her up out of the middle of the firefight. We took her to a safe area and dropped her off so we could return to Harry and the CSM. Unfortunately, it was beginning to get dark. It was still light when we reached them, but the light was fading rapidly. We hovered down to where Harry could grab the helicopter's skid. Then my aide and I grasped his wrists and pulled him in. We flew off to a safe place a few minutes away, dropped him off, and returned for the CSM. By the time we reached the area it was too dark to see him. He, however, surmised this and set fire to his map to attract our attention. We immediately spotted him and pulled him to safety.

The point I am trying to make is that my decision to go rescue Cathy was an emotional decision deriving from my background, my early training, and the values I took from my parents. It was not a decision based on the needs of the unit. My concern with having women in combat units is that, like me, some soldiers might make decisions based on their attitude regarding women rather than on the factors related to the safety of the unit and the accomplishment of its mission. In some instances, that could be disastrous.

The recent Department of Defense decision to open combat jobs to women is a perplexing subject to me. Am I just old-fashioned in my thinking that men naturally try to protect women, or does that trait still exist? I have read some things recently that make me think that today's macho males might say they treat women in peril just as they would men in peril, but that is not really true. Chivalry still beats in the breast of man.

As Deane mentioned, he was awarded the Distinguished Service Cross for a series of actions during a two-week spell from November 5 through November 18, 1966, during combat operations near the Michelin Rubber Plantation. The citation reads, in part:

> *Upon learning that elements of a light infantry brigade were receiving intense hostile fire from a numerically superior Viet Cong force, Brigadier General Deane immediately flew into the battle area, conducted low level passes while receiving hostile fire and identified the positions for the ground element. After landing in an insecure landing zone, Brigadier General Deane walked with his leg in a cast to the command post of the forward infantry elements which were about 30 meters from the main Viet Cong force. Brigadier General Deane repeated this process four times on 5 November and was present with forward infantry elements during four major Viet Cong attacks which carried to within yards of his position. His presence with the forward infantry troops and his repeated flights over the battle area contributed immeasurably to the successful conclusion of the operation and extraction of the American forces involved.*

> *On November 12, 1966 Brigadier General Deane was flying over combat operations when the battalion command group was hit with a claymore mine that immobilized it and caused difficulty for the command group in controlling the movement of their subordinate elements through the jungle. Realizing the seriousness of the situation, Brigadier General Deane, while receiving intense hostile fire, assumed command and control of the battalion from his helicopter. Brigadier General Deane landed in an insecure landing zone near an infantry element and personally directed its movements. When Brigadier General Deane observed that a flanking patrol was approximately 1,000*

meters behind the Viet Cong force and on the flank, he person-
ally directed this small group into a clearing and, while receiv-
ing intense hostile fire, landed on four separate occasions and
extracted all members of the group. Later in the day, he again
landed under fire and extracted a wounded Sergeant Major and
an Operations Officer from a nearby jungle clearing.

On November 18, 1966, Brigadier General Deane was flying
at low level over the battle area when he monitored a radio mes-
sage that a lieutenant and a small patrol were receiving hostile
fire about 1,500 meters from the battalion landing zone. Briga-
dier General Deane immediately established radio contact with
the patrol, determined that they had multiple casualties, utilized
his helicopter as a gunship and conducted fifteen to twenty low-
level passes while firing his personal weapon and door guns on
the Viet Cong. After the insurgents withdrew, he remained in the
area, vectored a company into contact with the patrol and skill-
fully directed the medical evacuation. Later, Brigadier General
Deane landed his helicopter deep in hostile territory to extract
a helicopter crew which had been shot down by hostile fire near
the headquarters of a Viet Cong division. Through the entire bat-
tle of Tay Ninh Province, Brigadier General Deane was present
on or over the battlefield whenever any unit was in contact. He
utilized his aircraft weapons system against the Viet Cong, per-
sonally directed innumerable small engagements, inflicted heavy
casualties on the Viet Cong and saved countless American lives.[11]

Ted deSaussure got relieved of his command when the battle was
over and went up to be the ADC in the 1st Cavalry. That was another
embarrassment. I always felt that he thought I probably had some role
in his being relieved. I didn't. I said nothing but good things about Ted
in any discussions of the battle. He was just not properly supported. The
25th Division was supposed to be supporting his brigade, which had just
come to Vietnam and was just getting under way. To give a guy a command and control ship like he had was inexcusable.

The fact is, as soon as I got out of his helicopter the first time, I called
mine forward and from then on he used it. I told Ted, "If you need to use
it, use it because of what you have." Then his people weren't good people. They hadn't been trained properly. He had taken the unit over when
he came to Vietnam; he hadn't brought it over. They weren't responsive
to him or didn't understand his methods of command. For example, I

called on his net to his brigade S3, who wouldn't answer me half the time. Finally, I got him on the radio and I said, "I have a message for you, which I'll get to in a minute. But I have another one for you first. If you ever fail to answer me on this radio again, when I call you—and I mean starting right now—you're going to be relieved. Start doing your job." So he shaped up.

Then he had a commander of one of his battalions that had not yet been engaged. We had the battalion going through some woods to clear the area, to give protection to Bill Barott's battalion. He started into the woods. After he had been there a while, I said, "Mark your right flank with smoke." So he had his company that was on the right marked with smoke and the smoke came up. Then I had his left flank marked and the smoke came up there. It wasn't half an hour later that I asked him to mark his flanks again, and the right and left flanks had flipped.

The two lead companies had crossed, one in front of the other. He had no control of his people. He didn't know where they were or anything. It got to be a mess. I suggested to Ted that this would be an opportune time to have the battalion pull back into a cleared area about a kilometer to its rear to regroup as Bill DePuy had directed. I suggested the battalion commander move one company at a time to minimize the chances of their getting into a firefight with each other. No one really seemed to know where anyone was. So I pulled them back out of the jungle to get him squared away and started again.

Later, when I was commanding the 82nd, the commander of the XVIII Airborne Corps thought very highly of this guy. He wanted to get him a brigade command, and he wanted me to take him in the 82nd. I said, "I won't take him. The guy doesn't know anything about troop duty." He said, "He's an outstanding guy." I said, "If I'm ordered to take him, I don't have a choice; but if you're asking me to take him, I'll tell you I won't. I'm responsible for preparing this division for combat. This guy cannot lead anybody in combat, as far as I'm concerned."

He said, "Well, why don't I send him down and let you talk to him." He thought I'd fold. The guy came down and I said, "Look, I don't want to hurt your feelings. You and I know that I saw you in combat, and you know I wasn't satisfied with what I saw. I'm responsible for having this division ready for combat. I don't have confidence that you can fit into that picture. Therefore, I don't want you in the division. It's as simple as that." It was one of those unfortunate things you have to say. I'm sure it hurt the guy's feelings pretty badly, but there were more important things to worry about than that. So I didn't take him.

As the commander of the 1st Division, Bill DePuy got a reputation, which I heard before joining the division, of being a ruthless guy, that he was relieving commanders—primarily battalion commanders—right and left when they made mistakes. I think that maybe included brigade commanders. This reputation spread throughout Vietnam, certainly among general officers. Many spoke disparagingly of Bill; others had questions on their minds.

When I went to the division, I talked to a couple of people I had known. One evening, after dinner, not long after my arrival at An Loc, Sam Walker and I were talking. I said I wondered how all the battalion commanders viewed being in the division when DePuy had this terrible reputation for relieving people. Sam said that every officer worth his salt relished being a commander under DePuy. They had the opportunity to learn under one of the army's best field officers, one of the army's most astute thinkers. They knew that they would always be supported by DePuy. If they performed well, their performance would be rewarded by an outstanding efficiency report. Sam said the only people who were fearful of DePuy were those who knew they were lacking in the skills necessary to perform as combat leaders. They knew they were deficient and they feared they would be found out. The only guys who would be afraid or unhappy to be there were guys who knew they were incompetent. Bill wouldn't put up with incompetence, because that meant that people got killed.

I had a couple of long talks with Bill. He took me through the experiences he had as a junior officer and later a battalion commander in the 90th Division in World War II. His experiences were much like mine. He was a regular officer who had graduated from the University of North Dakota. He had joined the division as a new lieutenant and found that most of the senior lieutenants, captains, majors, and lieutenant colonels were Reserve or National Guard officers who had never had any great experience or interest in learning their trade. They went to periodic meetings where poker games rather than training sessions were the norm. As a result, when the time came to lead troops in combat, these officers were sadly deficient and unable to meet the demands of the task.

They had a number of very incompetent senior commanders who were there simply because they had been in the army for so long that they had reached the grade of colonel or lieutenant colonel. Bill was appalled by the number of soldiers he believed died due to the ineptitude of these officers. He observed so many people being killed that it almost drove him out of the army after World War II.

The fact that this incompetence would be tolerated with no corrective action taken resulted in very few officers being relieved of their duties. He wasn't sure that he wanted to operate in that environment. But having made the decision to stay in the army, he also made, in essence, a vow to himself that he would weed out incompetence wherever he found it—particularly in areas where it meant people's life or death.

I must say that in my six months or so with the division, I never once observed Bill relieve an officer whom I did not feel deserved it. I observed him relieve several people myself. If he hadn't beaten me to it, I'd have relieved the same people. They were terrible. For example, we had an artillery battalion commander who, when I first encountered him, wouldn't even register the guns when he put his battalion in position. That's a basic thing that an artilleryman does by instinct, like locking the doors before you go to bed at night.

He had been a staff officer and proceeded up the ranks of artillery until he became a lieutenant colonel. He never knew what he was doing. He never kept abreast of his profession. He almost shot me down one day with artillery. Once, an artillery prep on a landing zone was started late, was off target, and continued on as the assault helicopters were making their final run for the landing zone. I immediately called for a cease-fire to get the firing stopped. Had I not been on the scene, there could have been a serious accident. I was furious, and ordered my pilot to head for the division artillery headquarters, where I intended to relieve him. Upon my arrival, I found that Bill DePuy had already directed his relief. Bill had been monitoring my radio transmissions and was well aware of what had happened. He was relieved—as he should have been.

The point I want to make here is that Bill had the self-confidence, the perseverance, the willingness to risk what people might say about him or how they might regard him in order to see that things were done properly. He would see that people who didn't have the competence to do things properly were removed from positions where competence was needed.

For this, he got a bad rap from a lot of people. There are still people in the army who talk about that. My personal reaction is that I had great admiration for him. I've defended him in every arena that I've heard him castigated for this business. He did relieve people and did it the best he could—not to hurt them personally, but to get them out of positions where they were causing problems.

Bill went on to become the first commanding general of the Training and Doctrine Command (TRADOC), where he had the opportunity to correct those deficiencies he had observed and that disturbed him so as a young officer. He became the "father" of the army school system, the system that provides realistic and effective training for the leaders of tomorrow. He had the vision to develop the doctrine that is the basis for organizational structure and action on the battlefield, the doctrine that determines the weapon system requirements for the army. I know of no other officer in my era who did more to shape our army of today than William E. DePuy.

When he took over the 1st Division, which was not really doing anything, he was given a mandate by General Westmoreland to get the division moving. His predecessor, Jack Seaman, was moved up to be the commander of the 2nd Field Force. Bill called him and said, "You have a lot of people in the division whom I think are not competent—at least, not competent to operate the way I operate. If you hold them in high regard—and I assume you do, since you kept them with you all this time—I suggest you find jobs for them someplace else so that they don't get anybody hurt."

Seaman did take some, but he left a lot of them in the 1st Division. There was nothing for Bill to do except relieve them or put up with them. A lot of people might say, "Take what you get and train it." That's all well and good. In combat you don't have all that luxury of time to train these people.

With a rapidly expanding army, the chain of command, by necessity, had to be more tolerant of mistakes. That's one of the things that I think characterized the army then, as opposed to now—or at least as I saw the army when I was retiring. If people are going to be innovators and leaders, if they are going to be the Terry Allens or George Pattons—they are going to make mistakes; and I can mention one example of the army's failure to accept mistakes.

When I was in Vietnam with the 1st Division in 1966, we had a battalion commander, Bill Hathaway, who was just outstanding. Later, when I was commanding the 82nd Airborne Division, in 1969, I asked for and got Bill to come, initially as the support commander, though I had intended to give him a brigade.

He came to me one day and said, "You know, I'm trained as an officer and my job is to do things in combat. That's what I have prepared myself for all this time. I want to go back to Vietnam." So he asked me if I would release him. I said, "I'll release you, if you can get a command over there. I'll not release you to go to the staff in Saigon, because I think you'll learn more here than you'll learn on a Saigon staff. I'll try to help you to get a command."

I did help, and he did get a command. He did so well in that command that he was selected for brigadier general. Prior to his actually being promoted or relinquishing command, one of his outposts was overrun.[12] The company commander was killed and the battalion commander was wounded. There was a big investigation and punishment was imposed. Not only was Bill taken off the brigadier general's list and relieved of his command, but the secretary of the army threatened to reduce him to his permanent grade of lieutenant colonel.

Bill had to write to the secretary saying why he felt the action reducing him was unwarranted, and he asked for my assistance. I wrote a letter on his behalf outlining his duties and his performance of duties as I had observed them. I wrote a second letter to the secretary of the army about failure to accept mistakes when something goes wrong, when a guy is generally conscientious and effective. I pointed out that if he would go to any Officers' Club, he would find everybody bellied up to the bar, saying, "I'd give my left nut to have a command." But when the time comes to assign them to a command, you find that they all have some reason why they can't take it: Their wife has asthma and can't go to that part of the world, or their son is in school and can't be moved, or they have a sick grandmother.

Command is such a risky job in terms of career that a lot of people won't take it. I pointed out that I had ten guys come to me when I took over the 173rd Airborne Brigade, none of whom I knew, all pleading for an opportunity to command a battalion. I told each of those guys that if they came to the 173rd and did a good job, they could expect to go away with the best efficiency report that they'd ever had; but if they had not kept abreast of their profession, were coming there simply to get their card punched, and began to get my soldiers killed because of their incompetence—they'd go away with relief from duty for cause.

Then I said, "I don't know you, and I'm not trying to insult you. I'm just telling you what the ground rules are. You go away and think about it. If you still want to come, let me know." Of those ten, only one came back. People are not so anxious to get a command because of exactly this: they knew that if they made a mistake, despite their being a competent, superior commander such as Hathaway, somebody was going to chop their head off and end their career.

If you make a mistake when you are a staff officer, it's not discovered until you are three grades higher and ten years older. So nothing happens to you. Plus, it has gotten to the point, in a staff job, that every decision gets the consensus of the entire staff. So if there is a mistake, then everyone is guilty. If you are the commander, you're standing out there all by yourself.

In my view, the army, in those earlier days, was far more tolerant of mistakes. People were encouraged to do their best, but if they made a mistake, somebody was going to take care of them. They might call him in and rake him over the coals a little, but they didn't end his career right there. Now, if you were a constant goof-off, didn't pay attention to what you were doing, and didn't study to improve yourself—that was a different matter.

I think being a commander is a tremendously important accomplishment to get ahead. It helps you in terms of what people see in your record when they put you before a promotion board. More importantly, it trains you to be self-reliant. It trains you to know what to look for in the staff, to know what you are going to demand out of your staff to get the information necessary to make the best possible decision under the circumstances. If you are going to rise to the top of the heap, at some point, you are going to be the guy making all the decisions. If you have never made them before, it's going to be a much more difficult job than if you had prepared yourself as you moved up. So it's important that during your career, you have served as a commander.

You know, when I wrote that letter to the secretary, a lot of people said they wanted to see it published in some army publication. I said, "I'm not trying to make a hero out of myself. I'm just trying to tell the secretary, who obviously had no experience along this line, what the situation is in the world." Well, the secretary got upset with this letter—and he was the guy who used to say, "Tell it to me like it is." When you did that, you were liable to walk away with your head in your hand.

Once I was having lunch with General Abrams when he was chief of staff. He was talking about two flamboyant leaders in the army, Jim Hollingsworth and Hank Emerson.[13] Both retired as lieutenant generals. They were always saying things in the press and getting in trouble. General Abrams said, "You know, you have to have leaders like Hank and Jim in the army. They inspire men. They are fantastic leaders and you have to have people like that. If you are going to have them, you can't expect that you are always going to be on a tranquil sea. Sometimes there are going to be some waves. Occasionally, there are going to be white-caps. Sometimes, you're going to have to go to the rail and puke." What he meant was that you have to protect those maverick leaders; you have to expect they are going to get themselves in trouble. Hollingsworth was always spouting off about something that he shouldn't have, because that was just the way he was. That's what made him great with his soldiers. They thought he walked on water.

I got the word from a friend of mine who was very highly placed in the army: "We are going to have to get you out of the army for a while, to keep you from getting really tromped on, because the secretary is incensed that you would write him a letter like this." He just couldn't face up to the truth. So I got sent to the Defense Intelligence Agency and got a promotion out of it. It was a funny way to get a promotion, but that's how it happened. I was out of the army for a year and then reinstated.

But people are very intolerant of mistakes today. That's unfortunate, because this intolerance dampens all innovation or risk. People begin to do everything by the numbers. They want to cover their tracks, so they can say, "That's what the manual says. That's what the regulation says." That's all bad news.

I technically assumed command of the 173rd Airborne Brigade in December 1966. When I left the 1st Division, I went directly back to the United States on my month's R&R, which you got after a twelve-month tour in Vietnam. While I was home, I was required to take a physical exam because I had a broken leg. I had been in a helicopter crash. It was never clear whether our tail rotor simply fell off or was shot off. We thought we heard shots but were never sure. Anyway, there was some concern whether I could take over and operate in the field, so I had to take a physical exam for that. Also, some general officers apparently had heart problems that had been concealed by friendly medics. The problems didn't become apparent until the guy got into combat. Then the stress caused their hearts to go. So they were getting particular about these things.

The chief of staff directed that I take a physical exam at Walter Reed. I had no intention of going to Washington, DC; I was going to spend my time in San Antonio, where my family was. I took my physical exam at Brooke General Hospital, Fort Sam Houston, in San Antonio. Then I called the chief of staff, told him I had taken it, and asked if that was adequate.

His reply was simply that my instructions were to take it at Walter Reed and they hadn't changed. I then had to go to Washington to take the exam to make sure that he was satisfied that I was physically capable of assuming command of the 173rd. I passed the exam. By that time, my leg was out of a cast and I was getting around pretty well. I went back to Vietnam and assumed actual command of the brigade at the end of December 1966.

At the time, Sergeant Zelner Houchin was serving as door gunner and crew chief of the 173rd Airborne Brigade Command helicopter. He recalled his first encounter with Deane:

> *Our CG was General [Paul F.] Smith; he kind of liked to stay up high. I mean, like we'd fly around at maybe 2,000 feet. I don't think he liked to get down in the combat. He would fly up high and observe. So, I thought this was a gravy train assignment I have here. I guess I did that for six months, and then it was time for General Smith to go back to the States.*
>
> *One day we flew over to the 1st Cav to pick up this General Deane, who is going to be General Smith's replacement. So, we pick him up and bring him back to the 173d. Well, it just so happened on that particular day we were having an assault mission going on. Deane wanted to fly over the area to observe, but he's more aggressive; he wanted to fly at treetop level, and he wanted to land on the LZs. While we were flying so low, we spotted some Viet Cong who were trying to escape and Deane shot one with his AR-15. And he hadn't been with the 173d for only a couple of hours. I thought, "Oh Boy, this guy's going to be interesting.*[14]

When I was informed that I was going to assume command of the 173rd, I was interested in doing some airborne operations. I thought we should attempt to demonstrate that parachute assaults were not a thing of the past and to revive that art as a means of conducting warfare. General Thieu, who later became president of Vietnam, was the commander of the Vietnamese Army at that time. Prior to that, he had been an airborne guy. So I suggested to him that it would be desirable to conduct some joint airborne operations.

I didn't particularly care about conducting the operations with the Vietnamese airborne, but figured if we had a joint operation, we would have a greater chance it might be approved. He, in turn, went to General Westmoreland and suggested such an operation. General Westmoreland picked a target area for me to make this assault. It was an abandoned airstrip that had been built by the Japanese during World War II and used afterward by the French. Situated a few miles north of Song Be, the airstrip lay astride an active Viet Cong and North Vietnamese troop infiltration route.

It was on the top of a ridge in the midst of what people refer to as triple canopy jungle. I flew a reconnaissance over the area. It was just as forbidding as could be. If you didn't put your troops and everything right on that landing strip, they would be hung up in trees for the rest of time. Any of our heavy drop, like our artillery pieces, that did not land on that strip would have gone down into ravines and never would have been brought out. I was very much concerned about whether we would have much success in that operation.

Anyway, we went ahead and planned it. Despite my strenuous protests, I was called upon frequently to brief this plan, which was classified as secret. I emphasized the importance of security in an airborne operation because of the vulnerability of the troops when they first were jumping out, landing, and getting organized. Even so, we found out sometime before the operation that the plan had leaked, and all the bar girls in the vicinity of the assault knew about it.

So I recommended that the operation be cancelled, and it was. Not long afterward, we were notified that we were going to do an operation that involved several divisions going into War Zone C. There was going to be an airborne assault in that area. JUNCTION CITY was going to be a horseshoe-shaped operation. The idea was to encircle the enemy on three sides. At the same time, large mobile armored forces would drive between the open legs of the shoe, toward the center of the area. The unit that formed the legs of the horseshoe would move in first, and those that formed the top, or curve, of the shoe had to be moved in fast in order to cut off any attempt by the enemy to flee toward Cambodia. To accomplish this, a parachute jump would be planned.

Initially, General Westmoreland directed a brigade from the 101st Airborne, which was there before the 173rd, to make this assault. He had told the brigade commander that it would probably happen, but hadn't provided a definite timetable. The brigade commander came to see me and asked me what I thought about it. I wasn't very happy that he, instead of our brigade, was getting the mission. I told him I thought he was very fortunate to get that assignment and that it would be a great thing to do. I pointed out that there were many possible perils involved which, if they became a reality, would really jump up and bite him. He had to plan very carefully and maintain great security. I told him of my experience with the previous operation and how it had been leaked.

I did all I could to plant a negative attitude in his mind and apparently was successful. He went back to General Westmoreland and told him he didn't think it was a feasible operation. When I heard that he had said this, I immediately volunteered to do the operation. My proposal was accepted, and we made the airborne assault.

In planning for the first one, I had learned my lesson. For this assault, I asked the air force commander, General Bill Moore, to assign three or four officers to work on the plans. Nobody else was to know anything about our operation. In turn, the battalion commander who was going to make the assault, Lieutenant Colonel Robert H. Sigholtz, a couple of guys on my staff, and I would be the only ones in the 173rd who would know about the mission. We planned very carefully and developed a deception plan. All briefings that I gave, including Westmoreland's, were the deception plan, which had us landing about twenty miles from our actual drop zone.

I made my pleas for security and decreasing the soldiers' vulnerability. I didn't really care because we weren't going to be in that location anyway. We were to jump at 9:00 in the morning and were supposed to take off at 7:30 or so. We were to fly around to give the air force some training in navigation at low level. The night before, the battalion was locked into a predeployment area, and the officers on my staff responsible for the planning personally typed up the real plan.

We delivered the plans to General Westmoreland's headquarters at approximately 3:00 in the morning. Of course, nobody of importance was on duty at that point in time, and a sleepy duty officer just tossed them into the "in basket," so the plans just sat there on the operations desk. In the morning, General Westmoreland was briefed that the operation was going to go, but his staff never briefed him on the location of the real drop zone. We had made the weather decision, but still didn't know where we were going to land.

At about 3:00 in the morning I had gone to the departure airfield and met the air force commander, General Moore. We got a weather briefing and decided that the operation would go. We then had the pilots come in for their briefing. They were told to discard the flight plans they made up, because they weren't going where they had previously been told. They were given an hour to recompute their route. We then went out to the departure airfield, loaded the aircraft, took off, and flew around for a while.

I was standing in one door of the lead aircraft. Bob Sigholtz, the battalion commander of the 2/503 Infantry Regiment, was in the other door. I kept looking at my watch as I was holding the edges of the door preparatory to jumping. When the green light came on, my watch read exactly 9:00. We jumped and landed right on the drop zone. It was a perfect jump. We had fewer broken legs or sprained ankles, I think, than in any jump I've ever experienced. We only had a couple of guys hurt. Usually we had more than that hurt when we jumped at Bragg.

The paratroopers took scattered sniper fire, but no one was hit. With the battalion now in a blocking position, helicopter-borne infantrymen were dropped in to close off the top of the horseshoe. Within six hours, more than five thousand soldiers were landed by 250 helicopters of the army's 12th Aviation Group.

In the meantime, having been briefed that we were going to jump about twenty miles away, General Westmoreland was circling our proposed drop zone in his helicopter with General Thieu. Apparently he kept saying, "Where are they?" He was still circling as 9:00 came and went. Then our heavy drop came to bring our artillery pieces, with great big one-hundred-foot parachutes.

One of Westmoreland's aides happened to spot one of these big parachutes on the horizon and said, "I think they have missed the drop zone. They are way over there." By this time everything was on the ground, so General Westmoreland went back to Saigon. I gathered Westmoreland was upset that his staff had not briefed him properly and that he missed the real drop zone. Several days after the operation, he visited my command post, but never said a word about the drop then or during the next couple of visits. He just studiously avoided any mention of it.

Finally, at one briefing when I was sitting beside him, he turned to me and said, "Did you jump first?" I said, "Yes, sir." It was a tradition that the commander is the first one out of the lead aircraft. That was the only discussion we had on this whole airborne operation. He was so mad that he couldn't stand it. We had perfect security. Later, when we traveled to where we had originally planned to jump, we found mines and booby traps like you wouldn't believe. The operation had leaked again. If we had not had the deception plan, we would have landed in something like that.

Sergeant Houchin observed,

> I was the CG's helicopter crew chief by now, and he was just a very aggressive leader. He would like to fly low, and he wanted to get involved with what's going on. After each battle he would fly off to the field hospital and go there and give those boys medals. You, know, he would pin them on their beds if they were knocked out or something like that. But he would go by and thank them, and tell them how brave they were and this and that. He kind of reminded me of old Patton.

Our helicopter got hit five different times with enemy ground fire. I forget what mission we were on, but we were flying into an LZ and we received gunfire and I got hit in the shoulder from ground fire. So they took me to a field hospital where I received a purple heart from Uncle Jack who came to see me while I was still on the operating table. He made me feel special. Deane was just a great general. He was an inspiration to everybody.[15]

My duty with the 173rd was really a tremendous experience. They were great soldiers and that jump boosted the morale tremendously. It was a great organization. I spent much of my time in a helicopter watching operations on the ground, something I did for hours on end almost every day. I carried a rifle with me and it wasn't for show. I shot a number of enemy soldiers from my helicopter during these operations.

We frequently drew fire during our flights. On one occasion while I was serving in the 1st Infantry Division, we were flying at about twenty feet above the ground due to fog when we received a volley of gunfire. The door gunner on my side of the chopper was killed. When we got back to the base camp, all of us were covered with his blood, which the wind blew around inside the cabin. After we landed, a mechanic on the ground counted some fifty bullet holes in the side of the chopper. On another mission, we received fire from directly below us. One of the several rounds, which had come up through the floor, ended up in my helmet, which was on the floor beside me. I had taken it off to accommodate my radio earphones.

Every now and then while observing operations under way, you'd see an enemy soldier running across a field, and if it looked like he was going to get away or if we needed a prisoner, I would shoot at him with my M-16 rifle. With all that movement, a helicopter isn't the best platform to shoot from. I'd load my weapon up every other round with a tracer so I wasn't using aiming fire or sitting on a stable platform, but as I fired, I'd bring the tracers up until they'd hit the guy. Then we'd land and grab him and take him back for interrogation and see what information he could provide us.

I'm well aware that some people say it's not a general's job to go into battles. If a patrol is down there fighting, guys getting wounded and others fighting for their lives—what can you do? I'll go down to help wherever I can. I'm not going to stay at twenty-five hundred feet and watch my guys in trouble. Sure, I'm emotionally attached to them. You don't stand on the river bank and watch a friend go under; you help if you can.

Soon after his arrival, Deane set about to demonstrate his command philosophy to his soldiers. His brigade sergeant major, Robert A. Mrsich, described his actions: "General Deane took command right from the start. He got with the troops immediately and that's where he stayed. I've wanted to serve with a man like him all of my career. He'll go anywhere he thinks he's needed; into a hot landing zone to pull out a wounded trooper, or right into a raging firefight in order to lay down suppressive fire on the VC." Within his brigade, he earned a reputation of being a "troopers general."[16]

Another testimonial of Deane's leadership came from Captain Chuck Utzman.

> *In January of 1967, I was assigned to the 173d Airborne Brigade as the Aviation Officer. One of my first adventures was flying with General Deane in his Command and Control helicopter. "Uncle Jack" received a call from one of his battalions telling him they had captured a POW—Deane responded with "we'll pick him up," and we did. The POW sat directly in front of me on the floor of the helicopter—hands tied behind him, black pajamas, barefoot, older, good looking man; clean, healthy, black piercing eyes. He looked unafraid! Our eyes met, and I thought: This is our enemy? We dropped him off and returned to the area of operations.*
>
> *That was the beginning of my adventures in the helicopter business with Uncle Jack. He loved and respected our crews. But most of all, he loved and respected his troops. And wherever they were, if it was possible, he was going to visit them. Most of the time we made it possible—fully understanding and accepting that whatever the risk—he was just as committed to the troops and their missions as they were. He proved it! Tight and hairy LZ's? Many! And we got him out of every one of them.*
>
> *"Uncle Jack!" Everyone knew that call sign. Everyone respected that call sign. Everyone welcomed that call sign. When we heard it, we knew one of our own was on the way!*[17]

Captain Jack T. Kelley, General Deane's aide, remembered one incident while they were flying over the area of operations and monitoring radio traffic. A recon element had engaged the enemy and suffered several casualties. They were calling for Dust Off (medical evacuation), but Deane determined the ETA was unacceptable, so he told his pilot to

*divert and pick them up. They landed in a confined area and picked up
several wounded, but the pilot thought that he couldn't lift out of the
tight area with the added weight. Deane told Kelley and the sergeant
major to remain with the recon patrol and followed up his suggestion
with a healthy push.*

*Lieutenant Charlie Brown, who reported to the 173rd Airborne Bri-
gade in June 1967, recalled his first meeting with his brigade commander.*

> *After a couple of weeks doing odd jobs in the rear area, I was
> assigned to lead the 3rd Platoon, C Company, 1/503 Infantry in
> Dak To. Soon into my new job, Uncle Jack flew into our triple
> canopy jungle site and walked around the perimeter. When he
> got to my sector, I saluted and began to escort him from foxhole
> to foxhole to talk to our tired and unwashed troops. In fact the
> couple of times that he visited us, he spent most of the time talk-
> ing to the junior enlisted kids, asking several of them, "Is Lt.
> Brown treating you guys okay? If you have any problems with
> him, you let Uncle Jack know."*
>
> *Needless to say, I was terrified that one of them would tell the
> CG that I had wire brushed him the day before for falling asleep
> on ambush patrol or something like that. I told my dad this story
> when I arrived home some months later and he was delighted to
> hear that a General Officer took the time to come into a very
> dangerous area like Dak To, spend time with the privates, and
> threaten to horsewhip any officer who treated them with other
> than great respect.*[18]

*A telling indicator of the good morale within the 173rd was related
by Captain Kelley. "One morning the 'old man' asked me if anyone had
been in his hooch for any reason during the previous day. I didn't know,
and asked if there was a problem. In good humor, he informed me that as
he got into bed last night, he discovered that someone had 'short sheeted'
his bed. My investigation determined the culprits were nurses from the
3d Surgical Hospital."*[19]

I've always felt that noncommissioned officers' responsibilities were
to take care of the day-to-day needs of the soldiers. To see that they were
properly equipped, had the right amount of ammunition, were wearing
their dog tags, had rations, kept themselves clean and, if it was necessary,
take malaria pills. NCOs saw to it that all this was done. The officer's
job was to plan the utilization of his resources—basically, at platoon and

company commander level. How were they going to be used to accomplish the missions that were assigned to them?

If the officers spent their time going around checking things like dog tags or rations or ammunition, they would not have time to do the proper planning. This lack of proper planning then results in poor operations. I made a major point of the fact that I expected the NCOs to do their jobs in the 173rd. I looked to the sergeant major of the brigade to see that the sergeants major in the battalions—and in turn right down through the NCO chain of command—did their jobs.

I would periodically check to see that this was happening. I wanted the soldiers to shave, for example, every day, even when they were in the jungle, unless it was just physically impossible to get water to them. I insisted on this because I felt that a clean man has better morale than a man who lets himself get slovenly and dirty. A man who is dirty soon begins to feel self-pity. He loses his pride in himself and therefore is not an alert, effective soldier.

I relieved one sergeant major who just didn't seem to be able to grasp the fact that he had certain responsibilities, and that I was demanding that he carry them out. I think his relief from duty had a positive effect on the brigade. The results demonstrated to me that the noncommissioned officers, knowing their responsibilities, could be trusted to fulfill these responsibilities.

I had a sergeant major in one battalion who arrived after I took command. I briefed him on my views with respect to the noncommissioned officers. He became the battalion sergeant major and subsequently became my brigade sergeant major. But one of the battalion executive officers told me later that when this fellow came down to the battalion, he went around and started checking soldiers to see that the NCOs were doing their jobs. He found that they weren't doing as well as the battalion he had just left.

He had them sit up all night making dog tags out of C ration boxes and commo wire, just to give them the idea that they were going to wear their dog tags. I can't overemphasize the importance of this sort of thing. It goes back to earlier statements I made that in World War II, people were moved ahead so fast that they couldn't let go of their old lower-level jobs. Instead of giving a man a job and demanding the performance, they went down and did the job for them. Too many officers feel that if an NCO can't do the job, instead of making them perform, they do the job for them. Then the officers are not doing their own jobs properly. This situation is detrimental to the operation of the entire army.

I started a Brigade Jungle School, which was simply a training camp back at our base camp. When any new replacements came in, they were required to go through it. It was similar to the school we ran in the 104th Division during World War II. All the new replacements came through the jungle school base camp. They were trained by combat-seasoned veterans. Then, when they went into the line, they had some idea of what to expect.

Obviously the shock of being shot at is something you can't fully comprehend before it happens to you. But we had a fairly extensive training course in which we showed them what the mines looked like and how they would be set up, booby traps, punji stake pits, what to watch out for in the jungle, and how to take care of themselves. They were taught that we demanded that soldiers dig in at night, if they weren't moving, in order to be protected.

That brings to mind a story. I had a platoon that had been fighting all day. They were all tired, so the platoon leader didn't require them to dig in. They were lying on the ground, sleeping. That night they got hit with a mortar barrage. They had about three guys killed and about six or eight wounded. I relieved the platoon leader because he hadn't followed our standard operating procedures about digging in.

I used to visit the hospitals a minimum of twice a week to see the wounded. On one visit I ran into three of these wounded soldiers sitting on a bench and stopped to talk to them. Finally one of them said to me, "Why did you relieve our platoon leader? He was really a great guy." I said, "Why do you think he was a great guy?" He said, "Well, he just was a great guy and we all liked him." I said, "You probably liked him because he didn't make you dig foxholes, right?" He said, "Yes, he was a pretty understanding guy." I said, "Do you know why you are here?" He said, "Yes, we got wounded." I said, "Do you know why you got wounded?" He said, "Yes, we got hit with a mortar barrage." I said, "You got wounded because that lieutenant didn't do his job. If you had been dug in, you wouldn't be here with a wound; and three other guys would still be alive today. I don't think he's a great guy. I think he's a terrible guy."

So they all looked at each other and I continued on my rounds. As I left the hospital, the three guys were still sitting on the bench. This time as I went by, they all gave me the thumbs-up signal and nods of the head. That said, "We understand." That's part of what I'm talking about: insisting that people do their jobs because that saves lives. It's important.

On June 22, 1967, one of Deane's units, the 2nd Battalion, 503rd

Infantry, commanded by Lieutenant Colonel Edward Partain, was oper-
ating south of Dak To conducting routine search-and-destroy opera-
tions.[20] *While moving toward the objective, Alpha Company was strung*
out on a ridge trail with steep sides and surrounded by heavy triple can-
opy foliage when it encountered a moving enemy force estimated at bat-
talion strength. The NVA forces closed in quickly and tightly on the Sky
Soldiers, which negated their superior fire support from air and artillery.
Before extra help could reach their position, the company had suffered
76 killed and 23 wounded out of their total force of 137 soldiers.

Sergeant Houchin remembered, "It took several days to get the casu-
alties down from the mountain. When reinforcements got there, they had
to make an LZ for the aircraft to go in and take out the wounded and
the dead. A Chinook helicopter brought in refrigerated storage units to
put the dead in. I later found out that all of the dead had been shot in the
head at close range by the NVA, who had apparently been executing our
wounded. During our flight up there, I noticed a look of anguish on Gen-
eral Deane's face that I had never seen before."[21]

I used to talk to the press and had a pretty good relationship with
them. I only had trouble with the press twice. Once we had a company
that really got hit badly; it had a tremendous amount of casualties. The
press descended upon us. I told the guys who came there that I was prepared to talk to them, but there were certain things that I couldn't discuss. That was the number of casualties. They would have to be briefed
on that by going to General Westmoreland's headquarters, because those
types of questions were answered back there.

Several of them would get you on TV and start beating around the
bush. Finally, they would start directly to ask you the questions you had
already said you weren't going to answer. Well, I would just say, "The
interview is terminated because you have violated the ground rules of the
interview. I told you where you go to get that information. So that's it."

The other problem I had with the press was back when I was with
the 1st Division, during the time of JUNCTION CITY. As I came out of
the jungle, the bodies that had already been brought out were awaiting
evacuation. Some of them had been shot in the head. I went over to see
if I could identify Bill Barott, the battalion commander, whose wife I was
concerned about. I was bending over, looking at these bodies, when I
noticed a newspaper photographer taking pictures of the dead. Perhaps it
was my concern about Bill Barott, maybe it was the strain of the day, but
I was incensed. I said, "Why are you taking pictures of this?" He said,
"I'm going to send them back to my news agency." I said, "Why would

you take pictures of people who have been wounded or killed? Don't you think that's a terrible thing for a mother or a wife or a sweetheart to see at home? To see this, and know that their son or loved one was killed in this battle, and maybe that mutilated person is their child or loved one? That's a terrible thing."

He said, "Well, they go through censorship. If they pass, I use them." I lost control. I grabbed him by his collar, because I was really hot by this time, and I said, "I have no use for people like you. I'll tell you this: if you publish any picture from this incident in which I appear, I'm coming after you. And I'll kill you. Get on a helicopter, get out of my area, and never come back!" He practically ran to the nearest helicopter. Several reporters standing around witnessed this incident. Almost all of them came over and complimented me on my action.

I thought about this after a while and thought, "Gee, I'm going to be in trouble again." I called down to the PAO people in Saigon and related what had happened. The officer, Brigadier General Si Sidle, as I recall, thanked me for calling and told me not to worry. They went to the head of whatever news agency that reporter was with—and he was on his way out of the country that night.

When we did the parachute assault, I was introduced to a French correspondent, Catherine Leroy. She only weighed about eighty-five pounds soaking wet, but she had been a sports parachutist in France. She parachuted in with us. Of course, that made her love the brigade and from then on she became a part of our brigade. So the stories we got from her were always great. I have corresponded with her since then; she lives in Paris. So other than that, we didn't have too many problems with the press.

Near the end of my tour, we moved to the base camp of the 4th Division, which Ray Peers commanded at the time. We were there very briefly. Then we moved to a Special Forces camp called Dak To. My brigade was responsible for that area. We were expecting North Vietnamese Army units to infiltrate, and we had several encounters with them. My responsibility was to ensure that the three Special Forces camps in the area didn't fall—Dak To, Dak Seang, north of there, and Dak Tek, the farthest north. We put a couple of battalions in there to do some search-and-destroy missions and to disrupt any plans that the enemy might have had. We used the best intelligence available to us. Usually it was from direction-finding equipment and signal intelligence.

Specialist Michael Del Monaco, who served as a door gunner on Deane's command helicopter, recalled

I sat on the right side of the ship about five feet away from him. This allowed me to watch his facial expressions and his intensity. I wasn't always able to hear what the General was saying, because the door gunners had to maintain communications with the pilots. But, I quickly learned to feel what was going on by watching Uncle Jack's eyes. Where he was looking, altitude, smoke, maps out, all indicators of what might lie ahead.

I think this created a special relationship between the General and Hooch [Sergeant Zelner Houchin] and especially me because of our eye contact during flight. Whenever the General left the ship, I had to follow him with the radios if he wanted them. That meant where ever he went, I went.

During one period, Dak To was our base camp and airfield, but we were flying daily missions to smaller bases in the vicinity. I remember one was a small, very secluded Special Forces camp called Dak Seang. As we approached the landing zone, the General signaled me to follow him with the radios. As soon as we set the bird down, we started taking heavy small arms fire. The General and I jumped out as the bird took off. The camp had a heavy iron type gate and the locals started to close it because of all of this incoming fire. As Uncle Jack and I are running our asses off toward the gate, the General slips and goes down on one knee. I thought he was hit. I reached down with my hand to help him up, and as he struggled to his feet, he yelled out to me, "Wanna dance?"

It was right after this incident that the General changed his call sign. It was like Charlie knew he was coming in.[22]

We had an interesting experience there. A Vietnamese airborne task force under my operational control, located at the camp called Dak Seang, got into a hell of a scrap in the hills west of there. General Peers, the senior guy in that whole area, showed up and called in a B-52 mission. Peers and a lot of other people had the idea that after you put in a B-52 strike, you should send troops into the strike area to perform a bomb-damage assessment.

I didn't agree with that. My experience and belief was that when you put in a large enough unit to protect itself, there wouldn't be anything there. If you put in a smaller unit, the enemy would attack it and gobble it up. I thought, "What's the sense in doing that? We don't go out and check what damage we do with our artillery firing. Why do it when we drop some bombs? You don't do it when attack air comes over and drops bombs. Why do we do it for the B-52 strikes? You might find one dead guy or something, but what did it mean?"

While I was working under General Peers, I never used B-52 strikes because I wasn't going to do an assessment. Anyway, as this battle drew to a close, Peers felt that the Viet Cong or the North Vietnamese, whichever, would withdraw across the border into Cambodia. So he thought we ought to put a B-52 strike, or even a couple of them, right in there on the border. It would hopefully hit them.

He told this airborne Vietnamese colonel, "Now, I want you to do an assessment." We weren't in a position to order the Vietnamese around. Ostensibly they were under our operational control, but it was a fine line. You weren't supposed to make them do things that they didn't want to do; you had to convince them to do it. Well this guy looked at Ray Peers and said, "Are you nuts? I'm not going to do that. That's crazy!"

So Peers directed the Special Forces commander to put a team in there. Well, just a small team, one helicopter load of five or six guys, went in. They landed in that area and the team began to go as fast as they could back to camp on the ground. A week or so later we captured some guys in that area. When they were brought back to the Special Forces camp, one of them pointed to this lieutenant who had led the team in there and said, "I know you." This was through an interpreter, so the lieutenant asked how he knew him and he said, "You landed out there." He described them landing and he described everything they did. He said, "We didn't attack you because we thought that you were bait, trying to trick us to show where we were. We couldn't believe that anybody would be so foolish as to go in there without having some big force behind them." They should have been gobbled up. That's just what the Vietnamese colonel thought was likely to happen.

11

Office of the Assistant Chief of Staff for Force Development

After my tour was up, I went back to the Pentagon and I was assigned as director of doctrine and systems in the Office of the Assistant Chief of Staff for Force Development (ACSFOR). My job was to monitor certain systems that were not really R&D projects. One of these projects was referred to as the TOS (tactical operation system). It was a matter of determining what computers were required, and the software you had to have in order to receive, collate, and produce information that commanders needed in order to make their decisions.

One software package dealt with your friendly forces and personnel strengths. Another dealt with logistics strengths. Those packages would give the commander, through the operations officer, the information he needed to make useful decisions regarding his operation. We had that system and a couple similar to it. That was a big part of our effort. Those packages went on for years in development but never were very successful.

I was also responsible for type classification of materiel. Anything that had passed research and development tests and was going into production had to pass through our office. We had to base our decision on the results of the testing agencies. We had to determine how they would be type classified before they went into production.

One of the jobs I did for ACSFOR gave me a lot of personal satisfaction, and again demonstrated a lack of vision on some people's part. That job concerned the Cheyenne—a very complex, state-of-the-art attack helicopter being developed by Lockheed. For example, it had sighting systems that, if you spotted a target, let you lock onto that target and then drop down behind a hill, move off one thousand meters to one side or another, and pop back up with the gun still locked on the target. These were really very advanced things for those days. It was also darned expensive.

I recalled a conversation I had with a soldier at West Point in 1941, almost three decades earlier. I was on the polo team at West Point and the Buffalo Soldiers of the 10th Cavalry Regiment, a segregated regiment of black soldiers in those days, took care of the ponies. One day, I arrived early for practice in the West Point Riding Hall. I was sitting on the tan-bark surface of the indoor polo field, leaning against the knee boards, a slanted wall bordering the playing field. One of the Buffalo Soldiers came over and we started talking. In the course of the conversation he said, "Mr. Deane, some day battleships will rise out of the ocean, lifted by pro-pellers on top of them. They will fly around and shoot their big cannons at targets on the ground." I thought at the time it might be a little far-fetched but I never forgot the vision of that soldier.

Now, in 1967, just before Christmas, Secretary of Defense McNa-mara had disapproved the army's request for authorization to initiate a program that would produce 375 attack helicopters. He did say, how-ever, that he would reconsider his decision in early January 1968 if the army, having heard the basis for his decision, could convince him that he was wrong.

My boss, Lieutenant General Arthur "Ace" Collins, called me into his office about December 23, 1967, just after I picked up my parents, who had come from San Francisco to visit me for Christmas. I was a major general at the time. He told me of the McNamara decision. He nailed me with the responsibility for developing the case to convince McNamara to approve the attack helicopter program at a meeting ten-tatively scheduled for January 2, 1968. Collins said, "You're in charge of getting him to change his mind." I protested the assignment, pointing out that I was not an aviator and that he had a whole division of his staff responsible for aviation matters. He said I had the job and he would give me all the aviators I needed to get it done.

I had a series of meetings with a number of army aviators. The theme of all their thoughts and suggestions was a bigger, faster version of the Cobra attack helicopter we were using in Vietnam, equipped with the same weapons we had on the Cobra—just lots more of them. Still, it was no major change. For several million dollars' difference in the cost of the aircraft you were only getting a slightly increased capability. This did not ring any bells with me, but I found it difficult to envision anything better.

Then I woke up in the early hours one morning with visions of the Buffalo Soldier in West Point Riding Hall, the guy who predicted battle-ships in the sky. I got up and rushed to the Pentagon. I began to list all of the weapons in the inventory or under development. Among them was the thirty-millimeter automatic cannon, the so-called chain gun, named for the mechanism that allowed it to fire on automatic mode. It was being developed for the Bradley Fighting Vehicle. Then there was the Hellfire missile, which was capable of knocking out any known tank. We had the .50-caliber machine guns in the inventory. The question was, "How many of these weapons could be mounted on and safely fired from the proposed attack helicopter?" This was the question I assigned to the aviators when they came to work.

The Buffalo Soldier had given me the idea of the armament and the needed lethality. Next, he gave me the tactical concept, shooting those big guns at targets on the ground—the enemy's armor. I conceived of attack helicopter platoons or companies becoming the maneuver ram of our divisions under the appropriate circumstances. When our attacking forces were held up by the enemy, the enveloping maneuver would be undertaken by attack helicopters. They could get to the scene of attack in minutes compared to hours, or even days, by troops on the ground or by armor units and not be impeded by rivers, woods, or blown bridges.

The first time I briefed the concept up the line, I met with really bad reactions because we had to do an equal cost trade-off. If we bought the helicopters, basically the armor division would have to give up some tanks. The armor people wanted me drummed out of the army, my uniform stripped of its buttons, because I was going to take some of their tanks away. I figured, "What the heck. If you give some tanks now, they are going to come back later. Two or three years from now McNamara will be gone; and, if we need more tanks, we can request them. Meantime, if we need the helicopters, we will have gotten them too." I wasn't meeting with much success, but I continued to polish up the concept.

The aviators determined how the weapons could be mounted and ascertained that they could, in fact, be mounted and fired effectively and safely. When we had the package together, we made our first stop at the office of the assistant vice chief of staff, then Lieutenant General Chet Chesarek. He allowed as how our concept was about as stupid as anything he had ever heard. However, we were faced with meeting the secretary of the army, Stan Resor, in a few minutes and there was insufficient time to make any changes in our presentation.

We marched into the secretary's office and Chet took over. He said that Jack Deane had come up with a wild-eyed, radical proposal. He said we were only presenting it to get some guidance from the secretary as to where we should be heading in our presentation.

When I finished my presentation, the secretary said it was the most imaginative thing he had heard since assuming office and he did not want any changes. He told us to polish it up and be prepared to present it to McNamara on January 2.

At this point, Chesarek decided we had a winner and wanted to be the guy presenting it from then on. Mr. Resor artfully edged him out of the picture. I had a rehearsal with Mr. Resor at his home on January 1, and made the presentation to Mr. McNamara on January 2. Mr. McNamara was equally enthusiastic about the concept and approved the Attack Helicopter Program. The armor people still didn't like it because I had given up some of their tanks. Of course, today they think attack helicopters are the greatest things since sliced bread. That was actually the beginning of the concept of utilizing helicopters to knock out armored vehicles.

This was an example of technology driving doctrine, and there has always been this conflict of thought. I've been on the operational side as well as the research and development side. So I have a perspective of that conflict. There has always been this idea that the requirements guy says, "Look, you technical guys. Go sit in your boxes until we call you. We'll figure out the requirements. Then you can go ahead and develop something."

It doesn't work that way in real life. The word *telephone* was not even in the lexicon when Alexander Graham Bell came along. Nobody called Alexander Graham Bell up and said, "Hey, we need a telephone." He saw that there was a need to communicate better. So he developed the telephone. God said, "Let there be light." He didn't say electric lights. It wasn't until Edison came along that electric lights were developed. Nobody said to him, "Hey, we need electric light." The same with Marconi and the radio; he thought it up.

Technology does drive requirements; there is no question in my mind about that. There has to be a close interaction between the requirements people and the technical people. Unfortunately, we never have developed a systematic way of managing that interchange. I'm not sure I really sat down and tried to figure that out myself. I should have done it in the past. I did in some respects, but not others.

I didn't do it very effectively when I used to encourage my lab directors to get out to the units and find out what their problems were, so that we would know what basic research we should be doing. You have to get out into the schools to say, "Look, we now have electricity. It's something new. Maybe it will do this for you." Then the guy at the school would hopefully see these possibilities and say, "Hey, we have a requirement for that. Let us write up how you can utilize electricity to help us."

Unless you hammer on that every day, it just gradually goes away. Initially there is an effort. You also have problems with jealousies, prerogatives, and concerns about people overdoing things. In Vietnam we had a senior scientific advisor to the commander, General Westmoreland. That guy had a direct pipeline back to Defense Research and Engineering. When he thought the army needed something, he didn't go through army channels. He pumped it in directly to the defense level and they told the army to get this into the field.

The army said, "We have other things that we have to do. That's low priority, as far as we are concerned." Well, they didn't like that to happen. While we were in Vietnam, I made a suggestion that got turned down. I recommended that we get technical people from the labs, Director of Defense Research and Engineering (DDR&E), or army staff over there and put them with the brigade or division. Let them stay there for six months or three months, see how the army operates in the field in a real war, and see what the problems are. Then they should know what to direct their engineering talents toward solving.

They tend to sit back in a sterile atmosphere of the lab and not understand the real needs of the army. People argued, "Yes, we are going to allow direct pipelines into DDR&E and then we will be directed to do all these things with our resources that we don't want to do." There is that fear that these guys will overstep their bounds, and their proposals get opposed.

I had an interesting experience while I was acting for a short period as the deputy ACSFOR under Bill Gribble, an engineer officer. He was really a brilliant and great guy. I couldn't comprehend what half of his papers, written by all these smart guys, were really talking about. If they didn't look really bad or too important, I'd sign them and send them up the line to save my boss the trouble of reading them. I always had a nagging fear that one of these things was going to bounce.

One day I was sitting in the office and Ace Collins, the ACSFOR, came in. He shut the door behind him and looked madder than hell. I said, "Uh-oh. One of those papers just jumped up and bit me." Art said, "I just came from the chief of staff's office." I thought, "Oh, gee!" He sat down and he said, "You're going down to command the 82nd Airborne Division." Then he smiled. I was sure worried up to that point.

12

82nd Airborne Division Commanding General

I called ahead to the division and told them that within one week after I arrived, I wanted to go to the field for a week so I could get a feel for what kind of training we needed and what our capabilities were. The only way I could do that was to spend time with troops in the field.

We quickly established several new things within the division that were in vogue in those days. One was junior officer councils. I used to meet with them. If they had good ideas, I implemented them. I was in New York not long ago and this vice president of some stock brokerage firm came up to me and said, "Do you remember me?" I said, "Frankly, I don't." He said, "I was on your junior officer council in the 82nd Airborne. Boy, I thought that was the greatest thing. You listened to us and we were able to express ourselves fully, and that was terrific."

Six months into his command of the division, Deane led thirteen hundred of his paratroopers on a planned air assault exercise, Operation FOCUS RETINA, in Korea. It was staged directly from Fort Bragg with only refueling stops en route. An unexpected snowstorm caused a twenty-four-hour safety delay on the ground in Okinawa before Deane became the first man out of the door of his C-141 transport on March 17, 1969. There were fifteen minor injuries during the jump, and Deane ended up landing in the Han River before being retrieved and escorted to the reviewing stand in his soaking wet pants to shake hands and greet the exercise observers, South Korean president Chung Hee Park and General Charles Bonesteel, commander of the 8th Army and United Nations forces in Korea.

Of course, the most important part of our division was the soldiers. In the 82nd, we had an incident with a black soldier in a psychological warfare battalion stationed at Fort Bragg. He was a PhD sort, a very bright kid. He came over into the division and tried to organize what he called the black brigade. He wanted to organize the black soldiers, obviously for rebellious reasons. They had a meeting one night. The MPs heard about it, went down there, broke it up, and identified three soldiers.

So I organized a meeting with these soldiers along with their brigade and battalion commanders and their first sergeants. Two of them wouldn't say anything; they were scared to death just being in my office with all these people. One guy, named Fuller, was a Black Panther. He wasn't scared, and he started telling us how he felt about things. He'd say, "The first pig," meaning the first sergeant. He was not saying it as an insult to us, the listeners, or the first sergeant. That's just what his name for the first sergeant was. Well, the first time he started, "The first pig said . . . ," his battalion commander interrupted, "You call your first sergeant first sergeant. You treat him with the respect that is due to him." Well, a big iron door went right down between the two of them, and we never got anything more out of Fuller that was worthwhile.

I could see the meeting was deteriorating rapidly. So I said, "Let's knock this off. I have some of the message. Let me think about it." I immediately got Fuller back up to my office, sat him down, and said, "Let's talk about these things." He said, "We don't have any black magazines in our company day room and I think we should have some." So that day, I put out a directive that within a week, every company commander would certify that he had ordered at least three black magazines for their day room.

Fuller told me some other things. Some of them were things that were not bad in themselves but appeared bad to him. I explained why they weren't bad in my view and explained my responsibilities. Then I got the division together and said, "Look, I was talking to this kid, Fuller, and he told me about these black magazines. Now if you go in your day room, you will find that every company in this division has a subscription." I tried to explain the things that I was not going to solve, or couldn't solve, and the reasons why.

Well, I got to know Fuller pretty well. He told me early on that he was not going to go to Vietnam; he was not going to fight the white man's battle for him. He told me about how he had burned buildings down in Chicago, where he was from. He had a braided band on his wrist, and I asked him, "What is that thing you have on your wrist for?" He said, "That means 'Black Power,' sir."

I said, "Suppose I wore one of those on my wrist. What would your reaction be?" He said, "If you believed in Black Power, I'd be glad. But if you didn't, I wouldn't like it. You know how I feel about white people.

I'd just as soon kill them as look at them." I was standing in front of my desk and I put my arm around his shoulder and said, "Son, when you decide to kill me, you had better kill me with the first shot. If you don't, I'll cut your black heart out." We established a rapport there.

From then on, we understood each other and got along. Because he knew that I was doing the best I could for him and our black soldiers, he supported me. Any time I had a black problem within the division, I'd say, "Go see Fuller," and he would solve it. When I got ready to leave the division, he asked to see me. We were sitting there in the office and he said, "I have a real problem and I'd like your advice." I asked, "What's the problem?" He said, "I have applied for and been accepted to go to college. But I don't think I'm going to be effective as a spokesman for my people if I haven't served in Vietnam. If I extend for a year to go to Vietnam, I don't know when I'll get to go to college. I don't know what to do."

Here was a guy whose whole attitude had changed. I'd told him that the way to fight for his people was in a progressive and reasonable way. He had said he wasn't going to fight the white man's war. He hated the white man. But by then he wanted to enter what he perceived as the white man's world. He wanted to be effective in that world by being educated and being a spokesman for his people. He also saw that, if he hadn't served his country, he may not be looked upon as an effective black spokesman.

He had a real problem. I told him, "I'm not sure I can give you good advice on that. First, why don't we see if we can get your college postponed for a year? Get them to accept you in another year." I called up whatever university it was and talked to the chancellor or the president. I told him something about Fuller and what his objectives were in life. The guy agreed this was the kind of person they would like to have at his college. They would hold an opening for him and permit him to come in the following year based on whatever he had done up to that point.

When I left the division, he was going off to Vietnam. I've never heard from him since, but it was a rewarding experience to have dealt with that young guy and to feel that I had changed his life so much. At the same time he'd been very helpful to me and taught me a great deal as well. Between the two of us, we had averted a lot of major problems that could have popped up in the division. This was during the time when black militants were beginning to try to cause trouble in the military. There was a major race riot that killed several people at Camp Lejeune. We averted that kind of stuff. Fuller was a PFC, a junior guy; but he was a big help. Getting to know your soldiers, being there at odd hours, is not only important in the execution of your job, but tremendously rewarding in a personal way.

There was another incident early on that was unfortunate in that it happened at all, but it proved fortunate from my point of view. I received word that two or three black soldiers had a complaint to register. After the complaint was described to me, I didn't feel that the action being taken in response was satisfactory. At least, the complainers were probably not going to be satisfied with the action or with the explanation given for it.

So I said, "Let me talk to them myself." They came in and told me that they had been in this bar downtown with the inelegant name of Pussy Galore. The black soldiers complained that the bar wouldn't serve them as rapidly as they served the white people, and the waitresses were rude to them. They felt like this was outright discrimination. I told them we would investigate the thing, find out the facts, and get back to them. I put a guy in charge of the investigation who I felt would be objective. He went down and came back with the feeling that this story had been a mixed bag.

These guys were calling the waitresses pigs. The waitresses were mad at them, and they were mad at the waitresses. Who started it and how it got going, nobody really knew; but there was a little bit of fire on both sides. The investigating officer recommended no action as far as the initial complaint, but he was concerned enough to bring up another point. The establishment had a sign above the bar that read, "The proceeds from all drinks served to niggers—and they used the word *nigger*—will be turned over to the Ku Klux Klan."

I said, "That's really bad. I want that place put off limits." My legal officer came in and said, "You can't do that." I said, "I'm going to do it." Then he presented me with the regulation, which I couldn't believe. I couldn't do anything. In essence, it said that if this type of situation happened, the local commander had to go down to the offending guy and tell him that it was offensive and indicated racial discrimination. If the guy agreed to correct the situation, that was the end of it.

If he refused to correct it, I still couldn't do anything. I had to send the case eventually to the secretary of the army, who had to make the decision. I said, "If that's the regulation, then we have to figure a way around it." The bar was in Fayetteville and I called the mayor about the situation because I was mad. The mayor said, "I'll support whatever action you take." About the same time we had another, lesser incident concerning a barbershop in a nearby town, Spring Lake or someplace like that.

I told my chief of staff that I wanted to talk to the 1st Brigade at 7:00 the next morning and the rest of the brigades on succeeding mornings until I had talked to the whole division. So we split the division up into five groups. Now, some officers who were present have told the story that I strapped on my pearl-handled pistols and gave a Patton-like speech. That is not true. I certainly was never able to emulate Patton as an inspirational leader. I couldn't even meet his level of earthy speech.

Each morning for five mornings before breakfast, I met with a large group of soldiers on the parade field and related the incidents involving the bar and the barbershop. I told them about the sign above the bar. I told them the owner of the bar related to me that he had a black guy working for him, a janitor, and he thought the sign was funny. So the owner thought the sign wasn't really a bad thing. I told them about the regulation and how it limited my ability to act.

I said, "As far as I'm concerned, I have no use for that guy. He is lousy and has insulted some of our buddies, our comrades in arms. They are a part of this division; they are paratroopers, just like the rest of us. I'd never spend a cent in that guy's bar. I'm not going to tell you where you guys can or can't go, but I'm telling you how I feel about it." Well, the soldiers started yelling, "Hooah! Airborne, airborne all the way!" and all those things that soldiers yell. Here again, I demonstrated that I was not a Patton. I was so excited by their reaction that instead of grinning through my teeth, slapping my leg with a riding crop and growling at my dog, I yelled, "Take the rest of the day off!"

Boy, the next thing you know, nobody went to that bar! The Special Forces heard about it. They are all airborne, so they wouldn't go to that bar. Then the XVIII Airborne Corps troops and the corps artillery troops all heard about it and they wouldn't go to the bar either. The bar owner was going ape. So he came out and asked if he could have an interview with me.

He came in and started defending himself and complaining that I was putting him out of business. When he got through, I said, "I've listened to you, and I've got no regard for you at all. I think you're slimy. If you go out of business, I'll be delighted. You can take whatever action you want against me, but you are really going to suffer for what you've done to my soldiers."

Well, he went out of business. But that incident really brought the division together, hard. The whole division acted together over this cause.

So, from that point of view, it was a very positive event. I would hold monthly meetings with the whole division in the stadium. I would talk to them about problems that I'd seen within the division, such as the lack of black magazines and eggs, and what we had done to make corrections. When you establish that kind of communication, soldiers are satisfied. So the bar incident really was a fortunate happening for me during my command of the division.

In September 1969, Brigadier General Henry E. Emerson reported to Fort Bragg as the 82nd Airborne Division assistant division commander. With this assignment, Hank Emerson was reunited with an old comrade from the Vietnam War.

The first time I encountered General Deane was when I was commanding a battalion of the 101st Airborne Division. My battalion was way up north in the bad country, when somebody decided we were needed somewhere else, and we had to withdraw. My brigade commander wanted us to get the hell out of there quickly.

We got to this river, and put out a single rope bridge across it; right close to a waterfall, and put snap connectors on it; and one by one, we went across that bridge. Apparently, one of my troopers didn't have his snap connector on right; slipped off; and went over that waterfall, and we lost him.

While we were searching for his body, my brigade commander was getting on my case, saying "you have to get out of there now; we can't afford to lose the whole company." I said, "By God, Sir, we all came over here together, and we're all going back home together." I always told that to my troops; one way or another, we're all going back together; alive or dead. That means, we don't go anywhere until we bring out all the dead bodies out.

So he was giving me a hard time, and Jack Deane, was flying overhead and he heard all of this; and he broke in on our conversation, and told this colonel to shut up; that he was coming down to join me. He landed and told me, "You're doing exactly the right thing, Hank. Continue your search. Go for it." So we did, and after two days, we finally found that soldier and got him out of there. All of the troops felt good about it. That's how I met Uncle Jack, and that's how, I think, I became the assistant division commander of the 82nd under him; because he was impressed with my decision to stay on the river until we found our lost trooper.

On another occasion, one of our helicopters crashed in the thick jungle, and there was no way you could land a bird in there. The pilots were stranded. So I told General Deane, "I'm going to go down there and figure out a way to get them out." I thought I'd go straight down the shaft and maybe clip off a couple of trees, because we had to get these guys out of there. Deane said, "Well, I'm coming in with you." I said, "No; that's not necessary." And he said, "Yes. I'm coming down with you, Hank."

And so, the fact that he was willing to go into what was really a dangerous spot just demonstrates his bravery and you can imagine how much that impressed me; that he insisted on going down there with me. We did chop off some branches and whacked off part of the rotor blade; but we were able to get those pilots out of there.

So I have never forgotten that; that he not only came to the scene, but that he wanted to engage with me to pick our guys up. He was always a very aggressive guy, completely willing to go into harm's way, no matter what. He was always with the troops, on the ground.

Jack Deane was an electrifying guy! A really bright guy. I don't know that I ever served under anybody that was more tuned in to soldiers and their well-being, and their welfare and morale, than Jack Deane was.

Jack was really a smart guy, really an appealing leader. So organized. He loved to speak to the whole division assembled in the football stadium. I've heard some pretty impressive guys get up and speak to troops, but never in such a large formation. He would have them in a football stadium, the whole division!

And Jack had a saltier tongue than I did, and he could get up and talk to soldiers in soldier expletives, in a way that soldiers talked to each other. And the soldiers just loved listening to him! The father of the airborne, as far as everyone in Fort Bragg was concerned, was Jim Gavin. I never had the honor to meet General Gavin, but he was a paratrooper guy that started that concept of jumping on the hood of a jeep. Come on; get around me, where you can see me up close! He would deliver inspiring soldier talk to them.

Jack Deane was just an expert at it. He got up there once, and got into a little trouble with Westmoreland because we were going to conduct an exercise somewhere in conjunction with the Marines. Jack Deane got up and started ribbing the Marines and said, "We're not going to have those fancy pants Marines show us up over here." There was a reporter from the Fayette Observer *present who put it all in the paper. So Uncle Jack—that's what everybody called Jack—got picked on a little by Westmoreland, for snide remarks about the Marine Corps. But the paratroopers loved it!*

I don't know how many times in the Army that I've seen where the commander is going to make a speech, and the troops are at parade rest way out there and they can't even see him. The commander gets up and almost reads the thing. There is nothing rousing about that.

When Jack Deane would talk to the troops, he would get interrupted about fifty times with a big yell. Once, we had a black soldier get barred from being served at a club on that highway between Fort Bragg and Fayetteville; the main route from post to town, with all the gyp-the-GI joints. Well, this black soldier wasn't served; Deane investigated the circumstances and called a division formation.

So Jack jumps up and says, "Let me tell what happened today. One of our men, a black guy down here was refused service at one of the clubs. That offends every damned one of us! Screw them! They are off limits. That's all there is to it. We won't tolerate that!" He just wasn't going to tolerate it. Commanders that do stuff like that, maybe they are stepping a little bit over the boundary, putting a civilian place off limits, but like he said; "you offended my soldier; you offended every soldier in the 82d, and you've offended me. I'm not going to have it."[1]

I spent much of my time fighting the ever-growing drug problems within the army. When I was in command of the 82nd, we worked very hard to try to do something about this drug business. I'm not sure how much we accomplished; it was a very difficult problem. We set up a course of instruction. We had five or six speakers go around and hit all the companies in the division. We had a chaplain who discussed dope from a moral point of view. The JAG discussed the problem in terms of what a dishonorable discharge meant to a soldier if he was caught. We had medical people who discussed it from a medical point of view.

A company commander discussed it from the point of view of the effectiveness of the unit. One speaker who was particularly effective was a disc jockey, known to the soldiers because of his radio program. He spoke the soldiers' language—all the lingo of the drug world—and had himself been a drug addict. He had also been an alcoholic and had been cured of both. He understood the problem better than you or I, because he had been through it all.

First, we established a program where there would be a counselor available in the chapel between the hours of 7 and 9, three days a week. Not many people came to those things. We concluded that they didn't come because they were afraid they would be seen and that this would indicate their involvement with drugs, which might lead to people really zeroing in on them, getting them in trouble.

But this disc jockey let people know where he was, what his telephone number was, and what his home address was. Anytime anybody wanted to come talk to him, they could. I understand a lot of people went to see him. When I say a lot, you just have to have 1 percent of the group we had, and you had a lot that were maybe getting off drugs. We did everything we could to keep these guys from throwing their lives away. My policy was, anytime that anyone went AWOL in the division, I was to know the reason. While we had a low rate of AWOLs, nonetheless, I was concerned that there might be some generic problem that was driving them out. I wanted to know what that problem was and how we could get it corrected.

One day a soldier came in who had charges preferred against him, because he had been AWOL for four months or something like that. I asked him, "How come you went AWOL?" He said, "I got involved with drugs, so I went home." He had a week's furlough and went home to California. While there, either on his own, or maybe because his family convinced him, he went to a drug rehabilitation program. That was a three-month course and he took another week off. Then he came back to the division.

Now his unit was going to court-martial him. I said, "I'm not interested in court-martialing you. That's not going to do a lot of good for anybody. How about if I transfer you out of your company, battalion, and brigade, and put you in a whole new environment so you can start over again?" I admired the guy, trying to cure himself and admitting why he had been away.

He said, "No, sir. I'd rather be court-martialed and get a dishonorable discharge." I said, "Don't you know what a dishonorable discharge means to you? You will never be able to vote. You won't have any rights." He said, "Yes, sir. I know. But as long as I am here, the people who push drugs know where I am, and I know I'll get back into drugs again. I just don't have the personal strength of character to resist it. I don't want to be back into drugs, but I know I'm not strong enough to resist it."

Maybe he was pulling the wool over my eyes. I don't know. He seemed pretty sincere. I said, "What sense is it putting this guy in jail? It's an administrative burden for the army if he becomes a drug addict again. Why not give him a medical discharge and let him out? Maybe he can take care of his life." So we got him out. I've always felt that if you can take care of people some way other than putting a blemish on their record, then you should do it.

I recalled that right after World War II, when I brought my battalion back from Europe to the United States, I met every soldier as he reported in from leave. I told him what the problems were around the area, the problems the other units were having, and what I expected of our guys. I told them they had done a fabulous job in the war and had a reputation of being one of the best battalions in the division. I said, "Let's not blow it, because we are only going to be here a short time."

We always had the fewest DRs within the division, but still had a few soldiers who would do something they shouldn't. Instead of court-martials, on Saturday, I would take the guy to the top of a mountain that was near us. It would take him about four hours to get up there. He was supposed to be at the top at a certain hour and have a white flag he carried with him. The duty officer would look through his binoculars to spot the soldier, who would wave the white flag, and then he would come down. He would repeat the exercise on Sunday. Those guys didn't like that, but they didn't get out of the service a few months later with a court-martial on their record.

So now, commanding the 82nd, I thought, "Why destroy this kid?" Maybe he fooled me. A lot of times these guys come in and give you a sob story that breaks your heart, but they are phonies. Anyway, I tried my solution.

The army has all these reports and things that you turn in in order to track division readiness, but I don't put much store in them. They are indicators to people and give some feel for things, but my method was to just spend a lot of time with the units. I used to spend all day out in the field when I was in the division, going around from one unit to the next, just watching them. Then you would get a feel for whether they knew what they were doing and whether their commanders were competent. If I saw something I didn't like, I would head them down the right track. Or talk to their next higher in command and say, "Here is something that I think your soldiers are a little short on. I think you ought to give them some help."

Once I had a new battalion commander join the division who was a "fight the system" kind of guy, a malcontent. You could see it right away. The first time he rendered a readiness report on his battalion, which was a month or two after he'd arrived, he turned in a C4. That's the lowest rating: not fit to go to combat and not fit to leave the barracks in the morning. I called the guy and his brigade commander in, and his brigade commander supported his position. He said, "If that's his judgment, I support it." I said,

> I'm not saying he's to change his rating. If that's the way he feels, that's the way he is going to rate it. But I think I've had more experience than this man and will tell you one thing: I belonged to the best-trained division that this nation sent into combat during World War II. It had a reputation. The training and the state of training in that division was no better than this, and probably not as good as in the 82nd today. If you talk about what's perfect and that's the only thing that you can put down, whatever the top rating is, there is no such unit in the whole army. Every unit that I've ever seen will go into combat and have problems initially. Just the shock of being shot at makes people a little different than they are in garrison. They remember in a hurry; but for the first two or three weeks, they mill around and do bad things, and a lot of people get hurt.
>
> But this division was no worse than that. If this readiness report had an A on it, or whatever the top rating is, then that means you have to be perfect. You're going into battle and you're going to win every battle you ever saw. You wipe out everybody and you never have any casualties. That's a stupid report sheet.
>
> I say that I think this division is as well trained as any unit I've ever seen. That should be an A, as far as I'm concerned. If you think that's a C4, I'm really concerned about the rest of the army, as well as your battalion. If you're starting at a C4 now, you're going to have a heck of a time getting above a C4, in my estimation. That's going to affect your efficiency report, because

you're saying that your unit is no good and you're going to make it better. Well, you had better make it a hell of a lot better, or you're going to be a total failure as a battalion commander.

What he was trying to do was get a high report card. He would say he had come in and taken over a battalion that was not fit to leave the barracks, and six months later had it passing all of its tests. This was a cover-your-ass operation. Well, he didn't last long. As a matter of fact, he was on his way within a couple of months. He was a malcontent—not honest—and didn't have any gumption. To me, that's a bum.

When you go out and look at units, you can get a sense of how well trained they are and what their deficiencies are. That's the way I did it. I spent time with them, got accustomed to seeing what they were doing, and compared them with other units.

On a typical day I'd get up really early, go in and eat breakfast with the troops. Some days I'd go in and do some paperwork. Once the troops had gone out to training, I'd go out to the units to visit and observe them. I'd maybe eat in the field, spend part of the afternoon out there, come in, then finish up paperwork or have meetings with some of the staff. Then I'd go home.

In the evenings, I used to go to the enlisted men clubs on post to talk to soldiers and find out any problems they might be having. The fact that I was going to these places would get other people going. I'd take my sergeant major with me from time to time. Other sergeants major knew the division sergeant major was going around their areas, so they would go around too. Next, the battalion commanders and company commanders would show up.

They were all seeing that things were going well, and the troops were seeing that somebody was concerned about them. You don't go in those clubs and start raising hell; you go in there and talk in a friendly way, show them you're interested in them and get them to talk about their problems. You have to convince them that you're concerned about their welfare, like those kids who were wounded when their platoon leader didn't make them dig their foxholes. Their welfare is in making them dig their foxholes—not always something that is pleasant, but something that is going to make them survive combat.

That means hard training and, sometimes doing tasks that are unpleasant; but again, it's all for the welfare of the soldier: to keep them alive. As a side benefit you may train him to be a better man and, when he gets out of the army, to be more successful. If he stays in the army, maybe he will be more successful than if you hadn't trained him or had concern for his welfare.

At Bragg, as I'd done in the 2nd Battle Group, I used to have outsiders come in and inspect us. In the 2nd Battle Group, which was a smaller unit and didn't require so much, every Saturday I would have what I called a command inspection of one of my five companies. I would pick a company at random.

I had a team that had supply experts, come over from the Berlin Brigade. They would inspect the arms room, the supply room, and the admin records of the company. That gave me a feeling if things were going pretty well. When we would come to the annual general inspection, the same guys would be inspecting us. They had been there all year long and made us look good. They weren't about to say we were bad, because they were the one who had been training us.

Similarly, at Fort Bragg, I used to have people come from outside to inspect, to make sure that we were doing things well and also to get an objective view. I'm not an expert logistician, so I didn't think up any great innovations. We just went along with the policies that you were supposed to follow. When there are supply problems, it's not a matter of supply or maintenance policy. It's just always been with me that if you have a problem, you should decide what the problem is, what the solution is, then go tell the next higher headquarters and ask for support. If we had supply problems, that's how we handled it.

Back during Vietnam, we received a directive that you wouldn't use smoke grenades except under certain circumstances. Well, I wrote a study for General Palmer, who was then the head of USARV (US Army, Vietnam). I demonstrated that for every airmobile assault we made, we needed the first aircraft to go in and mark the landing zone with smoke, so the following aircraft knew where to come in. Then, if you encountered enemy fire, you threw a red grenade out, which signaled to following helicopters, "We received enemy fire—don't go over that area but come in from a different direction if possible."

Then when we called the helicopters in to extract us, they had to find us, so we used smoke. I told General Palmer, "Here's the number and kind of grenades you use in a typical operation. It is an integral part of our operation, so I'm not concerned that a smoke grenade costs whatever it does. I need the smoke grenades to operate." Well, they wrote back to the United States and cranked up production. Soon we began to get the grenades and the problem went away.

For a while it looked pretty dismal, but I documented a very sound case for utilizing the smoke grenades. That was one of things that characterized the operations of the 173rd and the 1st Division, for that matter. We used to prepare for our airmobile assaults very thoroughly and beat the hell out of the area before we went in.

I had a commander of army aviation in Vietnam once complain to me that I was not exercising the principle of war called surprise by zipping in there with no preparation. I said, "There is another principle of war called mass. I put a mass of fire on the landing zone, and if there's anybody there, they don't hurt me when I come in. I have never lost a helicopter in an assault or an extraction." I asked the guy to name any other unit that could say the same thing. There weren't any. They had all lost helicopters; some lost a lot of them, which meant losing a lot of people too. They saved some ammunition and used surprise, but I thought that was a terrible way to save ammunition. Needless to say, I didn't get any more comments from him.

Colonel Paul O'Mary, one of Deane's officers from the 173rd, later commented on the standard operating procedures of a helicopter assault during Deane's tenure of command: "I can't help but reflect back on the way that the 173d prepped a landing zone—pounding the area with 105's, and after the 105's finished firing, throwing out smoke pots, and keeping the 8-inch and 155's coming on each side while the helicopters were discharging the troops. No one can say for sure, but I can't help but wonder if a lot of others would be living today if Uncle Jack's tactics had been used in all units. I can say for certain that some soldiers in other units were killed doing things that 'Uncle Jack' Deane would never have permitted."[2]

I believe that when you need ammunition, you use it and don't fiddle around counting beans; the same went for smoke grenades. In a peacetime garrison situation, as we had at the 82nd, the operational and maintenance (O&M) funds got short from time to time. Now here you come to a supply situation. When the O&M funds got short the first time, I told my artillery people to find out what other training devices the army had that we could train on artillery without requiring you to fire ammunition.

It turned out that right there at Fort Bragg, packed in cosmoline, were little devices that would shoot a pellet that had smoke in it maybe one hundred yards. You could practically use it right in the vicinity of the barracks. You didn't have to go way out in the country to fire artillery. You saved ammunition, and could train on gun drill and train forward observers to adjust fire. Your training was not quite as good, but it was something, and it was saving ammunition. Then, when you actually did go out and fire, you were already trained, so the ammunition was better used.

I also knew from my experience in Europe and in programming and budgeting that when we had O&M problems, you could cut back on a unit's gasoline allocation and save money. You saved money not only from gasoline that is not expended but because you don't wear out your tires and don't need as many repair parts. All of that adds up.

Whenever we had this shortage of funds problem, I said to cut the gasoline allocation to all units in half. We issued coupons to the company commanders, who would issue them out for their people to get gas. When he used up all of his coupons, he didn't get any more gas for the rest of the month, so he had to husband those coupons. Instead of his supply sergeant making a trip to the PX and somebody else going to the post office, they would all get in one jeep and cover all these places in one trip.

When it was possible to march to a training location, we marched instead of loading onto trucks and driving there. The marching was good. Sometimes we added little tactical problems, such as being ambushed, as we marched out. So we had some training included. Well, we found that, with 50 percent allocation, we were saving a lot of money but also losing a lot of training. So I pumped it up to 65 percent and still felt we were losing some training. I think we ended up using about 70 percent of the allocation we had the year before, but by then we were getting just about as good of training time as before.

This situation was forced upon us. We should have looked at doing it anyway but didn't, because we had the money before and just didn't pay attention. Once it was forced upon us, we began saving 30 percent of the gas allocation, plus attendant savings in spare parts. That's a supply and maintenance policy, if you want to call it that.

At the end of my tour with the 82nd, General Tolson, the XVIII Airborne Corps commander, called and told me that I was being sent to Washington. I would be in a job that an air force lieutenant general held and would soon be promoted to lieutenant general. I said, "I'm not so sure about that." It turned out that I was right. The position was not a lieutenant general's job; they downgraded it.

13

Defense Communication Planning Group

The title of the Defense Communication Planning Group (DCPG) was a cover name—the organization had nothing to do with communications. It was a special task force, formed at Secretary of Defense McNamara's direction, to develop electronic, seismic, acoustic, or magnetic sensors to detect the passage of North Vietnamese troops through various areas in Vietnam and Laos. The only communication was from the sensors back to us, to indicate they were being activated.

The name was chosen to hide the research we were conducting in this task force. The idea was to try to find enemy supply trails, so that our bombing would be more effective; to find where they were massing in Vietnam, so that we could concentrate troops against them. This was the so-called McNamara electronic wall.

The guy in charge was (Alfred) Dodd Starbird, a brilliant army engineer lieutenant general who knew how to wield power.[1] He had power in that job because he worked directly for McNamara. It was a job that all of the services hated. They didn't want McNamara's electronic wall. Worse than that, McNamara would say to Starbird, "How much money do you need to do the job?" Starbird would estimate what he needed and he never stood short. The services were given an allocation to put into this pot, right out of their hide, without any reference to the relative priorities between what Starbird wanted to do and what the army, navy, and air force wanted to do with their money.

Those monies were fenced off and his to spend. He did a fantastic job. He had a tremendously tight deadline to put this together. Because he was a very bright guy and also tremendously energetic, he got it done. He drove this thing and developed these sensors. An air force lieutenant general, Jack Lavelle, succeeded him. Lavelle was going to be the commander or deputy commander of PACAF (Pacific Air Forces), and I was to succeed him.

173

DCPG had a motley crew. I had some very good, bright people. We had a lot of technical services types who had been passed over for promotion. They knew that they weren't going to go anyplace in whatever service they came from, and they weren't so great. The group's morale wasn't very good because Lavelle, testifying before Congress, had said that he felt the Defense Communication Planning Group had completed its mission and should be disbanded. He did this for a variety of reasons, I guess.

I think he was pressured by the chief of staff of the air force which, like the other services, didn't want us in existence. The services were all going to Congress and saying that the DCPG wasn't doing any good, that it was all a waste of money. Congress didn't particularly want us around either. So I've taken over this organization, and my job was to preside over its funeral.

I didn't particularly like that job, but I was assigned there and didn't get a choice. On the other hand, there was a group of scientific guys who worked under the Defense Science Board who felt this was a very good organization. Because it had a "Manhattan Project" kind of authority, it could get things done. They felt we should retain this organization. Maybe they knew we couldn't continue to work, particularly on sensors, but there were other jobs. So they said, "Now, you figure out a job to do."

Well, we set about trying to figure out how sensors could be employed in a European environment and what they might be able to do for us there. We developed a whole scenario and show, and put it on at Wildflecken or Grafenwoehr for people from SHAPE and from the chiefs of staff of the German and British armies. They were quite impressed. A lot of those people wanted sensors and got them. Our army was still not very enthusiastic. They weren't sure that we needed sensors and, if we did need them, that they could handle the job.

While I was at DCPG, the Israelis had 175-millimeter guns that we provided them, and they would fire across the Suez Canal at the Egyptians. When the Egyptians returned fire, and knocked out or killed an Israeli soldier, it was a catastrophe because the Israelis had limited manpower. When they lost a soldier, it was like the United States losing a company. This was a big problem for them. They wanted to be on the banks of the Suez, but they were getting guys killed there. They wanted to make their 175-millimeter guns fire more accurately and were concerned about the type of observer aircraft to use in order to do it. They wanted to get some F-4s, but policy makers were concerned that Israel would use the F-4s not to spot the artillery fire but to attack Cairo. They didn't want to provide any more offensive capability to the Israelis than they already had.

Well, Dave Packard, of Hewlett-Packard, was the deputy secretary of defense at the time. He called me in and said, "What can you do to help them with the problem of spotting their artillery fire, adjust it, and make it more accurate?" I went back to my bunch of passed-over rejects and told them the problem; after a few days, they came back and outlined their idea. I didn't know if it would work or not, but they were enthusiastic. I said, "Sounds great. Go do it. How much money do you need?" They told me and I said, "Okay, you have it."

Those guys went out and bought a Tyler mount. That's a mount the motion picture industry uses to stabilize cameras on moving platforms. When a guy is driving with his arm around a girl in a convertible and the camera is right in front, panning in on them, the Tyler mount keeps the camera from jiggling. We started to buy a balloon to use as the platform, but I ran into a buzz saw in Congress on that. It was the worst session I ever had with the House Appropriations Committee; they really beat the hell out of me!

So we got ourselves an old C-47. They bolted the Tyler mount to the floor in this C-47 and put a tripod on that. Then they put a fifty-six-inch, folded Questar telescope on the top of the tripod. That, in turn, had an optical stabilization system developed out in California by a guy named Luis Alvarez. So the optics were stabilized. At the eyepiece of the telescope, instead of having a man looking through it, they had a television camera that went to a television set on the airplane.

A big pair of binoculars was coaxially mounted with the telescope so a guy could look through the binoculars and point the thing to where the bursts were. The burst would be picked up on the television screen. They would press the stop-action button, measure how far away they were from the target, and adjust the fire that way. In just three months, they had that thing operating in Israel. And these were a bunch of so-called rejects! But they didn't have any red tape; they didn't have anyone bothering them. Just, "Here's the money. Go do it." And they did. We did several jobs like that.

DCPG folded in accordance with the wishes of Congress after I had been there about two years. I was facing a period of bitterness. We were going to close our doors on a Monday and walk out. The Defense Mapping Agency was to take over the building we were in, on the Naval Observatory grounds, where the vice president lives now.

I hadn't heard what my next assignment was going to be, and this was a week before we were closing down. I didn't want to take leave, so I called the personnel people but didn't get any satisfaction out of them. I finally called Dutch (Walter T. Kerwin, the deputy chief of staff for personnel [DCSPER]). His attitude was, "Keep calm. Everything that should happen will soon." Typical personnel management!

Friday he called up and said, "Monday you will report to the assistant chief of staff for force development as the assistant to the assistant." I didn't even have a title; I guess it was the deputy assistant chief of staff for force development. "If you keep your nose clean, maybe some better things will happen to you." I got so darn mad! Here it is Friday, and I have to report on Monday, and nobody would tell me anything about my new assignment up to this point.

I said, "You get to be a major general and they treat you like this? How do they treat the privates?" First of all, I went home to talk to my wife. I said, "I'm really mad and I'd like to retire at this point. If they treat people like this, I don't want to be a part of this organization." She said, "Fine." She didn't really like the army, and she never had. Then I thought, "Before I submit my papers, I'm going to talk to two guys who have really supported me over the years and get their opinion."

One was Ken Belieu, who was the undersecretary of the army. We had been colonels together earlier in life and good friends over the years. He had continued to be a great supporter. The other guy was the vice chief of staff, Bruce Palmer, whom I'd been very close to in the Dominican Republic and subsequently. Ken Belieu was very sorry to hear about the situation and said, "I think that's a shame, because I'm sure you're going to be up for a third star before long." Bruce Palmer said, "You can't do this. We have plans for you." I said, "The plans aren't very good, the way they handled me." He said, "I'll tell you. You submit your retirement papers and I'll tear them up. I'm not going to let you retire. Look, General Abrams is going to become chief of staff of the army and things are going to change. Stick around until he gets his feet on the ground. If you don't like the army then, I won't object to your retiring. Give it a year."

So I said, "Okay, I'll give it a year." I then reported to Bob Williams, the ACSFOR, who was a lieutenant general I had known for many years. Bob said, "I'm delighted to have you here, but you're not going to be here for long. This is just a holding spot for you. I don't know where you are going, but you are going to be a lieutenant general."

Well, about that time I did two things that really put me in bad with the secretary of the army, Bob Froehlke. I wrote that letter pertaining to the punishment of leaders who had made mistakes, such as Bill Hathaway. The point I was arguing in my letter was that if he took these relief actions, in essence, we weren't going to have any leaders; people would avoid command duty. The secretary was incensed.

Also, I visited him one day on a courtesy call, just before I came to ACSFOR and not too long after he had come to office. Just at that time, the North Vietnamese were conducting a major attack in a town called An Loc, where I had been when I first joined the 1st Division. That was during the time when I was the commander in the northern front. Enemy hordes had swept down and surrounded An Loc. General Hollingsworth, the senior guy in the 3rd Military Region now, had a very flamboyant personality. He used to be a blocking back for an all-American football player at Texas A&M, and never worried about the facts getting in the way of a good story.

I remember one time during Vietnam I went in and picked up old Holly when his helicopter had a power failure. His pilot auto rotated and landed into a clearing just large enough for two helicopters to get in. My pilot was able to move in next to him and get Holly out. Several helicopters had to go in later to get the whole bunch of them out.

When we got back to the CP, there were a lot of reporters around. Holly put his arm around my shoulder as we walked in and said, "They shot my ass out of the sky, but Uncle Jack came along and rescued me— just like I rescued him three weeks ago!" He was talking about when I had crashed in a helicopter. He hadn't rescued me; I walked out of the jungle from that crash with a broken leg. He hadn't been shot down; he just lost power. But those were just minor details. The press ate it up. There were big articles in the paper, "General Saves General in Return for Earlier Feat" or something like that.[2]

Well, when the North Vietnamese attacked An Loc, the press asked Holly, "Are you going to be able to push them back across the border?" Holly answered, "We are going to kill every damn one of them before they can get to the border!" It was probably a little more colorful than that, but words to that effect.

That happened just before I went in to see the secretary and was in the morning's news. The secretary was very upset. He felt that generals should be people who sat around and drank tea, spoke gently and nicely, with great grammar and diction, and all that kind of crap. He told me, "I think this is disgraceful for an army general to talk like this. Bloodthirsty!"

I said, "Mr. Secretary, An Loc, from what I read, is in dire straits. If An Loc survives, it will be because Holly has inspired his people, with just those words, to fight and knock those guys off."

Not only did An Loc hold, but I'll bet you there is not a guy who survived who doesn't say it was because of Hollingsworth and his leadership. They were outnumbered and in terrible shape. Holly used to go in there every day himself. When the advisors wanted to get out, he said, "This is your duty station. You stay here, fight, and win." The secretary didn't like the way he talked, but he inspired soldiers by making bold statements like this. His men loved it.

Holly saved that place, just by dint of leadership. I said, in essence, that he was a great leader; and if An Loc held, it would be because of how he talked. Well, the secretary didn't like this, so that was my second black mark. That's when Ken Belieu came to my rescue. He was the undersecretary and knew that the secretary was really upset with me. So they had to get me out of the army some way.

14

Defense Intelligence Agency

They put me in a holding place in ACSFOR briefly. Then I got promoted to lieutenant general and went to DIA (Defense Intelligence Agency) as the deputy director. I found that assignment to be interesting in some respects but disappointing in others. My boss (Vincent DePoix), the director of defense intelligence, was a navy vice admiral and a man who believed in power. He expected to be the chief of naval operations someday or get some other four-star billet. He didn't want to jeopardize that. The more power he could get, the better he liked it.

In the first place, I believed this job should never have been a lieutenant general's position. I said, "This job should be downgraded to a major general." That upset the heck out of him, because it was more prestigious for him to have a deputy at the rank of lieutenant general. I also said, "I think we can cut back on a large number of personnel," and showed him ways to do it. That would have reduced the size of his empire, so he just ignored it and was mad at me for that suggestion. He did a lot of things that I just didn't think very highly of. From that point of view it was not a very pleasant assignment.

The work itself was interesting. It was interesting to sit in the briefings in the morning with the chairman of the Joint Chiefs of Staff and all of his staff, and hear what was going on. I had some interesting relationships with the Central Intelligence Agency as a result of my position there and occasionally sat on the United States Intelligence Board. One day Secretary of Defense Schlesinger was invited to meet with the Army Policy Council, led by the army chief of staff, General Abrams, and of which I was a member. As a part of his usual and unpleasant style, Schlesinger launched into an entirely uninformed criticism of the army's actions over the years in moving from the M-1 rifle of World War II through the M-14 and then to the M-16 used in Vietnam. He contended that the lack of imagination of the army leadership in failing to move directly from the M-1 to the M-16 was costly in time, money, and capability.

As the deputy director of DIA, I had some considerable interaction with Schlesinger, which did not engender a great amount of admiration for his leadership style. He was one I would have termed a bully. Few stood up to him because retribution was swift and unfailing. I recall going up to his office in the elevator at the CIA one day. One of the passengers had a bag of what I assume was a costume for an office party. In the top of the bag was a wig. Another passenger peered into the bag and reverently asked, "Whose head is that?" Great times at the CIA.

So much for the diversion. I was annoyed with Schlesinger's unfounded criticism of our rifle procurement and launched into an impetuous dissertation on why the army, specifically my idol General Gavin, had made the decision leading to the procurement process described by Schlesinger. I had been Gavin's planning and programming chief during that period. I pointed out that at the time the decision was made to procure the M-14, the army inventory of M-1s was so low that a major procurement had to be made. There were three options available.

First, we could buy more M-1s, thus tying the army to an obsolete weapon for another decade or more. Second, we could buy the M-16 then being developed by the Advanced Research Projects Agency (ARPA, later DARPA), a Department of Defense agency. Our tests of this weapon showed that the advantages of the lightweight characteristics designed into the weapon were more than nullified by its inferior structural design and its unacceptable performance in field conditions. It broke easily and jammed consistently when fired under the hostile environment found in the field. Third, we could buy the M-14, which would give us an advanced weapon, compared to the M-1, and would tide us over until the M-16 or some other more advanced rifle was perfected.

Gavin made what I thought was the right choice; going to the M-16 at that point in time would have been a disaster. The army would have been saddled with thousands of inferior, almost useless, weapons. That stopped the discussion on the rifle situation. I thought I had struck a blow for freedom, but Abe did not see it that way.

A few days later, I got a call from General Elmer H. (Hook) Almquist, the assistant chief of staff for force development. He said that Abe wanted to see us. He did not know why. Abe had not told him. This was not unusual. It was Abe's practice not to tell you why he wanted to see you. Abe told me he did this because if he mentioned what he wanted to discuss, the staff officer would spend hours preparing for the meeting, most of which time would be wasted on issues not related to Abe's questions.

Hook and I were ushered into Abe's office. He was reviewing a paper and continued to do so for a minute or two while we stood in front of his desk. Then he looked up at Hook and said, "You do not seem to know Secretary Schlesinger." Hook responded, "No, sir. The first time I have ever met him was at the Policy Council meeting the other day."

Abe continued, "He seems to know you pretty well, Jack." I responded that I had spent a lot of time with Schlesinger when he was at CIA and I was in DIA. Abe added, "He seems to think highly of you. I don't know why." I said something like, "Aw, come on, Chief." Then he said, "If you continue blurting out the truth as you perceive it, he is going to think you are just as dumb as the rest of us. That's all."

Hook and I left. As we walked down the E-Ring hallway to our respective offices, I said to Hook, "I have been chewed out many times in my life, but that was a classic and it was probably the most effective of all."

I've always said, "Wherever your job, you always try to make something out of it." I got some useful things out of that assignment, but I felt I was in a holding pattern there until I could get back into the good graces of the secretary and be brought back into the army staff. Vince DePoix, the navy director, of course had his own desires in terms of building his empire and his power. So he didn't do anything to alleviate these confrontations. It wasn't all that bad; it was just something that went on and on.

I'd been at DIA for a year when the Office of Chief of Research and Development (CRD) opened up. As I recall, Bill Gribble retired. I was a natural for the position. I had worked in R&D for several tours prior to that time. General Abrams, the chief of staff, knew that, because we sat on the Program and Budget Advisory Committee together. He had been the principal guy for Reserve forces, which he was in charge of at the time, and I was the backup.

Second and maybe more important was Bill Potts, who had been General Abrams's G2 in Vietnam. General Abrams wanted very much to make Potts a lieutenant general. Potts was the ASCI (assistant chief of staff for intelligence), just coming home from Vietnam as a major general, and Abrams wanted to reward him for his loyal and effective service. Here was an intelligence job, and Bill Potts had been an intelligence guy for many years. So it was a natural for him.

Potts took my place. That shifted me down to CRD. I bid Admiral DePoix a fond adieu and left. While I was at CRD, there were some things of note. At the time, the assistant secretary of the army for research and development (ASA[R&D]) was Norm Augustine. He later became under-secretary of the army, and after his government service went to Martin

Marietta as a senior guy. Norm and I got along very well. He was a person who I admired very much. He was hardworking and an intellectual, and we made a point of becoming disarmingly honest when we went up on the Hill to testify.

We gained a lot of respect, and the army gained some points on the Hill for being straightforward and not trying to hide things. Still, some of those creeps on the Hill, both elected officials and staffers, just don't like to play anything square. You tell them that you did something wrong, and they blow that into a million reasons why you didn't get appropriations for this or that.

You're slitting your own throat when you're honest with those types of people. Being honest isn't part of politics, I guess, and makes politicians suspicious of you. Anyway, we tried honesty and my successor and friend, Howard Cooksey, carried on that policy as well. I think that the net was probably beneficial, but it sure was distasteful at times.

Norm Augustine and I also started a system of flash reports. Anytime anything significant—generally bad—happened in any of our programs, particularly the major ones, a flash report went directly to us from wherever it happened, with copies to other people. We gave those to the people on the Hill and in the Defense Department.

These reports had two purposes. First, we wanted to know before other people knew, when things went wrong. This went back to my time from Korea in the 17th Infantry. This report let us gather some facts about the case and inform the people who would normally find out ahead of us through some back channel. Instead of them coming and hitting us over the head, we could go tell them we had this problem, where it was, and what had been done about it. That put out the fire before it became a conflagration. The second purpose in presenting these flash reports to people like Congress was to demonstrate that we weren't trying to hide things, as they had the feeling that we were. I presume these feelings still persist to this day.

I mentioned that I had been impressed with the rejects and the passovers when I had worked at DCPG, and with how well they had done when given some money and a little bit of encouragement. Really, very little money. On that apparatus for spotting artillery fire in Israel, I think that we may have spent $50,000, total. And they put a system in the field. If you assigned that job to one of the army labs, it would have become a major project with an initial budget of $10 million. You couldn't get the $10 million appropriated for a year. The next year, you might be able to justify it. So you get $10 million, write a contract, and let another year go by. Just all kinds of time and money!

I told Bill DePuy, who was now the commander of TRADOC (Training and Doctrine Command), "I'll bet you down at your schools there are a bunch of bright guys who have ideas about how we should do things. If they had a few bucks to buy a little piece of this and a piece of that, they probably could rig up something that could demonstrate their theory. I'm willing to make some money available to you." I think the total was $10 million a year.

"If you start making a lot of money, then it's going to balloon into big projects. I just want some guys to tinker around in their garage." Because people don't like you to tinker, I said, "We are going to call it the SAM fund." For those of us in the know, the acronym really meant screwing-around money. People who don't know think its surface-to-air missile funds.

I used to give Bill DePuy about $10 million a year while I was chief of research and development, and he distributed it to the schools according to projects they wanted to do. That's how we came up with the improved anti-armor TOW vehicle. The Armor School took an M-113 vehicle and got that articulated arm, which they fabricated, that would put the missile pods above a mask. Then you could fire over the mask; the people in the vehicle remained behind the mask. We started that project through the screwing-around money.

There were other such little projects, but that was the idea: Give some bright young guy an opportunity to tinker, come back later, and show the boss, "Here's what I have." You're not always going to win, but some good things will come out of that kind of operation. I felt it was worth a few bucks each year to do that.

15

Army Materiel Command/ Development and Readiness Command

During the last half of 1965, there were four major policy decisions regarding deployment levels of troops to Vietnam. For the army and its logistics command, Army Materiel Command (AMC), each decision called for increased procurement actions, the backbone of the supply effort. Pre-buildup planning had been based upon at least a partial mobilization of Reserve Forces. When this did not materialize, the imbalance of Regular Forces became apparent. With no firm guide as to either the size or composition of the forces to be supported, or their mission, AMC planners were left in a difficult position.

General Besson, the AMC commander, wryly noted, "Anytime we start a war in which we're going to have the policy of escalating our action as necessary to meet the demands of the situation, rather than an all-out attempt to crush the enemy with a bold plan to do it; we should be sure and start at the beginning of a fiscal year."[1]

Outside events impacted AMC's management plan almost from its inception. Besson noted,

Our full-scale involvement in the war in Vietnam began in April 1965, when the American economy was operating at an unparalleled level of prosperity. Prior to that time, the Army—and other services—had been marching to the tune of "cost reduction." Our dollar resources within AMC were at a minimum. We weren't buying much equipment, and the stocks on our depot shelves were low. Our maintenance activities were slogging along with a heavy backlog of care and preservation work. Then the bottom fell out. The President decided to increase the US commitment to Vietnam. By mid-summer 1965 we had the equivalent of a combat division in Vietnam, and two more divisions were on the way. Almost before we knew it we were tangled up in a full-scale war, and we were already behind the power curve.[2]

General Ferdinand Chesarek, AMC's second commanding general, recalled the urgency in getting supplies to Vietnam as quickly as possible:

We used the push supply technique in Vietnam. The most wasteful war we have ever fought. I remember going to Vietnam any number of times on various missions and in many instances the purpose was to figure out what we could do to reduce the cost.

The waste was indescribable, absolutely indescribable. Huge areas, piled to the sky with stuff that came there under the push technique. Nobody knew what it was or anything else. Most was never used; finally ended up bulldozing it into big holes and burying it. It was awful! So when somebody tells me that push is the way to go, they are telling me that somebody here in their wisdom, in Washington, knows better what is required and in what quantities and where than the people in the field, and I say "nuts." I have seen it in action.

My career, following Frank's [Besson], who was there basically at the apex of the Vietnam War, which was starting to wind down, was to support the war. If there is combat involved, that is where your attention is. That consumes the bulk of your concerns, your time and effort and everything else. We tried very, very hard to reduce the costs of the Vietnam operation. We took the supply system out of "push" and probably saved a couple of billion dollars. And the mere thought of going back to it again gives me the chills.[3]

While I was CRD, the army came under major criticism with respect to its acquisition process. The secretary of the army, to try to improve and stave off some of the criticism, created the Army Materiel Acquisition Review Committee (AMARC), headed by Air Force Reserve Major General Wendell Sell. This board was to review current procurement policies and procedures and recommend any changes, if warranted. Sell was a West Point graduate, class of 1939, who had left active service but remained in the Reserves. He was the president and chairman of Hoffman Electronics, a company in the Los Angeles area that made radio gear, beacons, and various electronic items.

Sell headed up the committee, which had a bunch of people from industry and some people from government on it. One guy was brought in because he had been at China Lake when the Sidewinder missile was developed. He had participated in that development. That was always thought of as an outstanding example of an acquisition of a weapon system—and it was despite of the navy, despite everybody.

It was a wonderful thing. An engineer named Bill McLean designed and built it, scrounging the money from here and there. Nobody knew what he was doing. Every time they found out, he changed the name of it and continued. He produced a missile at a fraction of the cost of the Sparrow, and it has been a tremendously effective missile. It's by far the fighter pilots' choice, when compared to the Sparrow.

This developer, whose name was Amile, turned out to be a real pain in the butt on this committee. Then we had Ollie Boileau, a very senior vice president of Boeing, and later the president of General Dynamics. I had a lot of contact with him and other people like that. They were tasked with reviewing the army's acquisition process.

Their major finding was that we had one leader at each of the commands, like Missile Command (MICOM) and Electronics Command (ECOM), in charge of both logistics and R&D. Logistics, the support of systems in the field, concerned the commanders in the field and the message brought home daily was: "I don't have enough repair parts." So that's where the emphasis was going. The acquisition part—R&D and the initial procurement—was being ignored.

The AMARC review committee concluded that one guy, running both the logistics and the R&D process, was paying attention only to the logistics; that, not the acquisition process, was the problem. They rated us as worse than or possibly equal to the navy system, which they thought was terrible. They said we should have a system like the air force, which has the separation in command all the way to the chief of staff. He has one four-star general in charge of the Air Force Systems Command, which handles R&D, and another in charge of the Air Force Logistics Command. They recommended this separation.

I was called in to meet with the secretary of the army; the chief of staff, who was Fred Weyand after General Abrams had died of cancer; Undersecretary Herb Stout; the vice chief Dutch Kerwin; Norm Augustine, the assistant secretary for R&D; and Harold Brownman, the assistant secretary for installation and logistics (ASA[I&L]). The secretary had approved the findings of the AMARC; now was the time for implementation.

The AMARC basic conclusion, the one that sort of set the tone for everything, was that the army's major problem was materiel acquisition: the fact that you had, at the commodity commands, a commander who was responsible for the acquisition process, the research, development, procurement, and also responsible for the business of keeping the equipment operational in the field—repair parts, training teams, et cetera.

Deane's predecessor at AMC, General Henry Miley, came to the same conclusions. He described the chairman of the AMARC, Wendell Sell, as

sort of a self-made man. He was a very capable individual doing a considerable amount of business with the Government. Sell had been recently engaged in a bitter procurement controversy with Electronics Command (ECOM). I sensed in the beginning of the process that he, if the words "bore a grudge" were wrong, it was something along those lines. He had his own thoughts about the way AMC, or at least ECOM, did its business, vis-a-vis, the Hoffman Electronics Company.

The AMARC people had sessions with Secretary Schlesinger, and there was little doubt in the minds of the Army staff and the Secretariat that Mr. Schlesinger regarded AMC, and particularly the ordnance part of AMC, as pretty much a sad show.[4]

The AMARC conclusion was that the most demanding part of this job was management of the day-to-day mobile training teams. So the daily struggle of keeping the army running in the field was what was taking his attention, and consequently diverting his attention from the acquisition part. They felt that both the army and the navy were very far behind the air force in acquisition. This was not just an AMARC finding; it was also the general perception at the Pentagon as well. The air force acquisition was way ahead of the army or the navy. So their recommendation, as a result of this conclusion, was that these two functions should be separated and headed up by different people.

I was given the task and was told that I was going to become the commander of Army Materiel Command. They told me that they wanted certain things accomplished. One, which they wanted immediately, was to change the name of the command to Development and Readiness Command (DARCOM), to try to create a new frame of mind there. The secretary told me that I was going to come down here and take command,

and that he wanted me to work out a plan to implement the recommendations of the AMARC, which he had approved. Then they wanted to know how I was going to organize it. I was to come back with a study and brief Mr. Schlesinger, the secretary of defense, who was personally interested. He had to be kept abreast of what I was doing.

"Very few people understand that [the background behind changing the name of the command from AMC to DARCOM]. It was Secretary of the Army, Marty Hoffman, who directed it, and I was there!" related Lieutenant General George Sammet. *"He told Jack Deane you will change the name; you will change the flag; you will change the stationery. AMC had a poor image with OSD and Marty Hoffman came from OSD, and therefore, to change the image, let's start from the very top and change everything. The commander; the name; the flag; everything. Jack Deane did not originate the impetus for change. He merely managed it."*[5]

I went home and just stayed there a while to put my thoughts on paper. I wrote a study on how I thought the command should be reorganized and put down some alternatives. The first, which I thought was the best solution, was to go the way the air force had gone, to a definite separation. I spent a lot of time on the air force and the navy. I examined how they did things and contrasted those with the way we did them. I tried to pick out the good things that they were doing, as I perceived them, and to ignore the bad things. The best way, as I saw it, was total separation.

Requesting an additional four-star general in the army made people gag, because it's hard to get those billets. My next solution was to retain the headquarters of AMC but to have a chief of staff, a three-star general, with two additional three-star generals assigned. I demonstrated that the air force had tremendous numbers of senior generals involved. They had Air Force Systems Division at Wright-Patterson Air Force Base with a three-star. Electronic Systems Division at Hanscom Field also had a three-star. They had three-star generals all over the place; and here we were at AMC with one chief of staff who was a three-star general!

Our job, dollar-wise, was not as big as theirs; but, in terms of the numbers and diversity of systems, our job was far greater. I recommended that we have three three-star generals: one to be chief of staff, one to be the principal deputy for R&D, and one to be the principal deputy for procurement.

Down through the commodity commands, they would handle those things that support the commodity commands. Instead of US Army Missile Command with one major general, we would have a missile R&D command and a missile readiness command, with a major general in charge of each. They would report not to each other but up through the chain of command to my principal deputies and to me.

The best I could get out of this whole deal was two three-star slots—one more than I had—which went to the two principal deputy positions. Initially, the procurement guy was a major general. That was because my chief of staff, Woody Vaughn, was already a three-star general and stayed in that position. When Woody moved on to the Defense Logistics Agency (DLA), we got a major general as the chief of staff; Gene D'Ambrosio became the three-star general for procurement.

There was tremendous resistance to all of this. People were comfortable as it was, and they feared change. The changes did cost people jobs; I was also trying to save people. My headquarters at DARCOM had twenty-one hundred people in round numbers, which I immediately cut to fourteen hundred. We attritted people over several months. When we finally reached the target date, we only had two or three people who hadn't either retired or gotten jobs someplace else. The personnel people did a pretty good job in working the cuts and transfers, but people still moaned and groaned.

The union was unhappy, but I always had somebody who knew what the union's reaction was going to be. So when the union tried to embarrass me in front of the audience, I always knew how they were going to do it and came right back with factual information. The union ended up looking bad and wasn't very popular either. Their leadership had gotten in through the apathy of people who hadn't voted.

People weren't very happy with the union after it came in because it wasn't doing the job for the people. I could overcome that, but there was a resistance to the change in the command which never went away. Today, the command structure is back to the way it was before the changes. Maybe, at this point, it's all right to be that way. Instead of trying to make this concept work, there was continuing resistance to it all.

At the time they were doing their AMARC study, I didn't know I was going to AMC. Fred Weyand had told me that the secretary and General Abrams, while he was living, wanted me to take it over. Whether that was going to be possible, because I was a combat arms officer, was questionable. So I wasn't sure about it. When Fred became chief, he wanted me to take over Forces Command (FORSCOM), but I said I didn't want to. He reiterated that it might not be possible for me to take over AMC.

When the AMARC had finished its recommendations and all those changes had been approved, I was then told that I would be going to AMC. I had the job of trying to prepare the implementing plan. That's what I spent a couple of weeks at home preparing, getting air force and navy briefings, and talking to a lot of people at defense and various places. I spent quite a bit of time on that.

I went to see Gene Fubini, whom I've mentioned before. He was a very brilliant scientist and an outspoken critic of the army. I said, "I want to talk to you about the army's lab system because I'm going to be taking over AMC." He gave the old cliché: "The army's labs are terrible!" I said, "Let's go down the labs, one by one, with MICOM first." He said, "Those guys are really pretty bright." As we went through them, one at a time, thinking about the details, he could really be critical of only a very few labs.

Before, his comments were always generalizations. That was pretty heartening to me. So by and large, we had very good labs and people. Unfortunately, we had some people who were not so good, and some who did not have the vision to look forward. We had a lot of people trying to protect their "rice bowls"; that was more important to them than the job at hand.

So that's how the reorganization of AMC ended up the way it did. Dividing the two functions of logistics and research was a way of doing what the AMARC report was saying we had to do. But how do you put two guys in charge of separate functions without making two separate commands? You can't put two guys in the same command and one occupies the office today and one occupies the office tomorrow. You could have called it one command, but had, in fact, two separate organizations for each commander. I don't know how you could implement what AMARC told us to implement without dividing them.

We really didn't have to do it at MICOM because MICOM was functioning well in that respect. MICOM had a guy named John McDaniel who was a very strong technical leader. It didn't matter who the commander was it could have been a guy who never even heard of missiles— John McDaniel would have carried out that part of the function and made it successful; the R&D function was what made MICOM successful. George Turnmeyer was the commander. Whether the guy paid any attention to him or even came to work, John McDaniel would have made MICOM successful. It didn't work that way in other places. Now, if you could only pick up a bunch of John McDaniels. He was a very, very capable and a very independent guy.

John was the kind of guy that you knew if you got on his back improperly and you lost your temper he's liable to just walk out and leave you. He could get a job in industry just like that; he was sought after. But he liked where he was, he liked it in Alabama, he was mentoring the senior class of engineers from Alabama, he was bringing them to his place and he was just having a ball down there. He loved it, he loved what he was doing and he was doing it very effectively. He and I got along just beautifully. There was never any question in my mind that if John didn't like what I told him to do, he'd just tell me to stuff it and he'd walk away. Now he never did anything to ignore the command channel—who was the boss and all that stuff. But if he'd get in a very serious disagreement with me, he'd walk; I was sure of that. He was a strong guy who ran a good shop.

But to get a military guy, or even another civilian, of that quality who could have the independence that John had was almost impossible. A military guy couldn't have; he's chosen to be a military officer, so if you bring a brigadier general in and he's under this major general and he's going to go to the major general to get things approved and the guy says, "I disapprove; go and do something else," it won't work. So you can't; the only way I could see was to separate them.

The only reason I did separate the functions at MICOM was to give some balance to the command because it was distasteful enough as it was, and if I had to say, "Well, MICOM's the only good command in all of AMC," then what would that have done to all the other commands? They'd say, "Gee, what is this guy telling us?" I didn't want to do that, and so I split that command even though I thought it wasn't necessary.

I don't think it did any damage to split it. We had growing pains and all that, but had I not split it, it just would have been terribly difficult psychologically to explain to all the other commanders why they were being split and MICOM wasn't. I just didn't want to go out and say, "You guys don't shape up; that's the reason you're getting split." What would that do to you for the next five years?

Now, I don't know if the solutions AMARC had in mind were solved once the board's recommendations were implemented, but they said to divide the functions. To divide the functions, I didn't know how to do it except have one guy in charge of one function and one guy in charge of the other. We had them divided prior to that; we had deputies to the commanders at the commodity commands who were responsible. But the commander is the guy who is wielding all the power, and the guys below him, particularly in uniform, were usually cautious and conservative.

In splitting out logistics from the research and development functions, AMARC hoped it would shorten the development cycle. They talked about that subject, but I don't recall any firm recommendations for how to improve it. I recall the general feeling was that if you had a guy responsible for research and development, when decision time came, he would make decisions. It wouldn't be, "Well, I'm busy today. Get those spare parts out to the 1st Division. Come back and see me next week." This was his baby; he'd make the decisions. That was a major cause of delay seen in all of these things. The AMARC hoped that when you separated R&D and readiness, there would be more focus, that decisions would be made more rapidly, and that things would progress faster. Well, they haven't.

As part of my preparation for assuming command of AMC, and preparing to implement the AMARC directives I received from the secretary of the army and the chief of staff, I took a couple of weeks of leave. I spent much of this time with my future colleagues in the navy, Admiral Ike Kidd, and the air force, Generals Bill Evans and Mike Rogers.

One of the most impressive things I observed during this learning period was the personnel management of officers following a career in the Air Force Systems Command. Bill Evans had a room in his headquarters to which only a chosen few had access. On the walls of this room were the names of the officers selected for "special grooming" in order to assume important positions within the command. These positions included those of program and project managers. With each name was a listing of his past assignments, the comments of his superiors on his performance, and judgments as to his potential in various positions within the activities of the command.

Every quarter Bill met with his senior leaders of various components of the Systems Command in this sacrosanct room. They went over the status of the officers nearing reassignment and decided what these officers needed next in terms of experience and responsibility to groom them for higher levels of responsibility or command. The decisions made during these sessions led to their next assignments. Largely as a result of Bill's control of the development of these officers, the air force program and project managers were considered to be far and away the best within the services by the senior civilian leaders in the Office of the Secretary of Defense.

Serving as a colonel, while previously working in the Office of the Director of Defense Research and Engineering (DDR&E), I heard firsthand how highly regarded the air force program and project managers were when compared to those of the army. Later, as commander of AMC, I had close contact with the DDR&E and his senior people. They all highly praised the quality of the army's program and project managers, and in general rated them above those in both the air force and navy. This credit belongs solely to my deputy for research and development, Lieutenant General George Sammet.[6]

George was one of the finest officers I have ever met in my entire career. He was intelligent, smart (they are not always the same), dedicated, energetic, hard-driving, modest, and unassuming. He did not seek fame or glory. He did not seek personal acclamation. He was a team player and making the team successful in every aspect was his only goal.

When I went to AMC, I tried to establish a career management system along the lines the air force used in its Air Force Systems Command. We wanted to find the really bright majors, and maybe even captains, throughout the army logistics community. Pick out maybe two hundred and begin to see that they received the best possible training and jobs in the logistics field. I tried to do this with the army logisticians, but got so much opposition from Lieutenant General Fred Kornet, the DCSLOG (deputy chief of staff, logistics), that I could never get it approved.[7] They probably didn't want combat arms officers making career decisions on technical service officers. Perhaps they were right.

The system we have today says that everybody is equal, so everybody should get the same kind of training. We felt, however, that under the existing system, the promising officers, the shining stars, were just as likely to be assigned to command an ammunition depot, such as Sierra Army Depot out in the desert on the California-Nevada border, as a complex depot such as Anniston Army Depot or Pine Bluff. At a depot such as Sierra, the commander could put on his robe and slippers when he woke up in the morning, walk out on the porch, pick up the morning paper, scan the horizon, count the ammo igloos, and if they were all still there, go back in the house and read the paper and have a cup of coffee. That was essentially his day. At Anniston, where badly damaged tracked vehicles were restored to near-mint condition, you have a job that has more responsibility than a senior vice president of Chrysler.

At the time, Chrysler Corporation was building our M-60 tank. Now, the guy in charge was a senior vice president who had a major division of Chrysler under him. All he did was get hulls that somebody else had cast, road wheels that somebody else had made, and wiring harnesses that still another organization had made. He would test all these things and put it together. That would become a tank, and he sent it out the door.

The guy at Anniston tore it completely apart, recovered about 60 percent of all the parts to be reused or refurbished, and got new wiring harnesses. All those things had to be replaced and made new. He then put the old tank back together, but now with parts he had scrounged from various vendors and things that could be rehabilitated. He put the tank back together and sent it out the door. That tank was just as good as a brand-new tank coming off the line at Chrysler.

This Anniston colonel had a lot more responsibility than the colonel at Sierra Depot. Commanding the depot at Anniston is a tremendous educational experience for an able colonel, and that colonel should be a guy that you expect, someday, to be a general. Someday you should expect him to be the DCSLOG of the army or the commander of AMC— maybe even the chief of staff of the army.

The guy who went to Sierra doesn't get that kind of experience. Now, why put your best guy out in Sierra, where he is not going to get the experience, and put some guy who has no capability to go to the top at Anniston? Why waste that kind of experience on him? That's not the attitude I see from the personnel people. Their attitude is, "He's a colonel; he has to do a colonel's job." So whatever colonel's job comes up next, they give it to this guy, without any regard for whether he is someone who really ought to be receiving top-notch training.

Anniston Army Depot was a far more important job, and thus a far greater learning experience. Both assignments called for colonels. In the career management system that existed in the army in those days, a colonel was a colonel. There was little differentiation between those who would become the leaders and those who would always be the worker bees. There appeared to be little effort to ensure that the most promising officers were assigned to the jobs that would provide them the experience needed to groom them for positions of major responsibility. I consider this failed effort one of my major disappointments while I commanded AMC.

The personnel people who are running the current system will tell you that they are getting the same results that I was seeking. But while I was at DARCOM and they were saying that it was happening, it wasn't. I know that because I had a guy assigned to command Sierra who should not have gone there; he was too good to go to Sierra. You know that certain guys have to be the post commander, the athletic officer, and the postal officer. Still, you don't put the guy who you think is going to be a future chief of staff running those jobs. You just shouldn't do that.

You probably can't really start to identify a top-notch guy before he is a major, with maybe fifteen years or so of service. If you can do it a little earlier, say twelve years, that would be better. The officer evaluation reports (OERs) can be a screen. I always try to err on the side of the guy even in writing efficiency reports. You take Hillman Dickinson, the guy I put in command up in CERCOM (Communications Electronics Readiness Command).[8] Hill was a colonel when he worked for me, but he had a civilian supervisor in the chain of command between us. The civilian wrote an evaluation report on him that was pretty good but included a couple of derogatory remarks.

I called the civilian in and said, "I don't want to influence you on what you say in your efficiency report, but let me ask you a question. Do you think Hill Dickinson should be a general officer?" He said, "Without question. Technically he is very fine; he knows his business. Dickinson has been doing a fabulous job around here." I said, "Well, this evaluation report you have written has just guaranteed that he will never be a general officer." He said, "Well, I didn't intend that." I said, "Well, that's what it says and I'll tell you why it says it." So I explained it to him. Then he went back and rewrote it, and Hill Dickinson retired as a lieutenant general. Hill Dickinson would never have gotten beyond colonel if that OER had been in his records.

John Lucas, who went on to be the president of the Communication Satellite Corporation, used to be DDR&E up in the secretary of defense's office when I worked there. His executive officer was a guy named Bob York, who was a brigadier general at the time.[9] He wrote an evaluation report on York and, for some reason or other, asked me to review it. I was a colonel. I went back and said, "Let me tell you my impression, based on how a promotion board will look at it: Bob York is doing a very good job here but he has reached the level of his capacity and should go no further in the army. Is that what you are trying to say?" He said, "No, I wasn't trying to say that." So he rewrote it.

Bob York later became a major general, commanded the Infantry School at Fort Benning, and later commanded the 82nd Airborne Division and the XVIII Airborne Corps. He retired as a lieutenant general. Now, that's one of the problems with evaluation reports. Some guys, civilians, for example, don't really know the system—how crucial every word in the OER is for a career.

Before I went to AMC, I had a couple of experiences that influenced my activities once I got there. First, when I became the chief of research and development, there was a project run by some mad inventor in New England. He had designed an artillery shell with a rocket-assisted motor (RAM) instead of a RAP (rocket-assisted propulsion), but his shell could get about as much range as we got with RAP.

His shell was also far cheaper to build and far more reliable. Art

Trudeau, the former chief of research and development, was aware of this RAM and what it could do; maybe he was a consultant to that company. He had been rapping on all the doors in the Pentagon trying to get people interested in it and was getting nowhere. Finally, he talked to me about it. I said, "Well, let me see what I can find out." I looked at it and it seemed pretty good. When I started making courtesy calls to the representatives on the Hill, one of the congressmen from New York brought the subject up. I said, "As a matter of fact, I have just begun to look into that. I'll assure you that, within the limits of my ability, this will get a good honest review."

Well, I was pretty naïve. I didn't realize how that lab was going to screw me. I put it to AMC that I wanted this round reviewed. I wanted a briefing on both the good and bad features, and on why we should or shouldn't do something about it. I told General Miley, then the AMC commander, "If the guy comes in here and gives me a lot of baloney, I'll expect you to do something about it."

This guy came in and gave the most biased, dishonest briefing I'd ever heard. Even with my limited technical ability, I could see how bad it was. The people on my staff who had technical ability were livid. That was what I was stuck with and I couldn't do anything about this round. I'm not sure anything could have been done about the RAM, but that briefing did convince me that something should have been done.

I learned that you had a lot of people who fought to protect their projects, and I had to figure out how to get around that. Boy, that's not easy. I asked Miley to relieve the briefing guy. I said, "He just lied to me. I can't accept this kind of thing." Well, Miley never did relieve him, but when I became AMC commander, I did. I just told him, "You lie. You're not honest. You're not objective. I don't need a guy like you around. You're finished."

Another experience was a briefing in General Miley's conference room on a Saturday morning. I happened to be over at AMC for another reason, and this briefing by a guy named Tom Stultnagel followed. Tom, who I had known for many years, was the president of Hughes Helicopters. Present at that briefing were Major General John Raaen, who commanded Armaments Command (ARMCOM), and his expert gun maker. We were having trouble with the Bushmaster gun, which was supposed to go on the armed helicopter and on the new armored personnel carrier we were developing.

The development wasn't coming along too well. Tom sat at a table right in front of us with a 7.62-millimeter machine gun called the chain gun. It didn't operate by gas pushing the bolt back and slamming forward, but by a chain that had a motor on it. A similar type gun had maybe two-thirds the moving parts, so maintenance was simpler. He said, "We did the first drawings of this gun in January; in April of the same year we were firing it successfully. It wasn't jamming and it wasn't doing anything bad. I would like to make you a model of this in 30 millimeter"—whatever the Bushmaster was. "I can do it for $10 million and will deliver five or ten working models to you in two years for that amount of money on a fixed-price contract."

John Raaen and his expert both said, "You can't develop guns like that in that time and for that money." I said, "Here is a gun in front of you they developed in three months. Why can't you scale it up and maybe have some success. Isn't it worth trying? There would be a two-year instead of a seven-year development." "No," they said. "We can't do that. It's impossible." The basic problem was that they didn't like anything being designed anywhere other than their lab. I made up my mind we were going to change that, and that led to what I later called our Skunk Works procurement.

So regarding the issue of developing expensive and sophisticated equipment versus developing less capable but cheaper equipment; it's a mixed bag. It's something that people generalize about. They say, "Buy a lot of cheap tanks. So what if you lose a few?" The fact is, if you buy a lot of cheap tanks, you're going to lose a lot of people as well as a lot of tanks. People are not going to want to ride in them.

Once we developed a system that was supposed to be cheaper and do a big job: the Sheridan vehicle. It had a 152-millimeter cannon on it—an odd caliber. We could shoot the Shillelagh missile out of that same tube. When they first developed that system, they had problems with the cannon. The shell had a combustible cartridge case that sometimes didn't burn out completely. Smoldering residue would remain in the tube; then when you'd stick the next round in, the residue might set off the combustible cartridge case. There was also an issue of noxious fumes in the turret that made the crew sick.

Here was an example of a cheaper vehicle that was going to knock out tanks. It was going to be light, so you could air drop it, but it was never successful. The money that went into that vehicle was, in my mind, completely wasted. During this time, I was in type classification. The Sheridan had so many problems I didn't even want to type classify it.

General Besson, who was the AMC commander at the time, wrote a letter to the Department of the Army saying that the Sheridan should be type classified, but you should put caveats in the operational manuals. For example, "Don't fire a round more than once a minute." That gave time for the burning residue to burn out completely. I said to General Besson, "In battle, a guy can't take a stopwatch, fire a round, and say, 'Hey, man, don't fire another one,' and all this stuff. You don't do that. Boy, you start shooting as fast as you can when you're under fire." That was a just totally impracticable solution to the problem.

He said, "Well, you really can fire it as fast as you want." I said, "Okay. I'll tell you what we'll do. We'll put a Sheridan vehicle out at Fort Knox. I'll have all the armor people, the user, sitting back about three hundred or four hundred yards behind it. You put one of your crews in there with a whole basic load of ammunition and fire one round after another as fast as they can. If it blows up, we won't buy it." He said, "I don't think we should do that."

We didn't buy that vehicle until all of those problems had been corrected; but when we did finally buy it, it was still a dog. This was an example of our attempt to do things cheaper and faster. Because we have a limitation on numbers of personnel and units, we have to go with our advantage of technology. We have to have guns that will fire faster and more accurately. We have to have systems that will acquire targets more rapidly and accurately, that can translate what they found into an identification of the target being a friend or foe, and that give quick data to get the first round of fire on the target as opposed to having to adjust for ten minutes.

That's technology. If we don't want to take advantage of technology, we're going to be undone, in my view. Now, you do have to examine how deep into this you want to go. You don't want a tank that's so complicated and sophisticated that it doesn't run half the time, or requires a PhD to run it. Some kind of balance has to be struck. But any kind of technology that can make the soldier's job easier and allow him do it more effectively ought to be taken advantage of.

When I took command at AMC, we had a bad image in a couple of places that were in some ways unrelated. First, the people in the Office of the Secretary of Defense and on the Hill felt that we were a cumbersome, unresponsive organization. In their view, AMC didn't look to the future, didn't care about innovation, and was not effective in managing programs.

Second, people in the operational forces looked on AMC as an organization that wasn't even a part of the army. They felt that AMC did not support them well in the field and was not responsive to their needs.

There were lots of reasons for this feeling on the part of the operational forces. For example, shortly after I became the commander, I visited the Air Defense Command in Europe—I think it was the 32nd Air Defense Group. In talking to the commander, I found that they were having trouble passing some of their tests because they had not received certain repair parts. Therefore, some parts of their missile systems were not operational.

When I got back to the United States, I called the Missile Command, told them this finding, and said, "Let's get it corrected." The answer I received from MICOM was that the people over there didn't know how to submit requisitions; until they learned, they weren't going to get repair parts. Their attitude was, "The hell with whether we are ready or not out in the field. You have to have your paperwork right first!"

Well, this practically sent me through the roof! I told the commander, "I want you to go over there personally and find out what repair parts they need. Make notes of those parts, then call up your command, and tell them to get them on their way. The paperwork will follow. From now on, I don't want that sort of thing ever to hold up supporting a unit in the field. That's why we have such a bad reputation. Some of us think we are not a part of the army; some of us think we are not interested in the readiness of the army."

Our major emphasis at AMC should be finding out what the soldier in the field needs, determining what's wrong with the equipment we put out there, and getting it improved so he's capable of fighting. Having been a company and battalion commander, I think I have some appreciation for what the tactical soldier faces.

For example, I received a comment from the commander of an armored cavalry unit at Fort Bliss. He said the clothing used by his unit was just too hot when worn in the desert in the middle of the day and too cold at night. I sent some clothing experts down there and told them I didn't want them to just visit with the troops during suppertime. I didn't want them to come back to the base camp at night but to stay out in the field for a week. Then they'll get an appreciation for what these soldiers face. I don't know if we solved that problem, but at least the experts started to get a better feel for the kind of clothing to develop.

AMC was responsible for the materiel readiness of the army and I wanted the command to feel that way. That's why we changed the name from Army Materiel Command to Development and Readiness Command, as opposed to Materiel Command, Logistics Command, or something like that. I wanted them to feel they were a part of the army—that they, too, were soldiers. They had just as much responsibility for winning the war as anybody else, and I wanted them to take some pride in that.

When I came on to the Army Staff after World War II, as a lieutenant colonel, at twenty-six or twenty-seven years old, I hadn't had much experience. I had only been commissioned for four or five years, but while on the Army Staff, I worked with a lot of officers who had been in the army since the 1930s. Prior to World War II, and well beyond it, the technical services had their own budgets; the chief of ordnance had his budget, the chief of engineers had his, the chief of signal, whatever they called him, had his, and so forth.

These organizations had their own budgets, and control of the purse strings gives you a tremendous power. There was some resentment on the part of the combat arms guys that the equipment they were getting in the field was something that the ordnance guy, or signal guy, or quartermaster guy, or whatever, felt they should have. Whether they wanted it or not was sort of immaterial; and if it was made in a way they didn't like, that was immaterial also. So the chief of ordnance said this is the best kind of gun you can have, so this is what you got. There was a sense of resentment about all of this; and the feeling was that if the so-called user had more to say in this whole situation, then maybe we'd get something in the field that was better for the soldier, easier for him to use, or something he can learn to use more efficiently.

I remember listening to discussions that were sort of over my head at the time, but I can remember a guy named Frank Young, who worked in the same shop I was in, the Pentagon Internal War Plan Office, and he was an ordnance officer. I remember his talking to some guy who was an armor officer. Well, both of them were from the pre–World War II period; they both had served in part of the war. The armor officer was saying the ordnance guys gave us such a lousy tank and Frank Young was trying to defend why the tank was the way it was, and so forth. The armor guy said he didn't know that much about it. So I could see that although these were two top-level young action officers, in their midthirties, there was some kind of resentment there.

They were two bright guys—we had a lot of bright guys there. Underneath this sort of resentment, we were all friends. We had a very congenial group. The tanker felt that he had a tank in World War II that was not comparable to the German tank and that we had failed in the ordnance arena to produce a tank that had the modern kind of technology in it and so forth. I don't know what the problem was, but this armor officer felt that the ordnance officer hadn't given him what he needed in the field to fight the German tank.

That was the theme I preached: we were in this together. If somebody couldn't make out a requisition properly, we had to get over there and teach them how to do it. In the meantime, we would take care of the problem. Of course, it's important to do the administrative work properly, because it makes the whole thing flow smoother, and you don't have to take special measures to get people up to a good state of readiness. Until that was accomplished, we had to take these special measures and keep people up to snuff. That was the thought I tried to inject into my command. Some people liked it. Others didn't like the way they had been looked upon in the past, but were willing to change. I don't know how you change people like that. You have to be a miracle man; I'm surely not that.

We had a situation that caused me to travel out to Rock Island to the Armaments Command. At that time we were having a lot of problems with the machine gun on our tank. It was practically useless and we were looking into substituting a new weapon for it. They fired a number of machine guns for me, and two machine guns really caught my attention. The M-60 machine gun, which they had a part in designing, was being produced by Maremont, up in Maine. The other option, a machine gun made by the Belgian Fabrique Nationale, or FN, seemed far superior. The FN machine gun sounded like a Mercedes; it was a fantastic-sounding gun. The Armaments Command commander, John Raaen, told me they had chosen the M-60 to put in the tank. I said, "Your test results don't indicate that the M-60 is any better. In fact, it doesn't indicate that it's as good. You've never had a stoppage with the Belgian gun. You have had stoppages with the M-60."

Raaen defended his decision by saying that the Belgian gun cost too much; it was going to cost more than the M-60. I said, "It's not really your business to decide that. If somebody has to decide what's best for the army regarding what it can afford, you're not the one. You are making a very far-reaching decision that is going to decide if a guy gets killed or lives, because his gun jams or doesn't. I don't think that's your decision to make." Then he made a lot of other excuses. One of his big things was that the Belgian gun was handmade. Another was that TRADOC was insisting that this gun be procured and fielded immediately. It would be faster if we took the M-60.

I came back to Washington and said to George Sammet, who was my deputy for research and development, "George, I think we should do something about this." We kicked around some ideas. One thought, eventually implemented, was to tell ARMCOM to buy ten of these Belgian guns, dismantle them, put the parts in a bushel basket, mix them all up, then pick out the parts and put them back together. Obviously, if it's a handmade gun, they won't go back together, or the gun won't shoot when you put it back together.

In the meantime, I called Bill DePuy, who was the TRADOC commander, and said, "I understand from my guy at Rock Island that your fellows at the Armor School are insisting that we get this gun into the tank without delay. If you want it bad, you'll get it bad. We can give you the M-60. But it's not as good as the Belgian gun. It's going to take us longer to get the Belgian gun. If you can stand to wait another year or whatever it is going to be, I'll get you the Belgian gun." He said, "We want the best gun. Time is not important. We have had this bad gun for so long now that it doesn't make much difference whether we keep it for another year." So that excuse went by the board.

Eventually ARMCOM got the ten guns. They couldn't get a stoppage even when they mixed up all the parts! This gun was fantastically made, and that's the gun we now have on the tank. That previous attitude, to me, was inexcusable. ARMCOM was not interested in what's best for the soldier; they were only interested in the gun that they designed or had a part in. That was the attitude I tried to change.

Here is another example of the type of practices that gave AMC a bad name. Bill DePuy from TRADOC decided what was needed in the army in terms of requirements, and I decided on producing what he said he needed. He and I went to Aberdeen for a demonstration of everything we had in the way of smoke for battlefield obscurants. One of the items demonstrated was a British system that projected smoke grenades from an armored vehicle. Well, when they blew these grenades out from a tank, a smoke screen obscured that tank from our view in just a few seconds. Our system sent out little strings of smoke. While it was a pretty picture, you could clearly see the tank for quite a while before the smoke spread. Right on the spot, Bill and I made the decision, as an interim measure, to buy the British smoke. We would get their permission to let us manufacture it on a royalty basis. We would learn how to make their grenade launcher and manufacture those. Interim, we would buy it from the Brits to equip our fleet.

We made that decision and told the people there, "That's our decision. Get with it." Well, you have a lot of things to do and can't keep checking on everything. I stayed involved with the smoke a little bit in

the interim, because there was word that the British were a little reluctant to go along with us on this. I called my counterpart in England, who
jammed them in the butt and got them going. So that problem went away.

About six months after we made the decision, I called the people
in and asked, "How are we coming on that smoke stuff?" They said,
"The study is almost complete." I said, "What study?" They said, "The
study about whether that smoke is satisfactory and cost effective." I said,
"There was not supposed to be a study. The decision was made that we
were going to buy it. What do you mean, 'a study'?" "Well, we don't
think that we should buy things without having a justification." I said,
"Look, that's my problem. If somebody gets on my back because I did
something without justification, let me defend myself. You don't need
to protect me. I said I wanted the smoke and I want it. Now six months
have gone by; you haven't done anything but sit around making a study.
I'm not sure how effective your study is."

They went away with a directive to get off the study and get on with
buying the smoke. What they were really trying to do was protect what
they were developing and bring it along to where it would compete with
the British smoke. Four or five months later I said, "How's the smoke
coming?" "TRADOC has almost completed its study." I said, "What
study?" "The study on smoke requirements." I said, "The commander
of TRADOC has already made the decision that we are going to buy the
British smoke."

I called Bill DePuy: "Do you realize your guys are making a study?"
He went through the roof. Our guys had convinced TRADOC that they
couldn't move ahead until they had a sound requirement statement. His
guys started putting together the normal requirement statement, which
takes months. That's criminal, but that's the kind of thing you found in
AMC. I don't know whether you still find it, but the people outside AMC
think you can still find it.

The next thing we did to try to improve our image, particularly
within the army, by starting a program that would put a warranty on our
products. This idea was George Sammet's—a heck of a good man. When
we introduced the new M60A3 tank into Europe, we sent a large team of
people from Tank-Automotive Command (TACOM), Armaments Command, Electronics Command, and whoever else had equipment in that
tank.

Those tanks were ours and didn't belong to Europe until the soldiers
were trained to operate them, operate the equipment in them, and maintain them. Anything that went wrong with the M60A3 during that ini-

tial period was our problem. We had to put new parts on them at our expense. When US Army Europe had the confidence they could handle the new tank and were ready to buy it, we turned it over to them.

There was a thirty-day extension for spare parts or something like that after they took over. All their spare parts and all the problems we had to solve, until they were satisfied that they could handle the new tank. Prior to that, all we did was ship them over. If they had a problem with the equipment, we said, "Requisition the parts." Now we were responsible for seeing that it was done and that gave us a huge boost. It was costly, but it allowed us to introduce a new major system into the field in a very smooth way.

People were happy with the tank and probably had more confidence in it as a result of having it introduced with a warranty. Before, when they had gotten new equipment, nobody was trained on it and couldn't maintain it—the thing would break down. Then they'd say, "This is a lousy tank."

I used to make speeches when I would go around to the logistics agencies or the commodity commands. As far as I was concerned, the equipment in the army was ours from the time we bought it until the time we scrapped it. It was up to us to see that it was kept up. The fact that we put it in the hands of some nuts out in the field was immaterial. We were interested in that piece of gear working, no matter what the guy did to it. We would overcome his problem. That was AMC and that was our responsibility.

A lot of people bought into that, and we began to get good reports from the field. The commanders in the field began to say, "Gee, we are getting a lot better support from AMC." We began to appreciate their problems. It was a very rewarding thing, but there wasn't enough of it. Our guys weren't getting with it enough. Mind you, I'm talking about the original AMC structure and name. I hope we haven't lost the progress we did make with the reorganization and with trying to instill a new spirit and outlook on the mission.

In the AMC structure you have a lot of good people. But you have a lot of people whose value and contributions are not well organized. It's difficult to recognize them all because AMC is so vast and widely spread. The commander in Europe, for example, has a relatively small geographical area. My command was spread across thirty-seven states and in seventeen foreign countries. No other commander in any part of the army has that kind of geographical problem.

How do you get around to all of those people? I visited many organizations that never had seen a commander from AMC before. If I was going to convey this new message, I felt I had to get around and see the people, so they saw face-to-face the guy from whom all this was coming, and so they could voice their opinions if they didn't like it. I felt it was important; some people didn't. I got criticized for being on the road as much as I was, and it wasn't any pleasure going on the road.

I spent a lot of my time trying to help contractors with their issues. One example was Cincinnati Electronics. The president of that company—I believe his name was George Mealy—used to bitch all the time about ECOM. At meetings and seminars we would have, he would, without exception, get up and blast off about something. He wrote me a letter one time when I was the AMC commander saying that the ECOM guys were on the take. I called him up and said, "I got your letter. I can assure you that, if what you say is true, some guys are going to jail. But when you make an allegation that the guys at Monmouth are on the take, you've got to be specific. There are probably twenty thousand people at Monmouth. What do I do—go there and ask each one of them, 'Are you the guy he is talking about?' If you have some evidence, come forward with it. I can't correct the situation without evidence. I don't have any basis for starting an investigation on bribery. Which of the labs are you talking about? What are you talking about?"

He said he would send me some further documentation. Apparently, he thought about it or looked into it, and the guys who told him this weren't willing to name names, or maybe they really didn't have any. It was just a generalization. He called me back and said, "Would you mind sending my letter back? I would not like to have that circulating around because I'm not sure it's true." So I sent it back to him and didn't hear from him for a while.

Then he called me and asked for an appointment. He came in and said, "Your people at Monmouth allege that I have illegally shipped some PRC-77s [portable VHF radios]." He had a contract with the Pakistanis, I think, to produce some PRC-77s for them. He was not supposed to ship any PRC-77s to them, under orders of the DCAS (Defense Contract Administration Services), until he had corrected deficiencies that were being found in his radios and he was up to snuff on his orders to the US Army. Anyway, he said, "They have alleged that I've illegally shipped some sets to the Pakistanis and they demanded a complete inventory of my plant. That's shut me down. In essence, I have to stop everything to go around counting parts, completed radios, and radios in process. That's really hurting me. That costs me money."

So I said, "If my guys ordered that, they must have had some reason. Let me find out what it's all about. Who should I call? Who is the guy who gave the orders?" He gave me a name at Monmouth. I didn't call the commander; I called the guy direct. I said, "Mr. So-and-so, I'm General Deane, the commander at AMC. I have this gentleman in my office who says that you ordered a 100 percent inventory of his plant with respect to the PRC-77. If you did order such a thing, I'm sure there is some reason for it. But I don't know and he doesn't know. I'd appreciate it if you would tell me."

The guy said, "I didn't order anything like that." I said, "Do you know of anybody who might have? This gentleman thinks your command did." The guy at Monmouth said he didn't know who had. I said to Mealy, "Those guys don't know what you are talking about." Mealy said, "Well, maybe it's so-and-so." So I think I probably called three or four guys at Monmouth and got the same answer, trying to solve Mealy's problem, to show Mealy that we were in fact interested in things being done properly.

Finally I said, "Who is in charge of the DCAS organization at your place?" The DCAS people worked for the Defense Logistics Agency (DLA), as I recall. I'm not sure if their people were in the plant all the time, but they come out of the DLA. He gave me the name and telephone number of some woman. I called her and said, "This is General Deane. I'm the commander at AMC and I have George Mealy in my office. He says that my Electronics Command, or somebody in the command, has directed that you ensure a 100 percent inventory of his plant is conducted with respect to PRC-77 radios."

She said, "General, I don't work for ECOM, and I don't work for you. I directed the inventory not because of anything you or ECOM said, but because I think it should be taken. I think Mr. Mealy is shipping radios out of his plant illegally. It's my responsibility to see that that doesn't happen." I said, "Thank you very much, madam. You have just solved my problem." I'd had her on the squawk box so he heard what she said. By this time I'd spent probably an hour or two telephoning people, talking to Mealy, and waiting for people to call me back.

I turned to Mealy and said, "Mealy, you didn't even have to leave Cincinnati to find this out. You could have just gone down the hall and asked her. Instead you get on an airplane, spend money, and come here to see me. All that money is going to be paid by the government somewhere in one of your contracts. You came here and wasted two hours of my time. Mealy, you're a small-time, lousy contractor. You haven't done anything right, as far as I can determine, since you have been the president of Cincinnati Electronics. Your radios are crummy. I've spent all this time on you. I don't ever want to see you again. Get out of my office!"

I never saw Mealy again. If he had been on the up and up, I would have solved his problem. But he came in with a bunch of allegations he hadn't checked out himself. If he had gone to the DCAS woman, he would have found out what was going on. He would have found out that ECOM had nothing to do with it. He jumped to unwarranted conclusions. He had a bunch of guys who weren't worth their salt working for him. They were probably covering their butts by making this story up and didn't think anything would really come of it. I hope he really jumped on them when he got home. At least I was trying to show industry, in the form of Cincinnati Electronics, which was a very poor contractor before Marconi bought them, that the army acted with integrity.

Anyway, those were my thrusts: one was to establish good relationships with industry and pay a guy a fair profit for work done. If you pay him a fair profit and treat him right, you're going to get his best engineers and the best floor space in his plant. If you try to make him do the job for nothing, he's going to do it in the part of the plant that he has shut down because it's no good. He is going to give you his poorest engineers. Try to establish a relationship that shows you're a good customer and that you expect service from a good contractor. It's a two-way street.

The other thrust was to demonstrate to the army as a whole that we were really interested in supporting the army and keeping it operationally ready at all times. We assumed certain responsibilities that AMC hadn't concentrated on in the past—that is, the materiel was ours from cradle to grave and we were going to see that it worked.

Although I had a strong background in research and development, I can't say that I ever did become an expert in materiel development. Many people spend their whole career doing materiel readiness and I was there for only a couple of years. As I mentioned early on, I group people into four categories and I always seek people in the second category. I try to find people who have the capabilities in the field I'm interested in at the moment.

My chief of staff, Lieutenant General Woody Vaughn, one of the finest men I ever knew. He was a first-class gentleman and probably as great an expert in logistics as the army ever saw. He knew the details but didn't mess around with them. He had a broad perspective of logistics, so I depended very heavily on him. He knew I depended on him, and I gave him the authority to do things. If it didn't require a decision from me personally, he could make the decisions.

Subsequently I got Gene D'Ambrosio, who was also a tremendous guy in logistics. He replaced Woody Vaughn as the expert, because he came in to get a third star and took the third star away from the chief of staff job. Woody went on to a three-star job at Defense Logistics Agency. Gene was a broad-gauge guy, willing to grab the reins and make decisions. He kept me informed through frequent meetings. If I had to make a decision, Gene could explain what I had to decide and what the pros and cons were. I had total confidence in him.

As you get into positions of importance, you surround yourself with people who can do these things. What you want are the guys who have the guts to go it alone, no matter how tough it is. They will go on and keep charging; those are category 2 people. Secondly, they have not just intelligence, but intelligence with energy. You can sit around, be intelligent, and think of a lot of good solutions to problems or innovations that should be implemented. But if you don't have the energy to put that into action, your intelligence is wasted. Gene had all of those qualities. He also had a vision. Leaders have vision and he was a leader. That's how I handled things—I took the advice of people I trusted. These leaders I pushed from the colonel rank to become general officers. It probably still works that way today.

They used to say that they appointed a promotion board to select brigadier and major generals, that the board should make the decisions, and that nobody should try to influence it. As the senior logistician in the army, although I wasn't an experienced logistician, I felt I should try to see that the guys best fitted to be brigadier generals were selected. There might be only one logistician on the promotion board and his judgment wouldn't prevail. So I tried to present the consensus of all the major logisticians in my command to the chairman of the promotion board.

I would always write a letter to the chairman for whatever use he wanted. If he wanted to throw the letter in the wastebasket he could, but at least he knew my input. In some instances he told the board. I've even had some boards come to me and say, "Your letter was really helpful to us because we didn't know any of those people." When you put those boards together, artillerymen, infantrymen, armor, and all are on it, and those guys have never met these logisticians. I hadn't met them all either. That's why I had to depend on people in whom I had confidence to tell me who were the comers in the logistics field.

Then we would rate them: if they are only going to make one, this is the one who they ought to make. I would send that order of priority to the chairman of the promotion board. When I was there, we got a better share of promotions in our command than anyone previous or since. You're not supposed to do anything; but if you think something is going to be better because you did something, you ought to step out and do it. And I did it. The people in the command knew it and appreciated that I was going to bat for them when others were not going to bat for their guys. That helped morale. I just depended on people in whom I had confidence. If people demonstrated to me that I shouldn't have confidence in them, from then on I didn't give them anything important to do.

General Jack Stoner, who commanded ECOM, was Chemical Corps. That slot would normally call for a signal officer. What seemed to drive the Signal Corps in those days was long-line communications. If you wanted to be a signal guy, that's what you wanted to get into. In my opinion, they didn't have any senior people who I felt were competent to take over the command at ECOM—which I, industry, and everybody else outside of ECOM saw as one of my major problem commands.

They weren't the only ones with problems, nor the worst, but they were pretty close. When I couldn't find people who I felt could deal with the morass up there, I selected Jack Stoner. We divided ECOM into three commands: ERADCOM, the Electronics Research and Development Command, then in Adelphi, Maryland; CORADCOM, the Communications Research and Development Command; and CERCOM, the Communications-Electronics Readiness Command. This goes back to trying to bring readiness into the logistics end.

I had met Jack Stoner only once, on one of my trips to Europe. Stoner had a support command at the time, the 7th COSCOM (corps support command). That was a logistics job. I spent the better part of a day and evening with him, and maybe had dinner at his quarters. I received command briefings and was really impressed with the gung-ho spirit of his organization, and I felt the commander gets some credit for that. When I needed a logistics guy at Fort Monmouth, I asked about Stoner to confirm my opinion. By and large, everybody thought very highly of him in that field—maybe in other fields, too, but that was the only one I was interested in.

I asked for, and got, Jack Stoner to take over that command. For the other two commands, again, I couldn't find any signal people. I initially found a guy, Al Crawford, who I thought would be good in the CORADCOM at Monmouth. Crawford had been the project manager for Army Tactical Data Systems and was a very good project manager. He went there but just didn't have the required background. He came to me and asked me to let him go to some other job. Because I felt that the job he had was a lot more important than the one he wanted to go to and because I couldn't see any other signal officer who might be able to handle the job, I refused. He later retired and went to work with industry.

Then I brought in an armor officer named Hillman Dickinson, who had a PhD in physics. He was not only a good operator but he maintained his proficiency in his technical field over the years. I had worked with Hill earlier and had seen him work with engineers from civilian life. Guys from Bell Telephone labs and people of that quality looked on him as an equal to them. That was a good mark for Hill.

The other was an artilleryman named Charlie Daniels. He also had a PhD, as I recall, in physics and had maintained his technical proficiency. He had also been an artillery battalion commander in the 1st Division when I was with the 1st Division. I put him in ERADCOM. These three people did a very good job, but to make a dent in that command was not easy. I think they made some strides toward improving its image, its capabilities, and its outlook on life. Although it has been brought back together to some extent, I think it's a much better command as a result of these three guys.

The fact is that in DARCOM (AMC), most of the organization is made up of civilians. This always makes change very difficult. The army commander in those commands may serve there for maybe three years; it's more likely to be two or less before moving on. Unless he has been in that sort of business all his life and has served at Huntsville, Monmouth, or Rock Island, he doesn't have any preconceived ideas about what should be going on, what the problems are, and what the good and bad points are. He probably spends the first six months jelling in his mind a course of action that he should follow to improve the command and its performance. At the end of that time he is prepared to tell his people what he wants to do and what the future course is going to be.

It takes them several months to even begin to assimilate what he is saying. In many instances there is a resistance and that stretches the process out. Now maybe he has a year left in which, hopefully, he can get things running smoothly. When he leaves, some of it may remain, but the resisters, who have already made plans, now start implementing plans to move back to where they were.

The new commander comes in and they say, "Here are ways we can improve the command." The ways to improve the command mean to go back to the old way it was, in their view. They convince him and it takes him a few months to realize he got duped. I think that's one of the bases for the reputation that AMC has had over the years. AMC has gotten a lot of bum raps in terms of their image, but a lot of it was justified.

One of the things I used to talk to young officers about, I think, applies to fairly senior leadership and management positions. If you are going to be in the army and be good, you should be a real professional—somebody who they refer to as a real pro. Being a real pro meant a lot of things. One was being concerned about the welfare of the people who work for you. It meant being proficient in your job. Above all, it meant giving 110 percent all the time. Not just when some superior is looking over your shoulder, but all the time. You do this all the time because your subordinates and your peers are observing you all the time.

Sometimes a guy might appear good to the people above him, but to the people below him, he is a monster. If he is, he is probably going to destroy the morale in your command or hurt you in some way. It's best to be forewarned about that. If he is just trying to please the people above, he doesn't have the right motivation or, at least, the form of leadership I want to have in my organization.

For instance, when I was running that espionage operation in Germany, the deputy G2 was an old, experienced colonel named Bobby Schow. Schow has been in the intelligence business for a long time. We kept getting, as the head guy, a broken-down G3 or division commander who had never had any intelligence experience. Schow was an expert, and whenever any questions came up that I had to get approval on, they would say, "What does Bobby Schow think?" If I said, "Bobby Schow approves of this," they would say, "Fine, go ahead." If Schow didn't approve it, it was dead in the water.

One day, while I was still a lieutenant colonel, I had to brief Alfred M. Gruenther, who was one of two lieutenant generals just below the chief of staff.[10] One was for operations; the other was for logistics and administration. Gruenther, who was working operations, was a brilliant man. He had a brain like a steel trap. After my briefing, I gathered up my charts and was about to leave his room when he said, "Jack, sit down for a minute; I want to talk to you. You have had some experience in intelligence; what do you think of an intelligence career?" I said, "Boy, that's something I don't want!" He said, "Why?" I said, "I have the ambitions I think a normal guy has. That is to progress, become a general officer, and go as far in the army as I can. I just don't think you get there if you've been in the intelligence business for any length of time."

He said, "Why do you say that?" I said, "Well, let me tell you about my friend." I related the story about Bobby Schow making all the decisions, really running the intelligence business in Europe, but nobody ever considering whether he should become a general officer. When I left Europe, Bobby had said to me, "Your father's in business in California and I'd like to live in California. I'm going to retire pretty soon, because I'm never going to get promoted. I would appreciate it if, when you speak to your dad, you would mention that I'm interested in going into business out there; and, if he can help me, I'd appreciate it."

I told Al Gruenther all about Schow. Very shortly thereafter Gruenther went to SHAPE as chief of staff. When it came time to select the intelligence officer for the command, it was Bobby Schow. He subsequently became a major general, worked for the CIA, and also, I guess, may have been the ACSI—assistant chief of staff for intelligence on the army staff.

I don't know if this would have happened without my discussion with Gruenther, but it happened soon after we talked. But here I was, his subordinate, describing Bobby Schow's talents. Bobby was senior to me by ten or fifteen years in age and was a full colonel of long standing when I was a wet-behind-the-ears lieutenant colonel. He never failed to impress me, his subordinate. He didn't slough off when I was around. He was working just as hard at being a first-class professional when I was around as when his boss was around.

In the managerial ranks you like to look for people like that—people who are putting out all of the time—just like you want to see in the leadership ranks. You find out about people not by talking to superiors, because you only see one side of them if you talk to the superiors. Find out something about them from the people who have worked for them. Did they really admire them or didn't they admire them? What did they think of them as leaders or managers? That's another facet in picking the right individual for the job.

When we selected the M-1 tank, the two competitors were Chrysler and General Motors. The competitors were told that they could use either a turbine or a diesel engine. General Motors chose to go with the diesel; Chrysler, the turbine. Why they chose the turbine, I don't know. About the same time the secretary of defense's office made a deal with the Germans. At that time there was a big hurrah about what gun was going to go on the various NATO tanks and whether that would be the gun that we would try to standardize in NATO. We had a big competition between the 105-millimeter rifled gun and the 120-millimeter smoothbore. The 105 was basically a British gun that we adapted years ago. The 120 was a German gun, which they were very high on. There was also a new rifled 120-millimeter British gun. We ran competitions. The German gun punched through more armor. The British gun was more accurate. Ours was close in both categories, and one of their guns or the other would fall down very seriously in some category. Overall, our gun was best and the people doing the test recommended it.

The Germans backed out and said that they wouldn't accept the results of the test. There was a big dispute about whether the 105 gun would be able to penetrate the armor that we saw coming along in a few years. Our labs kept contending that it would; some years later, they changed their view without knowing anything more than they did before. I think our guys were not too honest because it was their own gun. That was the problem with our laboratories: many times, I've seen them get a "not invented here" attitude and really distort the facts. Anyway, some people at the defense level agreed with the Germans that if they would accept our turbine engine in their tank, we would accept their gun.

We got politically committed to putting the 120-millimeter German gun onto the M-1 tank. That put us in a position that we had to have a turbine engine in our tanks that skewed the competition. When the proposals came in from General Motors and Chrysler, General Motors' was far better in many respects. One example was that they were very definitive about what it was going to cost us. Chrysler gave us nothing. They said they could not quote because they did not have definitive quotes from their vendors. "All we can say is it will be our vendors' costs plus 5 percent." This was not acceptable and our source selection board chose the General Motors tank.

Despite their highly lucrative M-60 tank business, Chrysler Corporation had suffered $52 million in losses during 1974 and $260 million in 1975. They were already starting to feel the effects that would become clearer in 1979 and 1980. Chrysler's tank division represented the only money-making operation within the corporation. Because of the cost-plus system of defense procurement, a winning contract would practically guarantee the corporation a considerable future profit.

Chrysler executives pulled out all the stops in their attempt to influence the M-1 award. On June 17, 1976, Chrysler chairman John Riccardo visited the White House to meet with William Seidman, the assistant to the president for economic affairs and executive director of the powerful Economic Policy Board. Seidman was a close friend of Gerald Ford, one of a select group of advisors who had personal access to the president. "The Chrysler people came in looking for help," recalled Seidman. "And when we looked into it, we saw that they were in some trouble.

We wouldn't give them any direct aid, but we did look to help them out within the regular decision process." With the M-1 award only weeks away, the direction of this help was obvious.

We went up and presented this finding to Bill Clements, deputy secretary of defense and later governor of Texas—a ruthless kind of guy, a real roughneck. He had been a wildcat oil man. He had founded SEDCO, a major oil drilling company, and became a multimillionaire, but had never lost his toughness. We presented the finding to him and Mal Curry, who was then director of Defense Research and Engineering. Mal Curry had made this deal with the Germans at the behest of a guy in his office named Bob Basil. Anyway, when the presentation was made, they began to lean on us about why we didn't take the turbine selection. We told them the price with General Motors for the diesel was firm.

Chrysler continued its lobbying effort right up through the day of the scheduled award to GM. Lobbyist John Keegan hand-delivered a letter to William Clements in which Chrysler, which should not have even known the results of the source selection, threatened to issue a formal protest if the army went through with the award to GM.

Well, they weren't going to accept our decision to go with General Motors. It was never clear to me whether they wanted Chrysler to win the competition or whether they simply wanted a tank with a turbine engine to win the competition. Anyway, we were directed to tell Chrysler to come in with bids of what they would do if they did a diesel engine, and General Motors to come back with bids on what it would cost us and how they would do it with a turbine engine.

That way, we were supposed to have two bids, one with a diesel and one with a turbine, from each competitor. You would have something to compare. This is what it was supposed to look like on the surface. We found that when they came back with the new bids, Chrysler was definitive with their costs, and under the cost of General Motors. Obviously, all of General Motors' figures had been leaked to Chrysler.

I can't prove that, but it was obvious. After this happened, I really didn't participate; it just turned me off. That night I got on a plane to California to meet Doctor Fubini, who was out there with the Defense Science Board on some studies I had to participate in. I was still incensed about this tank, and he wanted me to go into the consulting business with him. I called him up and said I'd like to see him that evening if possible.

I went over to the apartment he had rented, because he had taken his family to California with him on this trip. I talked to him and told him

I was just fed up. We determined that I would retire. Because of some of my wife's medical problems, I didn't actually retire until the following February. That delay gave her a chance to have those things squared away while I was still in the service.

The tank competition was a political sort of thing. I don't know what the motivation was, whether they had gotten themselves in a bind with the Germans and had to make good on that, or whether for some reason or other they wanted Chrysler to win. I wasn't privy to that. I don't recall Chrysler being in that bad of shape. Maybe their financial situation was a motivation. That sort of thing was never discussed.

On November 12, 1976, the Defense Department awarded the contract for the $20 billion program to Chrysler. When the M-1s began rolling off the assembly line in 1980, the army found that the turbine engines were seriously deficient. The air filter system had yet to be perfected and the engines broke down at an alarming rate, "We were still having tremendous problems in the late '70s with the turbine," remarked General Donn Starry. "We had to completely redesign the air intake system." Ultimately, the army had to slow down its production of the M-1, and spend hundreds of millions of dollars to implement needed changes.

When I retired, I had offers of jobs in industry that were attractive and fairly substantial in salary and potential retirement benefits, stock options, et cetera. I really felt that if I went into a job like that, I would just be doing more of what I'd been doing for so long and might as well have stayed at AMC. It would be the same problems and worries. You go home at night and think about what you have to do the next day, and how to make sure all your subordinates are doing a good job.

I thought to myself, "I'm retiring. Why do I want to continue doing the same thing? I'd rather keep my hand in and at the same time have some freedom to do what I want." The way to do that was to become a consultant. Then I could go to companies and talk to them on a schedule that I largely dictated.

Sometimes they would want me at a specific time because they had to get a proposal in and wanted me to work or coach or critique them on it. If I had to make a presentation of some kind and they wanted my reaction before they went to whatever army agency was involved, that dictated time sometimes. But by and large, I had my own schedule. That appealed to me.

Additionally, I had the good fortune of being involved with a number of companies that were doing different things in different management styles. It was interesting to observe these and be able to recommend to companies the strong points I saw in some other company and how they handled things.

I've been doing that ever since I retired. I'm on the board of directors of my own consulting company. I've also been on the board of directors of a not-for-profit organization designed to promote free trade throughout the world. I've spent a little time at that. They have a lot of distinguished people on their board: Davy Jones is a former chairman of the Joint Chiefs of Staff. Rubin Askew was an unsuccessful Democratic presidential candidate. Bill Ussury, a former secretary of labor, has also been negotiating the labor problems that Eastern Airline has had. Karl Bendetsen is former chairman and chief executive officer of Champion International. John Troups is the chairman and chief executive officer of Planning Research Corporation. It has been interesting to exchange ideas with them.

During my tenure as commander of AMC, one of the things I tried to instill in people was a feeling for their role in the support of all the equipment that we had in the field. To test whether it was happening, I would check with operational units from time to time. I asked what complaints they had made about the equipment, and what had been done about those complaints.

For example, I visited the 82nd Airborne Division and found that they sent in a complaint about the FAAR (forward area acquisition radar), which had a lot of loose cables and wires. When the radar was in the stowed position for movement, those wires were exposed. As you went through the woods, these wires became entangled in branches on trees and broke.

The 82nd had written the signal people at Monmouth asking for some kind of a cover to be developed to protect these wires. The answer received was that people in the field should train the drivers not to drive under branches lower than ten feet, eight inches above the ground. This solution was totally impractical and contributed to the bad image the operators in the field had of AMC. That was one of the things I was trying to correct.

I knew that I was going to become the commander of the AMC and I determined that I could blow $10 million out of a total budget of $2 billion on a mistake and really not be taken to task too badly. This gave me an opportunity to start a new R&D or acquisition methodology that would possibly shorten development time.

The gun was a good vehicle for the experiment. I had been familiar with a fellow named Kelly Johnson, a Lockheed aeronautical engineer of great fame. Johnson designed the F-104 Starfighter, the U-2 spy plane, and the subsequent SR-71 Blackbird, which flew at great altitude and at tremendous speed. Kelly Johnson had developed the latter two aircraft in what he called his "Skunk Works," where there was total secrecy.

Nobody bothered him. He didn't have any decision points to go through and didn't have to get approval at several levels of authority. When the aircraft was finished, he said, "Come look at it, and see if it's what you want." In both cases it was what the CIA wanted; and it was a fantastic job, done in a very short time for this complex aircraft.

After knowing Kelly Johnson, for whom I had a lot of admiration, I decided to try to do the same thing, as far as I could, within the framework of the regulations that governed me—even if I had to bend a few of them. I started what I called the Skunk Works methodology of acquisition.

We first went to a very briefly conducted competition, which saved a little bit of time. Hughes Helicopter won that competition. We gave them the money and had a project manager in charge. We told the project manager to go out there, make the decisions that had to be made, and do whatever was necessary to make things go along right. I said, "I don't want to hear from you until the weapon is finished and ready for delivery, unless you feel that you need my help. If you need help, call General Sammet, my deputy for R&D. But don't call anybody else; we'll get you the help you need."

Then we got the chief of staff of the army to agree that nobody would visit the project. We didn't want visitors making people stop their work to prepare briefings. We didn't want people making suggestions that would take the contractor off the track to do something he felt they wanted but wasn't sure should be done. We were giving him the money and were going to hold him to performance.

A little less than two years later, the contractor delivered the working models as promised, on cost, and actually a little under time. The models worked and became the weapons we now use on the infantry fighting vehicles and the attack helicopter. This is a way of shortening the procurement cycle, in my view. It cannot be used on everything, but it can help in some acquisitions.

The principle is eliminating decision points. If we can eliminate some, we won't get so many questions from Congress, the Office of the Secretary of Defense (OSD), the assistant secretaries in the Department of the Army, and the Army Staff. When questions come up, just say, "We haven't gotten to that decision point yet. When we get there, we'll give you the answers, but we don't know the outcomes yet." The fewer decision points you have, the less delay you have.

The other thing I did to save time in AMC Headquarters was establish what I referred to as the "air request net." If you are an infantry battalion commander and need an air strike because you're in contact with the enemy and need support, you get on the radio and call back on the air request net. Your radio transmission goes directly to a guy in the tactical air control center or someplace where they make decisions on what aircraft goes out for what strikes.

That air strike then comes to you, and they alert you that it is coming and when it is expected to be there. You don't go to your regimental or higher-level commander to get permission for this. Your request goes directly to the guy who can either grant it or deny it. Your brigade commander or somebody on his staff is listening on that net. If he has some objection to your getting that strike or he has some other comment to make, he comes up on the net and makes it.

Similarly, the division and corps staffs listen in; and, if they don't have something substantive to say, they keep quiet. When he comes down and tells you the time the air strike is coming and what it has, again, these intermediate guys hear all that. If they have something to say, they come up on the net. I established something similar to that system for questions we were constantly getting from Congress and OSD on things going on within AMC—specifically, at the commodity commands.

At AMC Headquarters, we didn't have all the material on hand necessary to answer those questions. Everything you had—if you got it this morning from MICOM, for example—might be outdated. They might have had a missile blow up in the meantime. The information you had this morning is not necessarily current when you get the question in the afternoon. You have to go back to MICOM anyway, so why not have a guy on the Department of the Army staff go directly to the right guy in MICOM and ask the question?

In the meantime, in my headquarters at AMC, somebody is listening to the net, so to speak. We get an information copy of the message that goes down or the Department of the Army staff is required to call over and say they've asked this question. If we have objections or want to add something because we don't think it's a complete question as stated, we come up on the net; if not, we keep quiet. We hear the answer and get a copy simultaneously. Again we review it. If we don't like the answer, we come up and tell the Department of the Army, "Don't take any action now because we are not in agreement with the response. We will get you something more complete immediately and then you can act."

A lot of people felt I was losing control. Well, I had sufficient confidence in my ability to command that I didn't feel I was losing control. If this thing got out of control, I was going to take action. It never did get out of control. There was only one time that it got out of hand. That was when they attempted to re-compete the options for the Dragon missile. In that case, the guys in my MICOM were working directly with the people in the Department of the Army and the defense staff, and instead of informing me of what was going on, they kept quiet.

I'm not sure I accomplished the goal that I set out of becoming a policy-making command, as opposed to a dabbler, but I think we made strides in that. Had I stayed in the job a few more years, maybe we would have gotten the thing solidified and it would have worked better, but I got as far as I could.

16

Retirement

Over the course of time since my retirement, I have tried to stay active in army affairs and help where I can. During the early 1990s, while I was reflecting on my fiftieth class reunion at the military academy, some classmates and I began to develop a mutual concern about the current state of affairs at our alma mater. It was our opinion that West Point was no longer the disciplined institution we had once known and that it was in danger of turning into just another Ivy League college. The military aspects at the academy appeared to be more of a veneer than a way of life. Worse still, the high standards of the honor code seemed to have deteriorated.

These discussions led to a group of retired graduates (Lieutenant General John Norton, class of 1941; Lieutenant General Dick Trefry, 1950; Major General John Carley, 1945; and myself) banding together to prepare a "Report to the Secretary of the Army" on the United States Military Academy at West Point. The report, submitted to the secretary of the army in 2003, required hundreds of hours of work by our group and was a thorough, highly professional document on the state of affairs of the academy at the beginning of the twenty-first century. This report is on file in the libraries of all senior army schools.

Our group continued to work on problems at the academy, updating its findings in the original report to the secretary, and in 2004 published "A Report on the United States Military Academy by Four Concerned Graduates." In September 2004, General Bill Richardson, class of 1951, who had recently joined the group, Norton, Carley, and I briefed the army vice chief of staff and key members of the Army Staff on our report.

After many delays, our group finally succeeded in bringing the problems we found to the attention of the army's senior leadership. The many-faceted message included our concerns that a decline in adherence to the highest standards of the honor system would lead to future ethical problems, and that a continuation of USMA graduate losses of 60 to 70 percent at or before reaching ten years of active service would result in an accumulating leadership deficit in the active army. The work by our group of dedicated graduates was of greater long-term importance than was accorded by the army at the time. The group's work is now being carried forward by General Richardson and two new members, Dr. Bob Sorley, 1956, and General Ed Burba, 1959.

I believe a serious flaw in the recruitment process of West Point is the emphasis on candidates who show marked superiority in the academic field. More important, in my view, are leadership qualities. I have known many brilliant people, both in the army and in business, who simply were not, and never would be, leaders.

I may have a fixation on the subject, but I believe we should be looking for leaders. In the process of identifying potential leaders, I do not believe we will be in danger of rejecting guys who are also brilliant academically—the Ed Rownys, the Andy Goodpasters, the Dodd Starbirds, the Lucius Clays, both Sr. and Jr., the Bill DePuys, and so on. I believe that those who are destined to be leaders are more likely to relish the leadership opportunities and challenges the army can and must offer to retain this type of person. I believe these grads are more likely to have what Ed Burba refers to as "the predilection to stay in the service beyond their mandatory obligation date or, at best, beyond the ten-year mark."

I also believe, based on the study done at Leavenworth at the direction of Ric Shinseki, which revealed flaws in senior leadership as seen by young officers participating in the study, that we have to get away from the zero-defect attitude. People are going to make mistakes. To the extent possible, these mistakes should be used as teaching points, not as career-ending events. Today, army officers seem to couch their thoughts in terms that are ambiguous, terms that give them an escape route if their views are challenged or proven wrong. Cut them some slack. Make them step up to their responsibilities.

After World War II, I found so many officers who didn't believe their subordinates could handle their jobs. Usually these were officers at the battalion commander level or above. They became company commanders, in effect, because they spent their time micro-managing their company commanders. Thus, company commanders were denied the "growth experience" of commanding, making mistakes, and learning. I fought this attitude in my outfits. I wanted squad leaders to be squad leaders, platoon sergeants to be platoon sergeants, platoon leaders to be platoon leaders, and so on. These guys had to be given the responsibility and the loose reins that would let them do their job, learn their job, excel in their job.

When you take away from the junior officers, the young West Point grads the initiative, the opportunity to excel, the responsibility of which to be proud, you destroy the joy they experience at the end of a day well done. Even I, a dyed-in-the-wool "lifer," would say screw it, under these circumstances.

I guess what I am getting to is that our army leadership has to take steps to change the culture that I am afraid exists today. When I was an infantry battalion commander in combat at age twenty-five, I made mistakes, but my regimental commander, Colonel John Cochran, and my division commander, Major General Terry Allen, would pat me on the back and say, "You're the greatest," or words to that effect. They didn't start micro-managing my battalion. I felt great every day. Every day was a challenge that enchanted me. I wanted to go out and conquer the world. That kind of leadership made me love the army even more. I am sure that kind of leadership would do a lot toward improving retention. Here, I agree totally with Ed Burba's contention that "there is something wrong with the nurturing. Our graduates don't feel they are the special breed that is bonded to long-time service in our army."

I also believe there has been an effort over time to eliminate the cost of the United States Military Academy from the budget regardless of the cost in lives, effectiveness in combat, and all the leadership intangibles that accrue from the training one undergoes at West Point, or for that matter, at VMI, the Citadel, and other similar institutions.

It is my firm conviction—derived from forty years of observation, not arrogance—that the average West Point graduate is a cut above the average graduate of the "independent military schools." This is not surprising. The majority of applicants to West Point apply not just to get an education but to serve the nation as an officer. I believe this holds true to a lesser extent with applicants to the independent military schools.

There are notable exceptions: Marshall of VMI, the builder of the Infantry School, the molder of our World War II army, a great soldier and statesman, one of the great Americans of the twentieth century; Terry Allen, my division commander in World War II, a superb leader whose qualities of leadership on the battlefield knew no bounds, a man who failed to graduate from West Point; Jim Hollingsworth of Texas A&M, another superb battlefield commander about whom our revered Creighton Abrams once said to me, "Men like Holly are indispensable in war," a leader whom I personally observed in combat; and Bill Hartzog of the Citadel, one of our most important four-star commanders, who had a large part in shaping the future of the army in terms of organization, doctrine, and training.

I am equally convinced the average graduate of the independent military schools is a cut above the average graduate of the ROTC program at other colleges and universities. Here again, there are notable exceptions: Fred Weyand, a former chief of staff; Colin Powell, a former chairman of the Joint Chiefs of Staff; and Bill Rosson, among others.

Please note, lest I antagonize or infuriate anyone, that I am speaking of graduates as a whole. There are poor leaders who come out of West Point, just as is the case with independent military schools and other institutions of higher learning. There are also great leaders.

The products described by my convictions stem in large measure from the differing levels of immersion in the varying degrees of Spartan, often harsh, military atmosphere found at the several types of college-level institutions. The student learns to cope, he learns to take orders and follow them without question, he learns to make decisions under extreme pressure, he learns to keep the mission foremost in his mind despite the distractions of his environment, and he learns to deal with adversity and to press on to his objective.

The tougher the training, the more trying the environment, the stronger a leader he is likely to become. I recall an outstanding officer who was a battalion commander in World War II, a Distinguished Military Graduate of the ROTC program at a major university. In the first battle in which his battalion became involved, the German artillery fire, the noise, the confusion were all more than he could take. He broke down and cried like a frightened child. I know. I was there. I guess I should have said, "Outstanding, except for one minor deficiency." He had not been morally and mentally hardened.

In this day and age, when it seems to be the fashion to reduce everything to a common denominator, which portends reducing quality to the *lowest* common denominator, we must fight to retain the quality of the force. We must insist on taking the best qualified, the best trained, and the most capable people available to lead our young soldiers. To do less would be criminal.

We must not rationalize. Statements like, "The Army says it is only seeking to be fair" make me retch. People who say things like this will probably never be faced with leading soldiers on the battlefield, and probably never have been. I would really like to know who made the statement, if accurately quoted, "I view this as an equity thing, and I don't view it as disadvantaging anyone." The only person disadvantaged, and apparently forgotten by the speaker, is the young soldier who may have to put his life in the hands of a nondisadvantaged, but somewhat incompetent, leader like my World War II colleague.

If the army buys into the arguments of equality and being fair, if it accepts the argument that the product of college ROTC is, on the whole, as good as the product of the independent military schools, then one must look at whether the product of West Point is any better than that of either of these other two types of institutions. It will be hard to make the case that it is or, if so, that it is sufficiently superior to warrant the expenditure of federal funds, my tax dollars and yours, to acquire this product. There goes West Point, perhaps the independent military colleges, and certainly the quality of the force that has made ours the most outstanding army in the world.

Looking back over my time in the army, I often think about one of my best friends, Hank Emerson. He was one of the greatest leaders I encountered during my career. He often told me that the modus operandi that I adopted in my relationship with my soldiers was the model on which he later based his. We speak on the phone frequently, and in October 2012, I was his guest at West Point. He was asked by the Army football coach to address the Army football team the day before the Army-Boston College game. He requested tickets for the game and we were seated in the superintendent's box in the stadium.

He wanted me to also speak to the team, but I declined. My voice is now so soft and quiet that no one in a group of more than four or five can hear me if there is no loudspeaker system. I did speak briefly with each member of the team after Hank spoke to them, telling them I was the greatest combat leader to graduate since MacArthur.

They won the next day in heroic manner. With about two minutes left in the game, Army was behind by four points. They were on the one-yard line, fourth down. They could not push it in. It looked like the game was over, but they fought even harder. They held Boston to three and out, got the ball back at midfield with just over a minute to play. They drove down the field and the quarterback, Steelman, then broke loose for twenty-nine yards and the winning touchdown. I don't know whether it was Hank's talk, but I cannot remember a more inspired performance in the face of overwhelming odds than that of the Army team that day.

Another great lifelong friend, Hugh Carey, and I met in the summer of 1942 when we both joined Headquarters and Headquarters Company, 3rd Battalion, 415th Infantry Regiment at Camp Adair near Corvallis, Oregon. At the time, we were both newly commissioned second lieutenants of the infantry. Shortly after joining the division, I was transferred to the Anti-Tank Company of the regiment and did not have close contact with him until the summer of 1943 when, as newly promoted captains, we were sent to the Advanced Infantry Officers Course at the Infantry School at Fort Benning, Georgia. I had an automobile at the time, so Hugh and I drove to Fort Benning in my car over a period of several days, during which time our strong friendship was born—a friendship that lasted the rest of our lives.

It was at Fort Benning that I first saw Hugh's great intellect and tactical vision. He stood out in our class of a hundred or so students, most of whom were older and more experienced than we. His responses to answers in our various classes were clear, concise, loaded with wisdom, and indicative of the notable future he was to enjoy throughout his life.

When we returned to the regiment, Hugh was assigned to the regimental staff as the S-3 (operations officer). I was assigned as the regimental S-2 (intelligence officer). In these positions, we worked hand in glove. His tactical concept of each of the regiments' operations dictated the specific intelligence needed to ensure success. My job was to see that we acquired the necessary intelligence to permit the regimental commander to assess the situation and judge the adequacy of Hugh's proposed plans to accomplish the mission assigned to the regiment at the moment.

Hugh and I were very close, both as friends and as colleagues, while we served on the regimental staff. We were in constant communication, discussing the operations of the moment as well as those we could foresee. When I slept, he took care of my duties and responsibilities; when he slept, I took care of his. My admiration and respect for this singular individual never ceased to grow.

It was obvious right from the start that the regimental commander was greatly impressed with Hugh's vision and analytical thought. He had complete confidence in Hugh and leaned upon him heavily in making his decisions. Over the course of our operations in Europe during World War II, mostly in Germany, it was clear that the division commander had unbounded confidence in our regiment. He consistently assigned us important and difficult missions. Without question, this confidence was the direct result of the competence of our regimental commander and the brilliance of Hugh Carey.

After the war, Hugh returned to civilian life, participated in his family's business, became a lawyer, and entered politics. He enjoyed success as a respected and outstanding member of the US House of Representatives, where he served seven terms. This success led to his running for election as the governor of New York. He served two terms as governor and is credited with having saved New York City, and thus the whole state, from financial collapse in 1975. During this period, I saw him from time to time in Washington, and we corresponded with each other. The final resurgence of our friendship came with his cardiac bypass surgery. He called me shortly after his operation, and I sensed his need for support from a fellow warrior, from a comrade whose friendship had been forged in the bonds that bind men sharing the dangers of combat. I wrote him immediately, and we had many telephone conversations and exchanges of letters in the weeks and months before his death on August 7, 2011.

As he wrote me in his final days, "General, in my life's travels, I have met many great leaders, but few have bonded in friendship and given me as much courage as you have." These are words that I shall never forget—words that I cherish because they come from a great man, a humble soldier, and a superb leader: my friend, Governor Hugh Carey.

I am now enjoying my retirement in our home on the coast of Maine, and I look forward to participating as a veteran and a member of the Greatest Generation in our annual Gouldsboro Memorial Day Parade. Along with some of the older fellows, I ride on a flatbed trailer float with folding chairs and a hand rail, draped in red, white, and blue bunting. It is drawn by one of the Gouldsboro fire engines. With impenetrable security measures, it is led by the local constable in his cruiser and trailed by Cub Scout Pack 101.

We start off at Fisher Field and go down Route 186 to the town offices in Prospect Harbor, one of the several little villages that make up Gouldsboro. The route is lined with adults, children, and excited barking dogs. Everyone waves, and the little kids are wide-eyed as they look on in wonderment. There are patriotic songs and speeches, followed by cake, ice cream, and coffee. The whole thing is vintage Norman Rockwell, and it makes your heart swell with pride and a tear comes to your eye as you witness the sincere patriotism of the people in our small town.

In December 2011, Jack Deane was diagnosed with melanoma. The surgeons operated, but the original spot had not healed as expected and more surgery was required in March 2012. His condition appeared stable until April 2013, when a series of unshakeable headaches sent Jack to his doctor and a brain scan revealed several tumors. Surgery for the largest tumor was followed by treatment. He faced this last battle with the same bravery, dignity, and determination he had displayed in the military encounters of his past. Jack was still handling his daily chores plus all finances up until two days before he died on July 18, 2013.

Appendix

General John R. Deane Jr.'s Service Career

Military Schools Attended

Infantry School, Basic Course, 1942
Infantry School, Advanced Course, 1943
Intelligence School, 1944
United States Army Command and General Staff College, 1953
Armed Forces Staff College, 1953
National War College, 1959
Harvard University, National Security Fellows Program, 1963

Educational Degrees

United States Military Academy: BS, military engineering, 1942
George Washington University: MBA, business administration, 1964

List of Promotions	Temporary	Permanent
Second Lieutenant	May 29, 1942	May 29, 1942
First Lieutenant	Nov 19, 1942	May 29, 1945
Captain	Jul 14, 1943	Jul 1, 1948
Major	May 22, 1944	Jul 6, 1954
Lieutenant Colonel	Apr 12, 1945	May 29, 1962
Colonel	Dec 6, 1955	May 29, 1967
Brigadier General	Aug 1, 1965	Nov 20, 1968
Major General	Nov 1, 1967	Jun 12, 1970
Lieutenant General	Sep 22, 1972	
General	Feb 12, 1975	

Decorations and Badges

Distinguished Service Cross (with Oak Leaf Cluster)
Distinguished Service Medal (with 2 Oak Leaf Clusters)
Silver Star (with 2 Oak Leaf Clusters)
Legion of Merit (with 3 Oak Leaf Clusters)
Distinguished Flying Cross
Purple Heart
Bronze Star (with Oak Leaf Cluster)
Air Medal (with V Device and the numeral 27)
Joint Service Commendation Medal (with Oak Leaf Cluster)
Army Commendation Medal
American Campaign Medal
European–African–Middle Eastern Campaign Medal (with 3 Bronze
    Service Stars)
World War II Victory Medal
Army of Occupation Medal (with Germany Clasp)
National Defense Service Medal (with Bronze Service Star)
Korean Service Medal
Armed Forces Expeditionary Medal (with Bronze Service Star)
Vietnam Service Medal (with 3 Bronze Service Stars and Bronze
    Arrowhead)
Korean Defense Service Medal
Meritorious Unit Commendation (with 2 Bronze Oak Leaf Clusters)
Combat Infantry Badge
Master Parachutist Badge
Army Aviator Badge
Office of the Secretary of Defense Identification Badge
Army Staff Identification Badge
Republic of Vietnam Parachutist Badge
Republic of Korea Parachutist Badge
Republic of Vietnam National Legion of Honor (5th Class)
Republic of Vietnam Gallantry Cross (with Palm Device)
Republic of Vietnam Gallantry Cross (with Gold Star)
Republic of Vietnam Medal of Honor
United Nations Service Medal
Republic of Vietnam Campaign Medal (with 60 Device)
Republic of Korea–Korean War Service Medal
Republic of Korea Presidential Unit Citation
Republic of Vietnam Gallantry Cross Unit Citation (with Palm Device)

List of Assignments

List of Assignments	From	To
Student, Officer Basic Course, Ft. Benning, GA	May 29, 1942	Sep 19, 1942
Anti-tank Platoon Leader, Executive Officer and Company Commander, 415th Infantry Regiment, Camp Adair, OR	Sep 20, 1942	Jun 30, 1943
Student, Officer Advanced Course, Ft. Benning, GA	Jul 1, 1943	Oct 12, 1943
Regimental S2, 415th Infantry Regiment, Camp Carson, CO	Oct 13, 1943	May 25, 1944
Student, Intelligence School, Camp Ritchie, MD	May 26, 1944	Jun 30, 1944
Regimental S2 and Battalion Commander, 415th Infantry Regiment, Camp Carson, CO; ETO; and San Luis Obispo, CA	Jul 1, 1944	Nov 16, 1945
Intelligence Staff Officer, G2 Intel Center USFET & EUCOM	Nov 17, 1945	Oct 9, 1947
Staff Officer, Special Operations Officer, and Operations Officer, General Staff, Washington, DC	Oct 10, 1947	Feb 4, 1951
Executive Assistant to the Secretary of the Army	Feb 5, 1951	Aug 20, 1952
Student, Command & General Staff College, Ft. Leavenworth, KS	Aug 21, 1952	Aug 24, 1953
Operations Officer, UNCMAC Far East Command (FEC)	Aug 25, 1953	Apr 10, 1954
Battalion Commander and Regimental Executive Officer, 17th Infantry, FEC	Apr 11, 1954	Sep 12, 1954
Operations and Training Officer, J3 Division, FEC	Sep 13, 1954	Jan 29, 1955
Student, Armed Forces Staff College, Norfolk, VA	Jan 30, 1955	Jun 30, 1955
Staff Officer, Washington, DC	Jul 1, 1955	Jul 27, 1958
Student, National War College, Ft. McNair, Washington, DC	Jul 28, 1958	Jul 9, 1959

Staff Officer and Assistant Chief of Staff for Programming and Analysis, Headquarters, USAREUR	Aug 6, 1959	Feb 23, 1961
Battle Group Commander, 2nd Battle Group, 6th Infantry, USAREUR	Feb 24, 1961	Jun 7, 1962
Military Assistant, Office of Deputy Director R&E and Executive Assistant to Assistant Secretary of Defense, Washington, DC	Jul 9, 1962	Jun 29, 1965
Assistant Division Commander for Operations, 82nd Airborne Division, Ft. Bragg, NC	Jul 1965	Jan 1966
Chief of Staff, Field Force I, US Army, Vietnam (USARV)	Feb 1966	Jul 1966
Assistant Division Commander, 1st Infantry Division, USARV	Jul 1966	Dec 1966
Commanding General, 173rd Airborne Brigade, USARV	Dec 1966	Sep 1967
Director of Doctrine and Systems, Office of the Assistant Chief of Staff for Force Development, Washington, DC	Oct 1967	Oct 1968
Commanding General, 82nd Airborne Division, Ft. Bragg, NC	Oct 1968	Jul 1970
Director, Defense Communications–Planning Group, Washington, DC	Jul 1970	Mar 1971
Director, Defense Special Projects Group, Washington, DC	Apr 1971	Jun 1972
Deputy Director, Defense Intelligence Agency, Washington, DC	Aug 1972	Jul 1973
Deputy Assistant Chief of Staff for Research, Development, and Acquisition, US Army, Washington, DC	Aug 1973	Feb 1975
Commanding General, US Army Materiel Development and Readiness Command, Alexandria, VA	Feb 1975	Feb 1977

Notes

Foreword

1. *Oral History of Lieutenant General Henry E. Emerson* (US Army Military History Institute, 2004), 88.
2. Interview with Major General John R. Deane by Forrest C. Pogue, October 31, 1960, tape 58, copy 2, p. 1, George C. Marshall Foundation, Lexington, Virginia.
3. Ibid., p. 5. During his interview, Deane relates an interesting story regarding the War Department notification of the attack on Pearl Harbor. Deane happened to be alone in General Marshall's office when a navy enlisted man rushed in with a piece of paper that read, "Pearl Harbor being attacked. This is no drill." General Marshall arrived shortly thereafter, and as the two men discussed what needed to be done next, the president called in on one of a battery of telephones alongside Marshall's desk. As Marshall and the president spoke, the telephone next in line rang, and Deane picked up the call. After taking a message, he accidentally hung the phone up on the receiver Marshall was using, cutting off his call with the president. Fortunately, they were reconnected quickly and everything worked out all right. Deane sheepishly described the incident as "my first official act of the war."
4. Brigadier General John Deane to his parents, January 26, 1943, Casablanca, Morocco.
5. Email correspondence between General John R. Deane Jr. and the editor, November 10, 2011.
6. Email correspondence between Lieutenant General Edward Rowny and the editor, June 5, 2012.
7. Email correspondence between Deane and the editor, November 10, 2011.

1. Growing Up as an Army Brat

1. Carl Fritzsche, from Cleveland, Ohio, was a graduate of West Point, class of 1928. After service in China in 1932–1935, he returned to West Point as an instructor for four years and then attended the Command and General Staff College. Following Pearl Harbor, he was assigned as intelligence chief to the 1st Armored Division, serving in the European theater. After the war, he became deputy chief of army intelligence in Europe. In 1949, Fritzsche was assigned to the Army War College, where he became chairman of the National Policy Group.

He went to Korea in 1952 as assistant division commander of the 25th Division, and served successively as chief of the Korea Military Advisory Group and chief of staff of the 5th Army. While serving as the commanding general of Fort Ord, Major General Fritzsche was traveling on an army plane carrying six persons when it crashed in the fog at Orinda Hills, California, killing all aboard on September 30, 1960.

2. Email correspondence between Kathy Crittenberger, daughter of Major General Willis D. Crittenberger Jr., and the editor, March 14, 2013.

3. Ibid.

4. Dudley G. Strickler, from Middletown, Indiana, was a graduate of West Point, class of 1927. At the start of World War II, Major Strickler served as commander of the 3rd Battalion, 45th Infantry Regiment, Philippine Scouts. His executive officer would later report, "Major Strickler was solely responsible for the enviable record of the 3rd Battalion, 45th Infantry Regiment. At every point where the battalion was committed, it met an enemy that was superior in numbers, equipment and supporting arms. Despite that disadvantage, his aggressive spirit carried us through to accomplish whatever mission we were charged with. All of the men who were near him until his luck ran out believe this." At daylight on February 1, 1942, in an effort to reduce the enemy beachhead established at Quinauan Point, an infantry attack was launched. The two center companies moved in quickly, but were halted after only a short distance. Major Strickler then went forward of the front lines alone to make a reconnaissance. In spite of active enemy snipers, Major Strickler persisted in moving about in the forward companies, shouting encouragement, giving personal directions and assistance, and by his courageous example motivating his men to a high degree of effort. His consistent and gallant concern for the welfare of the troops, transcending any consideration for personal safety, was a prime factor in the high morale and efficiency of his command, in spite of material battle losses. Just before clearing Quinauan Point, Major Strickler was killed by a bullet that penetrated his brain. He was awarded two Distinguished Service Crosses, a Bronze Star, and a Purple Heart for his service to his country.

5. George S. Brown, from Montclair, New Jersey, graduated from West Point in 1941. He joined the Army Air Corps and became a B-24 pilot in the 93rd Bombardment Group. In 1943, as executive officer, he took over and led the group after his commander was shot down during the Ploesti raid and was awarded the Distinguished Service Cross. President Nixon appointed him chairman of the Joint Chiefs of Staff on August 1, 1973. Brown was diagnosed with prostate cancer and retired due to ill health on June 21, 1978. He died on December 5, 1978.

6. Edward H. deSaussure Jr., from El Paso, Texas, graduated from West Point in 1941. He served in the Pacific theater during World War II in the 4th Field Artillery Battalion. In 1946, he served as aide to General Jacob Devers when he commanded army ground forces. He later served in Vietnam as assistant division commander of the 25th Infantry Division, commander of the 196th Infantry

Brigade, commander of the 1st Field Force Artillery, and assistant division commander of the 1st Cavalry Division (Airmobile). He commanded White Sands Missile Range before retiring in 1972. He passed away in Ponte Vedra, Florida, on July 11, 2002.

7. General Lucius Dubignon Clay (April 23, 1897–April 16, 1978) was an American officer and military governor of Germany after World War II. The son of a US senator and the father of two general officers in the army and air force, he acquired a reputation for being an exceptionally hard and disciplined worker, going long hours and even refusing to stop to eat during his workdays. Clay orchestrated the Berlin Airlift (1948–1949) when the USSR blockaded West Berlin. He retired in 1949.

8. Major General John D. Crowley Jr. was born in Boston in 1916 and enlisted in the army in 1934. He served in the 5th Infantry before winning an appointment to West Point, where he graduated in 1942 as the last man in his class. During World War II, he rose from second lieutenant to lieutenant colonel in less than three years while he commanded units in the 1st Filipino Infantry, the 2nd Armored Corps, and the 101st Airborne Division. He led reconnaissance teams in the Battle of the Bulge and a secret mission behind the lines in Germany that hastened the collapse of the Ruhr Pocket. He transferred from infantry to the Transportation Corps in 1952 and was promoted to brigadier general in 1963. This earned him, the last man in his class at West Point, the distinction of becoming the first one of his class to reach the rank of general. He passed away in San Francisco on July 25, 2004.

9. Lieutenant General Thomas Rienzi was born in Philadelphia and attended Lehigh University before graduating from West Point in 1942. He served as a company commander with the 96th Signal Battalion in China, Burma, and India during World War II. After the war, he was assigned to Sandia Base, New Mexico, working on atomic weapons planning and implementation. In 1966, he was promoted to brigadier general and assigned as commanding general to the Signal Center and Fort Monmouth. In 1970, he assumed command of the Strategic Communications Command Pacific. He retired from the army in 1977 as a lieutenant general assigned to NATO. Upon his retirement, Rienzi became an ordained deacon and served the Catholic Diocese of Hawaii, which included the hospital ministry at Tripler Army Hospital. He passed away in Hawaii on December 15, 2010.

10. Major General Robert D. Terry (September 4, 1920–July 13, 2006) was born in Indianapolis and graduated from West Point in 1942. During World War II, he served as a signal officer with the 6th and 13th Armored Divisions in Europe and the Philippines. He was later a communications officer during US operations in the Dominican Republic in the 1960s. He commanded the 1st Signal Brigade in Vietnam. He retired from the army in 1975 as vice director of the Defense Communications Agency.

11. Major General Daniel A. Raymond (December 1, 1917–May 12, 2010),

from Philadelphia, graduated from West Point in 1942. During World War II, he served in the 10th Engineer Combat Battalion, 3rd Infantry Division, in positions from platoon leader to battalion executive officer. Intermittently he served in the Amphibious Force of the Atlantic Fleet, participating in four D-Days in North Africa, Sicily, Salerno, and southern France. He commanded the 13th Engineer Combat Battalion in Korea and later earned a master's degree in civil engineering from Harvard University. During the Vietnam War, he served as theater engineer for the Military Assistance Command, Vietnam, followed by a three-year assignment working for the Marshall Space Flight Center testing rockets for the Apollo moon program. He retired from the army in 1975 and took a position with the World Bank. Among his awards for his army career were three Distinguished Service Medals, two Legions of Merit, two Bronze Stars for valor, and the Purple Heart.

12. Major General Willis D. Crittenberger Jr. graduated from the United States Military Academy in 1942. As an artillery officer, he served with the 10th Armored Division in World War II, rising to lieutenant colonel by the end of the war. During the Vietnam campaign, he was assigned as the military assistant to the deputy US ambassador and later as the commanding general, II Field Force Artillery. He retired as a major general, chief of staff, and deputy director for Defense Attaché Systems, Defense Intelligence Agency in 1978, and later served as a spokesman for the Daughters of the American Revolution. He resided in Washington, DC, until his passing on August 26, 2014 at ninety-five years of age.

Lieutenant General Willis D. Crittenberger (December 2, 1890–August 4, 1980) graduated from West Point in 1913. He served as the commander of the IV Corps after the liberation of Rome during the Italian campaign from 1944 to the end of the war. He went on to command the Caribbean Defense Command, the predecessor to United States Southern Command. He retired in December 1952. All three of his sons served in the army. Two were killed in combat: Corporal Townsend W. Crittenberger during the Rhine River crossing on March 25, 1945, and Colonel Dale J. Crittenberger during a midair helicopter collision directing combat operations in Vietnam on September 17, 1969.

13. Seventy members (19 percent) of the 374 officers who made up the graduating class of 1942 were killed in action during World War II.

2. Terry Allen and the 104th Infantry Division

1. Bryant Edward Moore (June 6, 1894–February 24, 1951) was born in Ellsworth, Maine, and graduated from West Point in 1917. During the early days of World War II, Colonel Moore commanded the 164th Infantry Regiment on Guadalcanal. After promotion to general officer's rank, he was assigned as assistant division commander with the 104th Infantry Division. He was subsequently promoted to major general and assigned the command of the 8th Infantry Division. During the Korean War, he commanded the IX Corps under General Ridg-

way. On February 24, 1951, during combat operations, his helicopter failed and crashed into the icy Han River. General Moore died a few hours later of an apparent heart attack, after having gotten help for the surviving pilot and crew members of the crash.

2. General Albert C. Wedemeyer (July 9, 1897–December 17, 1989) was born in Omaha, Nebraska, and graduated from West Point in 1919. Wedemeyer remained a lieutenant for almost seventeen years. After returning from a two-year assignment in Germany in 1938, Lieutenant Colonel Wedemeyer analyzed German Army tactical developments in the War Plans Division and became the chief author of the 1941 Victory Program, which advocated the defeat of German forces in Europe as the prime objective for the United States. He replaced General Stillwell as the China-Burma-India theater commander in 1944. After the war he was assigned as the army chief of plans and operations. During the Cold War, Wedemeyer was a chief supporter of the Berlin Airlift. He retired from the army in 1951.

3. Colonel John Hamilton Cochran was born August 13, 1893, in Chicago. His early schooling took place in Michigan and he graduated from Hartford High School in 1912. He received a degree in mechanical engineering from the University of Michigan in 1916. Cochran received a second lieutenant commission on August 15, 1917, and saw active service in France. He found the army much to his liking and made it his career.

He completed the company commander's course at Fort Benning, Georgia, in 1922–1923, and served in the Philippines from 1924 to 1925. In 1936–1937 he attended the Command and General Staff College and was promoted to colonel on January 1, 1941. In August 1942 he was appointed as commanding officer, 415th Infantry Regiment. During his service with the 104th Division, Cochran was awarded the Silver Star, Bronze Star with oak leaf cluster, and the Legion of Merit.

4. General Order #19, November 28, 1944, 104th Infantry Division.

5. "History of the 415th Infantry Regiment of the 104th Infantry Division" (unpublished MS, 1945), 111.

6. Major General Terry Allen's leadership success was summarized by a family member: "He was a remarkable man. He wore his accomplishments and greatness with humility. He possessed an amazing freedom which enabled him to be himself among the great and not so great. He was so secure in himself that he could be authentic and genuine, more than anyone I ever met. There was nothing fake about him; he didn't know how to pretend."

Allen was a proven fighter who could lead by example. During World War I, while in command of the 3rd Battalion, 358th Infantry, 90th Division, he was wounded by shell fire just before his unit jumped off in an attack west of Fey-en-Haye on September 13, 1918. He was knocked unconscious and slightly wounded from an artillery burst. He was carried to a dressing station and tagged for evacuation to the rear. On regaining consciousness, he left the dressing station, still dazed and weak, and followed his battalion forward. En route he organized stragglers and loose individuals, led them forward, and engaged enemy machine gun nests that were holding up the advance of the 2nd and 3rd Battalions, 358th Infantry. He engaged these machine gun nests with his detachment in hand-to-hand fighting and knocked them out. At one stage he used his fists in the fighting, so closely were they engaged. "I happened to swing and catch a Boche Noncom on the jaw," remembered Allen. The removal of these nests aided materially in the advance of the 358th Infantry. Major Allen was shot in the jaw during this fighting and was evacuated to a field hospital in the afternoon, before he could reach his own command post. "Our ammunition ran a little low and we took one strongpoint with fists and clubs. My only regret is that a couple of my dearly cherished back teeth were knocked out by a machine gun bullet," recalled Allen. He spent two weeks in the hospital before rejoining his battalion, which he continued to lead until the Armistice.

General George Marshall had his eye on Allen, whom he had met at Fort Benning. Marshall noted, "Terry Allen is one of a very few who are of that unusual type who enthuse all of their subordinates to carry through almost impossible tasks. He can do anything with men and officers, though unprepossessing in appearance and apparently casual in manner." Gerald Astor, *Terrible Terry Allen: Combat General of World War II—The Life of an American Soldier* (Presidio, 2003), 41–42, 87, 340.

Deane described him simply as "one of the greatest leaders I have ever known."

7. Email from General John R. Deane Jr. to the editor, February 10, 2013.

8. Thomas E. Ricks, *The Generals: American Military Command from World War II to Today* (New York: Penguin, 2012), 79.

9. "History of the 415th Infantry Regiment of the 104th Infantry Division," 111.

10. Gerald C. Kelleher was born in Albany, New York, on July 8, 1908, and died at age ninety-five in Port Orange, Florida, on November 23, 2003. He learned his trade as a battalion commander of the 1st/26th Infantry Regiment, serving under Terry Allen through the entire 1st Infantry Division North African campaign. Kelleher was initially captured by the Germans after his command post was overrun at Kasserine Pass. He later escaped and made his way back to American lines. He followed his division commander to the 104th Infantry Division, where he ended up commanding the 414th Infantry Regiment and earning the Distinguished Service Cross. He later commanded the 35th Infantry Regiment during the Korean War and was awarded a second DSC. He also served as a brigadier general on the army staff in Vietnam. In addition to his two DSCs, Brigadier General Kelleher was awarded seven Silver Stars, a Bronze Star with Valor Device, and a Purple Heart.

11. Deane learned later that he had been nominated for the Distinguished Service Cross for his actions at Liesen on March 31, 1945. The award nomination

was either not acted on or lost in the flurry of events following Germany's surrender and rapid transfer of 104th Division senior leadership at the end of the war.

12. Lieutenant General Fritz Bayerlein (January 14, 1899–January 30, 1970) served as an enlisted soldier and was wounded during World War I. After the war he remained in the army and was commissioned an officer, rising to major prior to World War II. He served on Guderian's staff during the invasions of Poland and France. After serving in Russia, he was transferred to the Afrika Korps as chief of staff, taking command on several occasions after his division commander, Major General Nehring, was incapacitated and Major General Von Thoma was captured.

Bayerlein developed muscular rheumatism and hepatitis and was evacuated before Tunisia fell. Upon his recovery, he served again on the Russian front and was assigned to command the Panzer Lehr Division, which was transferred to France in 1944. He spent the rest of the war fighting the Americans and British in Normandy, across France, Belgium, and Germany. He ended the war as a corps commander when he surrendered to the 7th Armored Division on April 19, 1945. Bayerlein was a prisoner of war from 1945 to 1947. While in captivity, he wrote the European battle histories for the US Army Historical Division. He was released on April 2, 1947.

3. Operation RUSTY

1. Major General Reinhard Gehlen (April 3, 1902–June 8, 1979) served as the chief of the German Army military intelligence unit on the eastern front. He was involved in a minor role of the bomb plot to assassinate Hitler on July 20, 1944, but his participation was not uncovered after the failed attempt. His unit's discouraging assessments in reporting led to his dismissal by Hitler in April 1945. Gehlen's vast store of knowledge made him very valuable to the Allies after the end of the war. His organization was eventually compromised by East Germany, and in 1956, the unit was turned over to the Federal Republic of Germany. Gehlen served as the first president of the Federal Intelligence Service. He retired from government service in 1968. He is considered one of the most legendary Cold War spymasters.

2. Mary Ellen Reese, *General Reinhard Gehlen: The CIA Connection* (Fairfax, VA: George Mason University Press, 1990), 73.

3. "Debriefing of Eric Waldman on the US Army's Trusteeship of the Gehlen Organization during the Years 1945–1949," September 30, 1969, in *Forging an Intelligence Partnership: CIA and the Origins of the BND, 1945–49; A Documentary History* (CIA History Staff, Center for the Study of Intelligence, European Division, 1999).

4. Reinhard Gehlen, *The Service: The Memoirs of General Reinhard Gehlen* (New York: World Publishing, 1972), 132.

5. "Debriefing of Eric Waldman."

6. Reese, *General Reinhard Gehlen*, 73.

7. Ibid.

8. General Drastamat Kanayan (May 31, 1884–March 8, 1956) was an Armenian nationalist known as General Dro. He fought in World War I as a battalion commander in the Russian Caucasus Army and was seriously wounded. He served as the defense minister of the short-lived Democratic Republic of Armenia from 1918 to 1920. After Armenia was absorbed into the Soviet Union in 1920, Kanayan immigrated to Iran, and later Germany. He sided with Nazi Germany in the hopes of establishing a free Armenia with the defeat of the Soviet Union. After World War II, Kanayan was arrested by American forces but soon released. He settled in Lebanon and died while in the United States for medical treatment in 1956.

9. Reese, *General Reinhard Gehlen*, 85.

10. *Forging an Intelligence Partnership*, xviii.

11. Major General Edwin L. Sibert was born in Arkansas in 1897 and graduated from the US Military Academy in 1918. He was commissioned in the field artillery and served as the military attaché in Brazil in 1940. During the war, Sibert commanded the 99th Infantry Division artillery in 1942–1943. He later served as G2 of the 12th Army Group in 1944–1945 and then as the G2, USFET, until 1946. Sibert was assigned as the assistant director for operations in the Central Intelligence Group in September 1946, a position that he held until mid-1948. After his return to the army from the CIA, Sibert served as the chief of staff of the Far East Command in Japan and later as commanding general of Camp Edwards in 1952. Promoted to major general in 1953, Sibert retired the following year to Martha's Vineyard, Massachusetts, where he remained active in the community until his death on December 16, 1977.

12. Major General Robert A. Schow, born in New Jersey in 1898, graduated from the US Military Academy in 1918. Commissioned as an infantry officer, Schow was assistant military attaché to France and then served on the staff of the Supreme Headquarters, Allied Expeditionary Force, in 1944–1945. He later served as G2 for the 15th Army from 1945–1946 and remained in Germany until his assignment to the CIA as assistant director for special operations (ADSO) in March 1949. Schow remained as ADSO until February 1951, during which time he was promoted to brigadier general. In 1951, Schow was promoted to major general and assigned to G2, Supreme Headquarters, Allied Powers, Europe. He returned to Washington, DC, in 1954 and served as deputy assistant chief for intelligence from 1956 to 1958. He retired in 1958 and died in April 1991.

13. General Hoyt S. Vandenberg (January 24, 1899–April 2, 1954) was the second chief of staff of the air force and the second director of the Central Intelligence Agency. He graduated from the US Military Academy in 1923 and became a pilot in the Army Air Corps. Vandenberg was instrumental in building up the Army Air Corps in Europe in World War II. He organized the 12th Air Force and flew missions in North Africa, Sicily, and Italy. He later commanded the 9th Air

Force in northern Europe. In 1946 he became director of intelligence on the War Department general staff until his appointment as director of the CIA in June. He returned to active duty in 1948 to become the second chief of staff of the air force. He retired in 1953 and died the following year of prostate cancer at age fifty-five.

14. Samuel B. Bossard was born in Pennsylvania in 1912 and graduated from Princeton University in 1933 and Columbia University in 1938. He studied in Germany during the 1930s and was a professor of German. During the war, Bossard served as an enlisted man and officer in the OSS, where he was assigned to X-2. He remained as a liaison officer with CIG and CIA and handled the Gehlen Organization at CIA headquarters. Bossard resigned from the agency in 1950. He died in 1996.

15. Hanna Reitsch (March 29, 1912–August 24, 1979) was a German aviator and the only woman to be awarded the Iron Cross First Class and the Luftwaffe Combined Pilots–Observation Badge in Gold with Diamonds during World War II. She set over forty aviation altitude and endurance records during her career. She was the first female helicopter pilot and was a test pilot for the Ju 87 Stuka and Dornier Do 17 projects. Reitsch recalled that during the war all other test pilots had been killed or gravely injured attempting to land a piloted version of the V-1 rocket. She volunteered for the mission and discovered the rocket's extremely high stall speed was thwarting the pilots, who had no experience landing at such high speeds. Reitsch's background with the very fast and dangerous ME 163 jet fighter led her to a successful landing of the V-1 rocket in 1944. She became close to General Robert Ritter von Greim and flew with him to Berlin as the Russians were closing in on Hitler's headquarters. They were in the last plane to leave Berlin on April 28, 1945, and were captured by the Americans at the end of the war. She continued to fly after the war and set several gliding records as late as 1979, when she died—according to rumor by the cyanide pill that Hitler had given her during her last visit to his bunker. She had never married.

16. Field Marshal Robert Ritter von Greim (June 22, 1892–May 24, 1945) was the last commander of the German Air Force during World War II. He entered World War I as an artillery officer, but transferred to the Air Service and became a pilot in 1915. By the end of the war he had scored twenty-eight victories. In 1933, he was asked by Hermann Goering to help rebuild the German Air Force. On April 26, 1945, with Berlin surrounded by Russian forces, von Greim was ordered by Hitler to report to him.

Accompanied by Hanna Reitsch, rumored to be his intimate companion, Von Greim was wounded in the foot by Russian ground fire upon his landing approach and Reitsch took over the controls and landed the plane. Hitler promoted von Greim to field marshal, making him the last German officer to achieve that rank, and appointed him to lead the German Air Force, replacing Goering, who had been dismissed for treason. He and Reitsch left Berlin on April 28, just managing to take off before the air strip was overrun by advancing Russian forces. He

surrendered to American soldiers in Austria on May 8, 1945, and committed sui-
cide on May 24, 1945, upon learning he was to be transferred to Soviet control.

4. Lessons Learned Serving as a Cold War Staff Officer

1. General Andrew J. Goodpaster (February 12, 1915–May 16, 2005) graduated second in his West Point class of 1939. During World War II, he commanded
the 48th Combat Engineer Battalion in North Africa and Italy. He was awarded
the Distinguished Service Cross, the Silver Star, and two Purple Hearts for his service, which was cut short due to a serious wound in 1944. Upon recovery, he was
assigned to the War Planning Office under General Marshall, where he served for
the remainder of the war. He earned a PhD from Princeton University in 1950
and served as commander of the 8th Infantry Division in Germany in 1961–1962.
During the Vietnam War, he served as the deputy commander of the US Military
Assistance Command, Vietnam (MACV) in 1968–1969. He ended his career as
commander in chief of USEUCOM and supreme allied commander of NATO from
1969 to 1974. After retirement in 1974, he was recalled to active duty and assigned
as superintendent of the US Military Academy as a lieutenant general from 1977 to
1981. General Goodpaster was seen by many as the quintessential "soldier-scholar."

2. Lieutenant General Edward Rowny was born April 3, 1917, and earned
degrees from Johns Hopkins University, West Point, and Yale as well as a PhD
from the American University in International Studies. He commanded the 317th
Combat Engineer Battalion in the 92nd Infantry Division during the Italian campaign in World War II. After his service in Europe, he was assigned to the staff
of General MacArthur, helping to plan the Inchon landings of the Korean War.
Rowny served as assistant division commander of the 82nd Airborne Division in
1961–1962 and commanded the 24th Infantry Division from 1965 to 1966. In
1971 he was appointed the US representative to the Strategic Arms Limitation
Talks (SALT) and held this post under three presidents: Nixon, Ford, and Carter.
He retired from the army in 1979. After the election of President Reagan, Rowny
was appointed to the rank of ambassador as the president's chief negotiator on
Strategic Nuclear Arms (START). He also served in this position under President
George H. W. Bush until his retirement from government in 1991.

3. Lieutenant General Jack Norton enlisted in the army in the mid-1930s
and won an appointment to West Point. He was named first captain and graduated with the class of 1941. As a member of the 505th Parachute Infantry Regiment of the 82nd Division, he parachuted into Normandy on D-Day. He also
saw action in Sicily, Italy, Belgium, and Germany. From 1950 to 1953 he was the
executive officer to Army Secretary Frank Pace Jr. As a member of the Howze
Board, he outlined the use of the helicopter in future operations, and commanded
the 1st Cavalry Division in Vietnam in 1966. His final assignment, from 1973
to 1975, was as deputy commander of NATO's Allied Joint Force Command in
Naples. He died on December 6, 2004, of cancer at his home in Basye, Virginia.

4. General Ted Conway (July 24, 1909–September 11, 1990) graduated from the US Military Academy in 1933. During World War II, he served with the 9th Infantry Division, VI Corps, and Headquarters, 5th US Army. His service included battalion and regimental commands and duty as aide-de-camp to British general Sir Harold Alexander. He also helped plan the commando raid on Dieppe and participated as a shipboard observer during the operation. He was promoted to major general and commanded the 82nd Airborne Division in 1961. In 1962, he was posted to Bangkok as the chief, US Advisory Group, and in 1963 was promoted to lieutenant general and assigned as deputy commanding general, 8th Army, Korea. His final assignment after his promotion to general was as commander in chief of the US Strike Command, headquartered at MacDill Air Force Base near Tampa, Florida. He retired in 1969, having completed forty-two years of service to his country.

5. General Robert Porter (April 9, 1908–April 22, 2000) graduated from West Point in 1930. He began his career in the cavalry and served with the 1st Infantry Division in North Africa and Sicily, and the II Corps in Italy during World War II. Returning to the War Department in 1945, he served as a strategic planner, and later became executive officer to the undersecretary of the army. He later commanded the 2nd Armored Cavalry Regiment and the 3rd Armored Division. As a four-star general, his last assignment was as commander in chief of Southern Command from 1965 to 1969. After retiring from the army, he became an award-winning tree farmer. He died of a heart attack at age ninety-one in Charlottesville, Virginia.

6. General Charles Bolte (May 8, 1895–February 11, 1989) graduated from Illinois Institute of Technology and was commissioned as a second lieutenant in the army in 1916. He saw action in France in World War I with the 58th Infantry, 4th Division at the battle of Saint-Mihiel and the Meuse-Argonne offensive. In 1941, Lieutenant Colonel Bolte traveled to London as head of a group of army observers and in 1942 assumed the position of chief of staff of US forces in the United Kingdom. As a major general, he commanded the 69th Division and later the 34th Infantry Division in Italy. During World War II, Bolte was awarded two Distinguished Service Medals, the Silver Star, Legion of Merit, and the Purple Heart. As a lieutenant general in 1953, he became commander in chief, US Army, Europe. Later that year, he returned to Washington with a promotion to full general and was assigned as the army vice chief of staff. He retired from active duty in 1955 and lived in Arlington, Virginia, until his death in 1989.

7. General Matthew B. Ridgway (March 3, 1895–July 26, 1993) graduated from West Point in 1917. He did not serve overseas in World War I. During tours in China and Fort Benning, he caught the eye of General Marshall, who assigned Ridgway to the War Plans Office prior to World War II. In August 1942 he was given command of the 82nd Airborne Division, which he commanded during combat jumps in Sicily, Normandy, and Operation MARKET GARDEN. In 1950, Ridgway received command of the 8th Army in Korea after the death of

Lieutenant General Walker. Following the relieving of General MacArthur, Ridgway was promoted to full general and assumed command of all United Nations forces in Korea. In 1952 he replaced General Eisenhower as supreme allied commander, Europe. In 1953, he succeeded General Collins as chief of staff, US Army, until his retirement in 1955.

8. James O. Curtis Jr. (January 25, 1909–December 2, 1978) was born in Portales, New Mexico, into a large Texas ranching family whose ancestors were pioneers during the time of the Texas Republic. He graduated from the United States Military Academy in 1930 and then was assigned to the 8th Cavalry at Fort Bliss, Texas. During World War II, he served with the Allied Force Headquarters in North Africa and later the 1st Infantry Division. He earned a Silver Star while fighting in Sicily. In the closing days of the war, he was responsible for rescuing the famed Lipizzaner stallions from behind Russian lines in Czechoslovakia. After the war he commanded the 3rd Armored Cavalry Regiment and served as executive and military aide to the secretary of the army, Gordon Gray, and later Frank Pace. He was promoted to brigadier general in 1955. He retired from the army in 1960 and moved to California, where he sold real estate and taught at the University of California until his passing in 1978.

9. It appears that Deane's former assistant division commander from the 104th Division, now Major General Bryant Moore, initiated a by-name request for his services while he commanded the IX Corps in Korea in 1950. Moore died of a heart attack after surviving a helicopter crash during operations on February 24, 1951.

10. Lieutenant General Stanley R. "Swede" Larsen was a native of Hawaii and graduated from West Point in 1939. He served in the South Pacific in World War II with the 35th Infantry Regiment of the 25th Infantry Division, going from company commander to regimental commander. He was awarded the Distinguished Service Cross and the Silver Star for his actions. After the war, he served at the Infantry School in Fort Benning, Georgia, and later as the aide-de-camp to General J. Lawton Collins, army chief of staff. Subsequent assignments were commander, 325th Airborne Infantry Regiment of the 82nd Airborne Division, and chief of staff of the XVIII Airborne Corps. He commanded the 8th Infantry Division in Europe before going to Vietnam. He later served as I Field Force commander, Vietnam, in 1965–1967. He retired from the army in 1972 and died in a car crash in Shelby County, Alabama, on November 1, 2000.

11. General Wade H. Haislip (July 9, 1889–December 23, 1971) graduated from the US Military Academy in 1912 and was commissioned in the infantry. He served at Vera Cruz, Mexico, in 1914, and with the American Expeditionary Force from 1917 to 1921. In World War II, he commanded the 85th Division and the XV Corps through Normandy, France, Rhineland, and central Europe campaigns. In 1949, he was selected as the army vice chief of staff and served in that position until he retired in 1951.

12. General Andrew P. O'Meara (March 23, 1907–September 30, 2005) graduated from the US Military Academy in 1930 and was commissioned in the

field artillery. O'Meara served as a battery commander with the 4th Armored Division in 1941, and in 1942 took command of the 94th Field Artillery Battalion. By the end of the war, he was the assistant artillery commander of the VII Corps. During the Korean War, he was the artillery commander for the 7th Infantry Division. He spent the years after Korea working in research and development for the army. He ended his career as a four-star general in command of SOUTHCOM. He retired from the army in 1967 and settled in the Washington, DC, area. He died of a stroke at age ninety-eight in Arlington and is buried in Arlington National Cemetery.

13. Lieutenant General James M. Gavin (March 22, 1907–February 23, 1990) was placed in an orphanage in Brooklyn at age two and adopted into a coal-mining family in Pennsylvania. He left home at age seventeen and joined the army. He passed the entrance exam for the US Military Academy and entered West Point in 1925. After graduation, he served in various units before becoming an early advocate for airborne tactics. He authored the first field manual on airborne tactics and techniques. Later, when asked what made his career take off so fast, he would answer: "I wrote the book." Gavin became commander of the 505th Parachute Infantry Regiment in 1942 and led the regiment in the airborne assault in Sicily in 1943, where he earned a Distinguished Service Cross. He was promoted to general and made the assistant division commander of the 82nd Airborne Division for the Normandy invasion and took command of the division after the campaign. He led the division during Operation MARKET GARDEN and the Battle of the Bulge. After the war he rose to lieutenant general and served as the army chief of research and development. He retired in 1958 and served as president and chairman of Arthur D. Little, Inc. and US ambassador to France under President Kennedy. He died on February 23, 1990, and is buried at West Point.

14. *Oral History of Lieutenant General Howard H. Cooksey* (US Army Military History Institute, 1981), 36–37.

15. General Williston B. Palmer (November 11, 1899–October 11, 1973) graduated from the United States Military Academy in 1919. During World War II, as a brigadier general, he commanded the VII Corps artillery from the Normandy invasion to the Elbe. After the war, he commanded the 82nd Airborne Division in 1950 and the X Corps in Korea in 1951. He served as vice chief of staff of the army from 1955 to 1957, and was the first director of military assistance, from 1959–1962. His brother, Charles D. Palmer, was also a four-star general, and his grandfather William E. Birkhimer was a brigadier general and a Medal of Honor recipient.

5. Korea

1. Major General Julius K. Lacey graduated from the University of Tennessee and enlisted in the army as a flying cadet in 1929, serving as a fighter pilot and earning his commission in 1930. He received an advanced degree in meteorology

from MIT and was sent to Europe to study weather conditions and research aircraft icing. At the start of World War II, he returned to Europe to analyze meteorological problems for the RAF. In 1943 he commanded the Flying Fortress group in the 8th Air Force and later the 94th Combat Bomb Wing. He was awarded two Silver Stars and two Distinguished Flying Crosses. During the Korean War, he became the vice commander of the 5th Air Force. In 1954, he was appointed J3, Far East Command. Returning to the United States, he was appointed commandant, USAF Institute of Technology, Air University, Wright Patterson AFB, Ohio, before retiring in 1957. He died on July 5, 1992.

2. General John E. Hull (May 26, 1895–June 10, 1975) graduated from Miami University of Ohio and was commissioned a second lieutenant in 1917. He fought in France, earning a Silver Star. Because of his primary role in planning Allied operations throughout World War II, he was credited with having more experience integrating strategy with overseas operations than any other army officer. From 1953 to 1955 he was commander in chief of the Far East Command following the Korean War Armistice. Extremely modest, he was highly popular with his fellow soldiers. He retired on April 30, 1955, and passed away on June 10, 1975.

3. Lieutenant General Lionel C. McGarr (March 5, 1904–November 3, 1988) was born in Yuma, Arizona, graduated from the US Military Academy in 1928, and was commissioned as an infantry second lieutenant. He served in command and staff positions of increasing rank and responsibility, with assignments in Georgia, Hawaii, and California. He saw extensive combat as commander of the 30th Infantry Regiment in North Africa and Europe and also served as acting assistant division commander of the 3rd Infantry Division. He served as assistant division commander of the 2nd Infantry Division during the Korean War and commanded the 7th Infantry Division in Korea after the armistice. In 1960 he was promoted to lieutenant general and named commander of Military Assistance Advisory Group, Vietnam until June 1962, when he retired after advising against the US military escalation. He died in San Francisco in 1988.

4. Major General Sidney C. Wooten graduated from West Point in 1930. Before World War II, he served in various infantry units and as an aide to the governor of Puerto Rico. He commanded the 5th Infantry Regiment in Europe during the war. He later served in Korea and commanded the 17th Infantry Regiment and was the chief advisor to the South Korean Army. He later commanded Camp Kilmer in New Jersey, where he directed the reception and resettlement of thirty thousand Hungarian refugees who fled their country after the Hungarian Uprising of 1956 and retired from the army in 1965. He died of pneumonia on December 26, 2003, at age ninety-six.

5. Email from Major General Willis D. Crittenberger Jr. and Ms. Kathy Crittenberger to the editor, January 24, 2014.

6. Lieutenant General John MacNair Wright Jr. graduated from West Point in 1940 and was assigned to the 91st Coast Artillery, Philippine Scouts. The bat-

tery he commanded fired the last shot in defense of Corregidor in 1942. He was awarded the Silver Star and Purple Heart and spent over three years as a prisoner of war. He later served in the Korean War as the executive officer of the 32nd Infantry Regiment. After promotion to brigadier general, he was assigned to the 11th Air Assault Division (Test) and evaluated airmobile concepts at Fort Benning. This led to reorganization as the 1st Cavalry Division (Air Mobile) and deployment to Vietnam in 1965. In 1969, Wright returned to Vietnam as the commander of the 101st Airborne Division. His final assignment as a lieutenant general was as comptroller of the army. He retired in 1972 and passed away on January 27, 2014.

7. 2nd Battle Group, 6th Infantry Regiment, and the Berlin Wall

1. *Oral History of Lieutenant General Howard H. Cooksey*, 53.

2. General Bruce Clarke (April 29, 1901–March 17, 1986) enlisted in the army in 1917 and graduated from West Point in 1925. During World War II, as a brigadier general, he commanded Combat Command A (CCA) of the 4th Armored Division. Clarke led the relief of St. Vith during the Battle of the Bulge in 1944 that slowed the German attack. Writing afterward, General Eisenhower credited Clarke's actions as the turning point of the battle. During the Korean War, Clarke commanded the I Corps and the X Corps. His final assignment was as commanding general, US Army, Europe, before his retirement in 1962.

3. Lieutenant General Howard H. Cooksey was a 1943 graduate of Virginia Tech and fought in World War II with the 158th Regimental Combat Team in the Philippines. He served in Korea with the 7th Infantry Division and as a general officer in Vietnam with the 23rd Division. Other notable assignments during his career included executive officer of the 2nd Battle Group, 6th Infantry Division, Berlin, and commander, Fort Dix, New Jersey. His last assignment was deputy chief of staff for research, development, and acquisition before his retirement in 1978. He owned and operated two farms in Berryville, Virginia, and died of vascular disease on December 22, 1999.

4. Frederick O. Hartel was born in New Jersey and graduated from the United States Military Academy in 1933. He served as a battalion commander in the 45th Division at Anzio. He later served as commander of the 35th Infantry Regiment and on the faculty of the National War College. He took command of the Berlin Brigade two days before the construction of the Berlin Wall. He retired in 1966 as the chief of staff of the 2nd Army, and lived in Williamsburg, Virginia, until his death on November 29, 2000.

5. Jack Paar, *My Saber Is Bent* (New York: Simon & Schuster, 1961), 201.

6. Lieutenant General Albert Watson II (January 5, 1909–March 19, 1993) grew up in Mount Vernon, Illinois, and graduated from the United States Military Academy in 1930. He was an artillery officer who fought in New Guinea, the Philippines, and Okinawa during World War II. He served as the commandant of

Berlin from 1961 to 1963. Following his promotion to lieutenant general, Watson took command of the United States 3rd Army followed by duty as the commissioner of the Ryukyu Islands before retirement. His military awards included the Distinguished Service Medal with oak leaf cluster.

7. *Oral History of Lieutenant General Howard H. Cooksey,* 54.

8. "Army Exonerates Two Colonels for Part in Paar's Berlin Show," *New York Times,* September 28, 1961, 12.

8. Office of the Director of Defense Research and Engineering

1. Dr. Eugene G. Fubini (1913–1997) was the son of mathematician Guido Fubini, who emigrated from Italy to the United States in 1939 and in 1942 joined the war effort, working for America despite his native nationality. He worked on research and engineering of radio and defense electronics. In 1963, he became assistant secretary of defense and a major voice for the policy of technological supremacy during the Cold War.

9. 82nd Airborne Division and the Dominican Republic

1. Major General Joe Lawrie (February 14, 1914–February 25, 2009) served as an enlisted man before earning a commission at the start of World War II. He served with the 503rd Regimental Combat Team in airborne operations in the Pacific theater. He also served in Korea and Vietnam, culminating his career as commanding general of the 82nd Airborne Division from 1965 to 1967. His decorations included the Silver Star, Legion of Merit, and Bronze Star. He retired to San Antonio, where he passed away on February 25, 2009.

2. Bruce Palmer Jr., *Intervention in the Caribbean: The Dominican Crisis of 1965* (Lexington: University Press of Kentucky, 2015), 103, 105–6.

10. Vietnam

1. Major General Arthur L. West (1919–1985) graduated from Oklahoma A&M in 1940 and served with the 4th Armored Division, rising to battalion command before being wounded in 1944. After the war, he returned to Germany and commanded a constabulary squadron. He served as chief of training for the 8th Army during the Korean War and served on the Army General Staff until his retirement in 1967. West's awards included the Distinguished Service Cross, Silver Star, Bronze Star, and Purple Heart.

Lieutenant General Welborn G. Dolvin (February 8, 1916–May 17, 1991) graduated from West Point in 1939 and commanded the 191st Tank Battalion in the invasion of southern France in 1944 through the end of the war. During the Korean War he commanded the 89th Medium Tank Battalion. From 1966 through 1968, he commanded the 3rd Armored Division in Europe. He also served in Vietnam before retiring in 1975 as the commanding general of IX Corps, Japan. His awards included the Distinguished Service Cross, four Silver Stars, and three Purple Hearts.

2. General William E. DePuy (October 1, 1919–September 9, 1992) enlisted in the South Dakota National Guard and received his commission upon his graduation from South Dakota State University in 1941. Assigned to the 90th Infantry Division during World War II, he served as an operations officer and battalion commander, and was awarded the Distinguished Service Cross during the fierce campaigns from Utah Beach through the Battle of the Bulge. He served as commander of the 1st Infantry Division from 1966 to 1967. He is best remembered for his efforts as commander of the United States Army Training and Doctrine Command, where he helped create an innovative fighting doctrine for the army. He retired in July 1977 and died on September 9, 1992. DePuy's awards included two Distinguished Service Crosses, five Distinguished Service Medals, three Silver Stars, two Purple Hearts, the Distinguished Flying Cross, and Bronze Star.

3. Lieutenant General James F. Hollingsworth (March 24, 1918–March 20, 2010) graduated from Texas A&M University. He rose to lieutenant colonel in World War II, earning a Distinguished Service Cross and three Silver Stars. He also served in Korea and Vietnam, where he was awarded two more DSCs and another Silver Star. During his service he also collected six Purple Hearts. He retired in 1976.

4. "Trooper's General Knows His Men and They Know Him," *Hobbs (NM) Daily News,* March 6, 1967, 14.

5. General Sam Walker (July 31, 1925–August 8, 2015), the son of General Walton Walker, graduated from West Point in 1946. He served in Korean War, earning a Silver Star as a company commander with the 24th Infantry Division. During the Vietnam War, he commanded a brigade in the 1st Infantry Division. He later commanded the 3rd Infantry Division followed by selection as the US commander in Berlin. His final command was as commanding general, Allied Land Forces Southeast, headquartered in Turkey. He retired in 1978.

6. General Al Haig (December 2, 1924–February 20, 2010) graduated from West Point in 1947 and served in Korean War with X Corps, earning two Silver Stars. In 1966, he commanded a battalion in the 1st Infantry Division, earning the Distinguished Service Cross at the battle of Ap Gu in March 1967. Following the Vietnam War, Haig was appointed military assistant to Henry Kissinger, serving between 1969 and 1972. He moved from that position to White House chief of staff from 1973 to 1974. This was followed by a five-year assignment as NATO supreme commander from 1974 to 1979. Haig retired from the army in 1979 and served as secretary of state under President Reagan from 1981 to 1982. He died at age eighty-five in Baltimore on February 20, 2010.

7. General Fred Weyand (September 15, 1916–February 10, 2010) gradu-

ated from the University of California at Berkeley ROTC in 1938. During World War II, he served as assistant chief of staff for intelligence in the China-Burma-India theater from 1944 to 1945. During the Korean War, he commanded the 1st Battalion, 7th Infantry Regiment of the 3rd Infantry Division. Weyand became the commander of the 25th Infantry Division, which he led to Vietnam in 1965. He became commander of II Field Force in 1967. He became commander of US Army, Pacific, in 1973 and army chief of staff from 1974 until he retired in October 1976.

8. Major General Guy S. Meloy (May 16, 1930–August 25, 2013) served in various command and staff positions over the course of his army career. He commanded four platoons, three companies, two battalions—one for six months as a major, the second for twelve months as a lieutenant colonel, both in Vietnam—and a brigade. He served as assistant division commander and commander of the 82nd Airborne Division as well as director of training in the Office of the Deputy Chief of Staff for Operations and Plans. He was awarded the Distinguished Service Cross and the Purple Heart for his actions during Operation ATTLEBORO.

9. Guy S. Meloy, "Operation Attleboro: The Wolfhounds Brave Stand," *Vietnam Magazine,* October 1997.

10. William Chauncey Barott (February 17, 1927–November 4, 1966) graduated from West Point in 1951. He served as a platoon leader with the 38th Infantry Regiment in Korea, earning a Bronze Star and the Combat Infantry Badge. Follow-on assignments included company command in the Berlin Brigade under Colonel Deane. He was posthumously awarded a Silver Star for gallantry in action on November 4, 1966. General Deane later wrote to Barott's mother, "I heard nothing but glowing praise of Bill, the job he did, and his great leadership. Everyone here had the greatest respect for him as an officer and was devoted to him as an individual. You can be extremely proud of Bill. There is none better."

11. General Orders #6470 Headquarters, US Army, Vietnam (November 23, 1966).

12. Fire Support Base Mary Ann, manned by 231 soldiers of the 1st Battalion, 46th Infantry Regiment and located in Quang Tin Province, was attacked early on the morning of March 28, 1971 by the 409th VC Sapper Battalion. The exact number of enemy sappers involved is uncertain, but most sources agree that there were at least fifty. In the months leading up to the attack, the level of enemy activity in the area was low and contacts infrequent. This had lulled the US and ARVN soldiers in the area into a false sense of security. The sapper attack was described as sharp and very successful, leading to US casualties of thirty-three KIA and eighty-three wounded. The events at FSB Mary Ann had repercussions throughout the chain of command of both the 23rd Infantry Division and the 196th Light Infantry Brigade. Major General James L. Baldwin, the 23rd Infantry Division commander, was reassigned; Colonel William S. Hathaway, the 196th Light Infantry Brigade commander, was removed from the promotion list for brigadier general; and the battalion commander, Lieutenant Colonel William

P. Doyle, was reprimanded. In the end, six officers received some sort of disciplinary action from the secretary of the army.

13. Lieutenant General Henry E. Emerson (May 28, 1925–February 4, 2015) graduated from West Point in 1947. Known as "the Gunfighter," he conceived of aerial reconnaissance and the combat method of rapid buildup of combat power to surround and destroy enemy forces. He was awarded a Silver Star in Korea, and two Distinguished Service Crosses and four more Silver Stars in Vietnam. On one occasion, observing five enemy soldiers fleeing the conflict area, he ordered his pilot to land; immediately leaping out and using only his pistol, he killed one of the enemy and captured another. He was seriously burned in a helicopter crash in the Mekong Delta in 1968. He served as assistant division commander of the 82nd Airborne Division under Jack Deane and later commanded the 2nd Infantry Division and the XVIII Airborne Corps. He retired from the army in 1977, and resided in Helena, Montana, until his passing on February 4, 2015.

14. Email correspondence between Zelner Houchin and the editor, April 2, 2015.

15. Ibid.

16. John Nance, "Uncle Jack, Fighting General," *Milwaukee Journal*, March 5, 1967.

17. Email correspondence between Chuck Utzman and the editor, March 4, 2013.

18. Email correspondence between Charlie Brown and John R. Deane Jr., November 26, 1998.

19. Email correspondence between Jack Kelley and the editor, April 12, 2013.

20. Lieutenant General Edward A. Partain (June 26, 1929–March 24, 1996) graduated from West Point in 1951 and was assigned to the 27th Infantry Regiment fighting in Korea, where he served as a company commander. He went to Vietnam as an advisor in 1964 and later commanded the 2nd Battalion, 503rd Infantry under Brigadier General Deane. In later years, he commanded the 1st Infantry Division and served as commanding general of the 5th Army before his retirement in 1985. He died of a heart attack in 1996. Among his military awards were the Silver Star, Distinguished Flying Cross, three Purple Hearts, and two Combat Infantry Badges.

21. Email correspondence between Zelner Houchin and the editor, April 2, 2015.

22. Email correspondence between Michael Del Monaco and the editor, April 1, 2015.

12. 82nd Airborne Division Commanding General

1. *Oral History of Lieutenant General Henry Emerson*, 76–78, 88.

2. Email correspondence between Paul O'Mary and John R. Deane Jr., May 5, 2007.

13. Defense Communication Planning Group

1. Lieutenant General Alfred Dodd Starbird (April 28, 1912–July 28, 1983), the son of an army general, was born at Fort Sill and graduated from the US Military Academy in 1933. For much of World War II, he was a strategic planner in the Operations Division of the War Department. He participated in the Allied landings at Oran and Normandy. He commanded the 1135th Engineer Combat Unit, which was the first to cross the Rhine River. After the war, he held key assignments in the testing and development of nuclear weapons and was involved with the atomic weapons test at Eniwetok Atoll in the Pacific in 1949. As director of the Defense Communication Agency, he was involved in research and development from 1962 to 1967. Lieutenant General Starbird retired from the army in 1971 and was appointed to civilian posts in the Department of Energy by both President Ford and President Carter. He died of cancer at Walter Reed Hospital at age seventy-one on July 28, 1983.

2. According to the account in the *Reading Pennsylvania Eagle,* November 10, 1966:

> A helicopter carrying one of the 1st Infantry Division's senior leaders, Brigadier General James F. Hollingsworth of Sanger, Texas, was shot down near Operation ATTLEBORO today but neither the general nor his crew was injured. Brigadier General John R. Deane Jr. of San Francisco, California landed by helicopter in a clearing and took Hollingsworth out, while a ground force moved in and fended off Viet Cong snipers until still another helicopter took Hollingsworth's damaged aircraft out by sling.
>
> Hollingsworth and Deane are assistant commanders of the 1st Division under Major General William DePuy. When he was shot down, Hollingsworth was investigating the crash of an armed helicopter a few minutes earlier. Four crewmen of that helicopter were all killed and the helicopter burned.

15. Army Materiel Command/Development and Readiness Command

1. General Frank S. Besson, USAMHI Senior Officer Oral History Program Project, 1973, 269.

2. Reflections of Former AMC Commanders, USAMC Oral History Program, AMC History Office, 1989, 86.

3. Former Commanders—Ferdinand J. Chesarek, USAMC Oral History Program, AMC History Office, 1986, 43.

4. General Henry A. Miley Jr. was the third commander of Army Materiel Command, from 1970 to 1975. December 19, 1975 interview with General Miley, AMC History Office.

5. Former Commanders—George R. Sammet, Jr., USAMC Oral History Program, AMC History Office, 1986, 14.

6. Lieutenant General George Sammet Jr. (September 18, 1919–January 18, 2012) graduated from the University of Illinois in 1940 and received a reserve commission from the ROTC program there. He was called to active duty in 1942 and was assigned to an artillery battalion in the 95th Infantry Division in Italy, earning a Bronze Star, Purple Heart, and Air Medal. After attending several service schools after the war, he was assigned as director of instruction at the Turkish Artillery School, followed by assignment to the Office of the Chief of Research and Development (OCRD), eventually becoming the deputy director of development. After commanding the 4th US Army Missile Command in Korea, he returned to the OCRD as deputy director of missiles and space. He became deputy director of development, Army Materiel Command, from 1968 to 1969. He returned to AMC in 1973 as deputy commanding general for materiel acquisition. He was promoted to lieutenant general in 1975 and assigned as deputy commanding general for materiel development. Upon the retirement of General Deane, Lieutenant General Sammet was appointed commanding general, AMC, until he retired on May 17, 1977. He joined Martin Marietta and served as a vice president of procurement. He passed away in Orlando, Florida, on January 18, 2012.

7. Lieutenant General Fred Kornet Jr. was born in Wortendyke, New Jersey, on October 2, 1919. He served in the Ordnance Corps throughout his career, culminating as the army's senior logistician. He commanded Watervliet Arsenal and later US Army Aviation Systems Command, where he was instrumental in bringing computer systems and programs to various logistics agencies. He served as deputy chief of staff for logistics from 1973 to 1975. Many improvements were spawned through logistic programs that he promoted.

8. Hillman Dickinson was born in Independence, Missouri, in February 1926. He attended Massachusetts Institute of Technology and, in 1949, he received his BS from the US Military Academy. His initial troop assignment was with the 14th Armored Cavalry on border patrol in Germany, 1950–1953. In 1966–1967 he attended the Army War College before being assigned to Vietnam. There he commanded the 3rd Squadron, 11th Armored Cavalry Regiment (Blackhorse) from June 1967 to January 1968. In 1968, he joined the Defense Communications Planning Group, charged with developing the sensor program for Southeast Asia known as the McNamara Line. In 1971, he returned to Vietnam as senior advisor to the 1st Vietnamese Infantry Division in the northern two provinces. He was promoted to brigadier general in 1973 and major general in 1977, becoming the first commanding general of US Army Communications, Electronic Research and Development Command. After receiving his third star, his final assignment was at the Pentagon, where he created the Directorate for C3 Systems of the Joint Chiefs of Staff. He retired in 1982 and started a consulting firm. He died of pancreatic cancer on September 2, 1994.

9. Lieutenant General Robert H. York graduated from West Point in 1938. During World War II, he initially served as a battalion commander with the 18th

Infantry Regiment, 1st Infantry Division. He took part in eleven major battle engagements and three D-Day landings, at Oran, Sicily, and Normandy. He was handpicked to take over the 331st Infantry Regiment, 83rd Infantry Division, a demoralized unit that had suffered tremendous casualties and had lost its two previous commanders in the Normandy hedgerow fighting. York transformed the regiment into a hard-hitting unit that went on to fight in five major campaigns until the end of the war. York later served as commandant of cadets at West Point and commander of Fort Benning and later the 82nd Airborne Division. His final assignment before retirement in 1968 was XVIII Corps commander. During his service, Lieutenant General York was awarded the Distinguished Service Cross, three Silver Stars, three Bronze Stars, and six Purple Hearts. He passed away in San Diego, California, on April 15, 1988. He once commented, "I feel my so-called success was due to the fact that I genuinely loved and respected the soldier and especially the Infantryman. I felt honored to lead that man in battle and felt obligated to give him my best. And I also felt obligated to share with him, at least to some degree, the dangers he faced and some of the pain and fears he endured. The things you see in me—in my character—are a reflection of what I saw in each of you."

10. General Alfred M. Gruenther (March 3, 1899–May 30, 1983) was born in Platte Center, Nebraska, and graduated from West Point in 1918. During World War II, Gruenther served as the principal American planner for the Allied invasions of North Africa in 1942 and Italy in 1943. He became famous for the quality of his staff and tactical planning work. After the war, he became deputy commander of US forces in Austria in 1945. He was appointed supreme allied commander (SACEUR) in Europe from 1953 to 1956. After retiring from the army in 1956, he served as president of the American Red Cross until 1964. He died in Washington, DC, on May 30, 1983, and is buried in Arlington National Cemetery.

Index